grzimek's
Student Animal Life Resource

• • • •

grzimek's
Student Animal Life Resource

• • • •

Mammals
volume 4

Dolphins to Antelopes

THOMSON

GALE

Detroit • New York • San Francisco • San Diego • New Haven, Conn. • Waterville, Maine • London • Munich

Grzimek's Student Animal Life Resource
Mammals

Project Editor
Melissa C. McDade

Editorial
Julie L. Carnagie, Madeline Harris,
Elizabeth Manar, Heather Price

Indexing Services
Synapse, the Knowledge Link
Corporation

Rights and Acquisitions
Sheila Spencer, Mari Masalin-Cooper

Imaging and Multimedia
Randy Bassett, Michael Logusz, Dan
Newell, Chris O'Bryan, Robyn Young

Product Design
Tracey Rowens, Jennifer Wahi

Composition
Evi Seoud, Mary Beth Trimper

Manufacturing
Wendy Blurton, Dorothy Maki

LIBRARY OF CONGRESS CATALOGING-IN-PUBLICATION DATA

Grzimek's student animal life resource. Mammals / Melissa C. McDade, project
editor.
      p. cm.
   Includes bibliographical references and index.
   ISBN 0-7876-9183-6 (set hardcover : alk. paper) — ISBN 0-7876-9184-4
(volume 1) — ISBN 0-7876-9185-2 (volume 2) — ISBN 0-7876-9187-9 (volume 3)
   — ISBN 0-7876-9188-7 (volume 4) — ISBN 0-7876-9234-4 (volume 5)
   1. Mammals—Juvenile literature. I. Grzimek, Bernhard. II. McDade, Melissa C.
   QL703.G79 2005
   599—dc22   2004015604

ISBN 0-7876-9402-9 (21-vol set), ISBN 0-7876-9183-6 (Mammals set),
ISBN 0-7876-9184-4 (v.1), ISBN 0-7876-9185-2 (v.2), ISBN 0-7876-9187-9 (v.3),
ISBN 0-7876-9188-7 (v.4), ISBN 0-7876-9234-4 (v.5)

This title is also available as an e-book
Contact your Thomson Gale sales representative for ordering information.

Printed in Canada
10 9 8 7 6 5 4 3 2 1

Contents

MAMMALS: VOLUME 3

Reader's Guide

Grzimek's Student Animal Life Resource: Mammals offers readers comprehensive and easy-to-use information on Earth's mammals. Entries are arranged by taxonomy, the science through which living things are classified into related groups. Order entries provide an overview of a group of families, and family entries provide an overview of a particular family. Each entry includes sections on physical characteristics; geographic range; habitat; diet; behavior and reproduction; animals and people; and conservation status. Family entries are followed by one or more species accounts with the same information as well as a range map and photo or illustration for each species. Entries conclude with a list of books, periodicals, and Web sites that may be used for further research.

ADDITIONAL FEATURES

Each volume of *Grzimek's Student Animal Life Resource: Mammals* includes a pronunciation guide for scientific names, a glossary, an overview of Mammals, a list of species in the set by biome, a list of species by geographic location, and an index. The set has 540 full-color maps, photos, and illustrations to enliven the text, and sidebars provide additional facts and related information.

NOTES

The classification of animals into orders, families, and even species is not a completed exercise. As researchers learn more about animals and their relationships, classifications may change. In some cases, researchers do not agree on how or whether to make a change. For this reason, the heading "Number of species" in the introduction of an entry may read "About 36 species" or "34 to 37 species." It is not a question of whether some animals exist or not, but a question of how they are classified. Some researchers are more likely to "lump" animals into the same species classification, while others may "split" animals into separate species.

Grzimek's Student Animal Life Resource: Mammals has standardized information in the Conservation Status section. The IUCN Red List provides the world's most comprehensive inventory of the global conservation status of plants and animals. Using a set of criteria to evaluate extinction risk, the IUCN recognizes the following categories: Extinct, Extinct in the Wild, Critically Endangered, Endangered, Vulnerable, Conservation Dependent, Near Threatened, Least Concern, and Data Deficient. These terms are defined where they are used in the text, but for a complete explanation of each category, visit the IUCN web page at http://www.iucn.org/themes/ssc/redlists/RLcats2001booklet.html.

ACKNOWLEDGEMENTS

Special thanks are due for the invaluable comments and suggestions provided by the *Grzimek's Student Animal Life Resource: Mammals* advisors:

- Mary Alice Anderson, Media Specialist, Winona Middle School, Winona, Minnesota
- Thane Johnson, Librarian, Oklahoma City Zoo, Oklahoma City, Oklahoma
- Debra Kachel, Media Specialist, Ephrata Senior High School, Ephrata, Pennsylvania
- Nina Levine, Media Specialist, Blue Mountain Middle School, Courtlandt Manor, New York
- Ruth Mormon, Media Specialist, The Meadows School, Las Vegas, Nevada

COMMENTS AND SUGGESTIONS

We welcome your comments on *Grzimek's Student Animal Life Resource: Mammals* and suggestions for future editions of this work. Please write: Editors, *Grzimek's Student Animal Life Resource: Mammals*, U•X•L, 27500 Drake Rd., Farmington Hills, Michigan 48331-3535; call toll free: 1-800-877-4253; fax: 248-699-8097; or send e-mail via www.gale.com.

Pronunciation Guide for
Scientific Names

Abrocoma cinerea AB-ruh-KOH-muh sin-EAR-ee-uh

Abrocomidae ab-ruh-KOH-muh-dee

Acomys cahirinus ak-OH-meez kay-hih-RYE-nuhs

Acrobates pygmaeus ak-CROW-bah-teez pig-MEE-uhs

Acrobatidae ak-crow-BAH-tuh-dee

Agouti paca ah-GOO-tee PAY-cuh

Agoutidae ah-GOO-tuh-dee

Ailuropoda melanoleuca AYE-lur-uh-POD-uh MEL-uh-noh-LYOO-kuh

Ailurus fulgens AYE-lur-uhs FULL-jens

Alces alces AL-ceez AL-ceez

Alouatta seniculus ah-loo-AH-tuh se-NIH-kul-uhs

Anomaluridae ah-nuh-mah-LOOR-uh-dee

Anomalurus derbianus ah-nuh-MAH-loor-uhs der-BEE-an-uhs

Antilocapra americana AN-til-uh-KAP-ruh uh-mer-uh-KAN-uh

Antilocapridae an-til-uh-KAP-ruh-dee

Antrozous pallidus an-tro-ZOH-uhs PAL-uh-duhs

Aotidae ay-OH-tuh-dee

Aotus trivirgatus ay-OH-tuhs try-VER-gah-tuhs

Aplodontia rufa ap-loh-DON-shuh ROO-fah

Aplodontidae ap-loh-DON-tuh-dee

Arctocephalus gazella ARK-tuh-SEFF-uh-luhs guh-ZELL-uh

Artiodactyla AR-tee-uh-DAK-til-uh

Asellia tridens ah-SELL-ee-uh TRY-denz

Ateles geoffroyi ah-TELL-eez JEFF-roy-eye

Atelidae ah-TELL-uh-dee

Babyrousa babyrussa bah-bee-ROO-suh bah-bee-ROO-suh

Balaena mysticetus bah-LEE-nuh mis-tuh-SEE-tuhs

Balaenidae bah-LEE-nuh-dee

Balaenoptera acutorostrata bah-lee-NOP-teh-ruh uh-KYOOT-
uh-ROS-trah-tuh

Balaenoptera musculus bah-lee-NOP-teh-ruh muhs-KU-luhs

Balaenopteridae bah-lee-nop-TEH-ruh-dee

Barbastella barbastellus bar-buh-STELL-uh bar-buh-STELL-uhs

Bathyergidae bath-ih-ER-juh-dee

Bettongia tropica bee-ton-JEE-uh TROP-ik-uh

Bison bison BI-sun BI-sun

Bovidae BOH-vuh-dee

Bradypodidae brad-ih-POD-uh-dee

Bradypus variegatus BRAD-ih-puhs vair-ee-uh-GAH-tuhs

Bubalus bubalis BYOO-bal-uhs BYOO-bal-is

Burramyidae bur-ruh-MY-uh-dee

Cacajao calvus KA-ka-jah-oh KAL-vuhs

Caenolestes fuliginosus kee-NOH-less-teez fyoo-li-JEH-noh-suhs

Caenolestidae kee-noh-LESS-tuh-dee

Callicebus personatus kal-luh-SEE-buhs per-SON-ah-tuhs

Callimico goeldii kal-luh-MEE-koh geel-DEE-eye

Callitrichidae kal-luh-TRIK-uh-dee

Camelidae kam-EL-uh-dee

Camelus dromedarius KAM-el-uhs drom-uh-DARE-ee-uhs

Canidae KAN-uh-dee

Canis lupus KAN-is LYOO-puhs

Caperea marginata kay-per-EE-uh mar-JIN-ah-tuh

Capricornis sumatraensis kap-rih-KOR-nis soo-mah-TREN-sis

Capromyidae kap-roh-MY-uh-dee

Capromys pilorides KAP-roh-meez pi-LOH-ruh-deez

Carnivora kar-NIH-voh-ruh

Castor canadensis KAS-tor kan-uh-DEN-sis

Castoridae kas-TOR-uh-dee

Caviidae kave-EYE-uh-dee

Cebidae SEE-buh-dee

Cebuella pygmaea see-boo-ELL-uh pig-MEE-uh

Cebus capucinus SEE-buhs kap-oo-CHIN-uhs

Cebus olivaceus SEE-buhs ah-luh-VAY-see-uhs

Ceratotherium simum suh-rah-tuh-THER-ee-um SIM-um

Cercartetus nanus ser-kar-TEE-tuhs NAN-uhs

Cercopithecidae ser-koh-pith-EEK-uh-dee

Cervidae SER-vuh-dee

Cervus elaphus SER-vuhs EL-laff-uhs

Cetacea sih-TAY-she-uh

Cheirogaleidae KY-roh-GAL-uh-dee

Cheiromeles torquatus ky-ROH-mel-eez TOR-kwah-tuhs

Chinchilla lanigera chin-CHILL-uh la-NIJ-er-uh

Chinchillidae chin-CHILL-uh-dee

Chironectes minimus ky-roh-NECK-teez MIN-ih-muhs

Chiroptera ky-ROP-ter-uh

Chlamyphorus truncatus klam-EE-for-uhs TRUN-kah-tuhs

Choloepus hoffmanni koh-LEE-puhs HOFF-man-eye

Chrysochloridae krih-soh-KLOR-uh-dee

Chrysocyon brachyurus krih-SOH-sigh-on bra-kee-YOOR-uhs

Civettictis civetta sih-VET-tick-tis SIH-vet-uh

Coendou prehensilis SEEN-doo prih-HEN-sil-is

Condylura cristata KON-dih-LUR-uh KRIS-tah-tuh

Connochaetes gnou koh-nuh-KEE-teez NEW

Craseonycteridae kras-ee-oh-nick-TER-uh-dee

Craseonycteris thonglongyai kras-ee-oh-NICK-ter-is thong-LONG-ee-aye

Cricetomys gambianus kry-see-TOH-meez GAM-bee-an-uhs

Cricetus cricetus kry-SEE-tuhs kry-SEE-tuhs

Crocuta crocuta kroh-CUE-tuh kroh-CUE-tuh

Cryptomys damarensis krip-TOH-meez DAM-are-en-sis

Cryptoprocta ferox krip-TOH-prok-tuh FAIR-oks

Cryptotis parva krip-TOH-tis PAR-vuh

Ctenodactylidae ten-oh-dak-TIL-uh-dee

Ctenomyidae ten-oh-MY-uh-dee

Ctenomys pearsoni TEN-oh-meez PEAR-son-eye

Cyclopes didactylus SIGH-kluh-peez die-DAK-til-uhs

Cynocephalidae sigh-nuh-seff-UH-luh-dee

Cynocephalus variegatus sigh-nuh-SEFF-uh-luhs VAIR-ee-uh-GAH-tus

Cynomys ludovicianus SIGH-no-mees LOO-doh-vih-SHE-an-uhs

Dasypodidae das-ih-POD-uh-dee

Dasyprocta punctata das-IH-prok-tuh PUNK-tah-tuh

Dasyproctidae das-ih-PROK-tuh-dee

Dasypus novemcinctus DAS-ih-puhs noh-VEM-sink-tuhs

Dasyuridae das-ih-YOOR-uh-dee

Dasyuromorphia das-ih-yoor-oh-MOR-fee-uh

Daubentoniidae daw-ben-tone-EYE-uh-dee

Daubentonia madagascariensis daw-ben-TONE-ee-uh mad-uh-GAS-kar-EE-en-sis

Delphinapterus leucas del-fin-AP-ter-uhs LYOO-kuhs

Delphinidae del-FIN-uh-dee

Dendrohyrax arboreus den-droh-HI-raks are-BOHR-ee-uhs

Dendrolagus bennettianus den-droh-LAG-uhs BEN-net-EE-an-uhs

Dermoptera der-MOP-ter-uh

Desmodus rotundus dez-MOH-duhs ROH-tun-duhs

Dicerorhinus sumatrensis die-ser-uh-RHY-nuhs soo-mah-TREN-sis

Didelphidae die-DELF-uh-dee

Didelphimorphia die-delf-uh-MOR-fee-uh

Didelphis virginiana DIE-delf-is ver-JIN-ee-an-uh

Dinomyidae die-noh-MY-uh-dee

Dinomys branickii DIE-noh-meez BRAN-ick-ee-eye

Dipodidae dih-POD-uh-dee

Dipodomys ingens dih-puh-DOH-meez IN-jenz

Diprotodontia dih-pro-toh-DON-she-uh

Dipus sagitta DIH-puhs SAJ-it-tuh

Dolichotis patagonum doll-ih-KOH-tis pat-uh-GOH-num

Dromiciops gliroides droh-MISS-ee-ops gli-ROY-deez

Dugong dugon DOO-gong DOO-gon

Dugongidae doo-GONG-uh-dee

Echimyidae ek-ih-MY-uh-dee

Echinosorex gymnura EH-ky-noh-SORE-eks JIM-nyoor-uh

Echymipera rufescens ek-ee-MIH-per-uh ROO-fehs-sens

Ectophylla alba ek-toh-FILE-luh AHL-buh

Elephantidae el-uh-FAN-tuh-dee

Elephas maximus EL-uh-fuhs MAX-im-uhs

Emballonuridae em-bal-lun-YOOR-uh-dee

Equidae EK-wuh-dee

Equus caballus przewalskii EK-wuhs CAB-uh-luhs prez-VAL-skee-eye

Equus grevyi EK-wuhs GREH-vee-eye

Equus kiang EK-wuhs KY-an

Eremitalpa granti er-uh-MIT-ahl-puh GRAN-tie

Erethizon dorsatum er-uh-THY-zun DOR-sah-tum

Erethizontidae er-uh-thy-ZUN-tuh-dee

Erinaceidae er-ih-nay-SIGH-dee

Erinaceus europaeus er-ih-NAY-shuhs yoor-uh-PEE-uhs

Eschrichtiidae ess-rick-TIE-uh-dee

Eschrichtius robustus ess-RICK-shuhs roh-BUHS-tuhs

Eubalaena glacialis yoo-bah-LEE-nuh glay-SHE-al-is

Felidae FEE-luh-dee

Furipteridae fur-ip-TER-uh-dee

Galagidae gal-AG-uh-dee

Galago senegalensis GAL-ag-oh sen-ih-GAHL-en-sis

Galidia elegans ga-LID-ee-uh EL-uh-ganz

Gazella thomsonii guh-ZELL-uh TOM-son-ee-eye

Genetta genetta JIN-eh-tuh JIN-eh-tuh

Geomyidae gee-oh-MY-uh-dee

Giraffa camelopardalis JIH-raf-uh KAM-el-uh-PAR-dal-is

Giraffidae jih-RAF-uh-dee

Glaucomys volans glo-KOH-meez VOH-lans

Glossophaga soricina glos-SUH-fag-uh sore-ih-SEE-nuh

Gorilla gorilla guh-RILL-uh guh-RILL-uh

Hemicentetes semispinosus hemi-sen-TEE-teez semi-PINE-oh-
    suhs

Herpestidae her-PES-tuh-dee

Heterocephalus glaber HEH-tuh-roh-SEFF-uh-luhs GLAH-ber

Heteromyidae HEH-tuh-roh-MY-uh-dee

Hexaprotodon liberiensis hek-suh-PRO-tuh-don lye-BEER-ee-
    en-sis

Hippopotamidae HIP-poh-pot-UH-muh-dee

Hippopotamus amphibius HIP-poh-POT-uh-muhs am-FIB-ee-
    uhs

Hipposideridae HIP-poh-si-DER-uh-dee

Hominidae hom-IN-uh-dee

Homo sapiens HOH-moh SAY-pee-enz

Hyaenidae hi-EE-nuh-dee

Hydrochaeridae hi-droh-KEE-ruh-dee

Hydrochaeris hydrochaeris hi-droh-KEE-ris hi-droh-KEE-ris

Hydrodamalis gigas hi-droh-DAM-uhl-is JEE-guhs

Hylobates lar hi-loh-BAY-teez lahr

Hylobates pileatus hi-loh-BAY-teez pie-LEE-ah-tuhs

Hylobatidae hi-loh-BAY-tuh-dee

Hylochoerus meinertzhageni   hi-loh-KEE-ruhs MINE-ertz-hah-gen-eye

Hyperoodon ampullatus   hi-per-OH-uh-don am-PUH-lah-tuhs

Hypsiprymnodontidae   HIP-see-PRIM-nuh-DON-shuh-dee

Hypsiprymnodon moschatus   hip-see-PRIM-nuh-don MOS-kah-tuhs

Hyracoidea   HI-rah-koy-DEE-uh

Hystricidae   hiss-TRIK-uh-dee

Hystrix africaeaustralis   HISS-triks AF-rik-ee-au-STRA-lis

Hystrix indica   HISS-triks IN-dik-uh

Indri indri   IN-dri IN-dri

Indriidae   in-DRY-uh-dee

Inia geoffrensis   in-EE-uh JEFF-ren-sis

Iniidae   in-EYE-uh-dee

Insectivora   IN-sek-TIV-uh-ruh

Kerodon rupestris   KER-uh-don ROO-pes-tris

Kogia breviceps   koh-JEE-uh BREV-ih-seps

Lagomorpha   LAG-uh-MOR-fuh

Lagothrix lugens   LAG-uh-thriks LU-jens

Lama glama   LAH-muh GLAH-muh

Lama pacos   LAH-muh PAY-kuhs

Lemmus lemmus   LEM-muhs LEM-muhs

Lemur catta   LEE-mer KAT-tuh

Lemur coronatus   LEE-mer KOR-roh-nah-tuhs

Lemuridae   lee-MYOOR-uh-dee

Lepilemur leucopus   lep-uh-LEE-mer LYOO-koh-puhs

Lepilemur ruficaudatus   lep-uh-LEE-mer ROO-fee-KAW-dah-tuhs

Lepilemuridae   LEP-uh-lee-MOOR-uh-dee

Leporidae   lep-OR-uh-dee

Lepus americanus   LEP-uhs uh-mer-uh-KAN-uhs

Lepus timidus   LEP-uhs TIM-id-uhs

Lipotes vexillifer   lip-OH-teez veks-ILL-uh-fer

Lipotidae   lip-OH-tuh-dee

Lorisidae   lor-IS-uh-dee

Loxodonta africana   LOK-suh-DON-tuh AF-rih-kan-uh

Loxodonta cyclotis   LOK-suh-DON-tuh SIGH-klo-tis

Lutra lutra   LOO-truh LOO-truh

Lynx rufus   LINKS ROO-fuhs

Macaca mulatta   muh-KAY-kuh MYOO-lah-tuh

Macroderma gigas ma-CROW-der-muh JEE-guhs

Macropodidae ma-crow-POD-uh-dee

Macropus giganteus ma-CROW-puhs jy-GAN-tee-uhs

Macropus rufus ma-CROW-puhs ROO-fuhs

Macroscelidea MA-crow-sel-uh-DEE-uh

Macroscelididae MA-crow-sel-UH-duh-dee

Macrotis lagotis ma-CROW-tis la-GO-tis

Macrotus californicus ma-CROW-tuhs kal-uh-FORN-uh-kuhs

Madoqua kirkii ma-DOH-kwah KIRK-ee-eye

Mandrillus sphinx man-DRILL-uhs SFINKS

Manidae MAN-uh-dee

Manis temminckii MAN-is TEM-ink-ee-eye

Marmota marmota MAR-mah-tuh MAR-mah-tuh

Massoutiera mzabi mas-soo-TEE-er-uh ZA-bye

Megadermatidae meg-uh-der-MUH-tuh-dee

Megalonychidae meg-uh-loh-NICK-uh-dee

Megaptera novaeangliae meg-uh-TER-uh NOH-vee-ANG-lee-dee

Meles meles MEL-eez MEL-eez

Mephitis mephitis MEF-it-is MEF-it-is

Microbiotheria my-crow-bio-THER-ee-uh

Microbiotheriidae my-crow-bio-ther-EYE-uh-dee

Microcebus rufus my-crow-SEE-buhs ROO-fuhs

Micropteropus pusillus my-crop-TER-oh-puhs pyoo-SILL-uhs

Miniopterus schreibersi min-ee-OP-ter-uhs shry-BER-seye

Mirounga angustirostris MIR-oon-guh an-GUHS-tih-ROS-tris

Molossidae mol-OS-suh-dee

Monachus schauinslandi MON-ak-uhs SHOU-inz-land-eye

Monodon monoceros MON-uh-don mon-UH-ser-uhs

Monodontidae mon-uh-DON-shuh-dee

Monotremata mon-uh-TREEM-ah-tuh

Mormoopidae mor-moh-UP-uh-dee

Moschus moschiferus MOS-kuhs mos-KIF-er-uhs

Muntiacus muntjak mun-SHE-uh-kuhs MUNT-jak

Muridae MUR-uh-dee

Mustela erminea MUS-tuh-luh er-MIN-ee-uh

Mustelidae mus-TUH-luh-dee

Myocastor coypus MY-oh-KAS-tor COI-puhs

Myocastoridae MY-oh-kas-TOR-uh-dee

Myotis lucifugus my-OH-tis loo-SIFF-ah-guhs

Myoxidae my-OKS-uh-dee

Myoxus glis MY-oks-uhs GLIS

Myrmecobiidae mur-mih-koh-BYE-uh-dee

Myrmecobius fasciatus mur-mih-KOH-bee-uhs fah-SHE-ah-tuhs

Myrmecophaga tridactyla mur-mih-KOH-fag-uh try-DAK-til-uh

Myrmecophagidae mur-mih-koh-FAJ-uh-dee

Mystacina tuberculata miss-tih-SEE-nuh too-ber-KYOO-lah-tuh

Mystacinidae miss-tih-SEE-nuh-dee

Myzopoda aurita my-zoh-POD-uh OR-it-uh

Myzopodidae my-zoh-POD-uh-dee

Nasalis larvatus NAY-zal-is LAR-vah-tuhs

Natalidae nay-TAL-uh-dee

Natalus stramineus NAY-tal-uhs struh-MIN-ee-uhs

Neobalaenidae nee-oh-bah-LEE-nuh-dee

Noctilio leporinus nok-TIHL-ee-oh leh-por-RYE-nuhs

Noctilionidae nok-tihl-ee-ON-uh-dee

Notomys alexis noh-TOH-meez ah-LEK-sis

Notoryctemorphia noh-toh-rik-teh-MOR-fee-uh

Notoryctes typhlops noh-TOH-rik-teez TIE-flopz

Notoryctidae noh-toh-RIK-tuh-dee

Nycteridae nik-TER-uh-dee

Nycteris thebaica NIK-ter-is the-BAH-ik-uh

Nycticebus pygmaeus nik-tih-SEE-buhs pig-MEE-uhs

Nyctimene robinsoni nik-TIM-en-ee ROB-in-son-eye

Ochotona hyperborea oh-koh-TOH-nuh hi-per-BOHR-ee-uh

Ochotona princeps oh-koh-TOH-nuh PRIN-seps

Ochotonidae oh-koh-TOH-nuh-dee

Octodon degus OK-tuh-don DAY-gooz

Octodontidae ok-tuh-DON-tuh-dee

Odobenidae oh-duh-BEN-uh-dee

Odobenus rosmarus oh-DUH-ben-uhs ROS-mahr-uhs

Odocoileus virginianus oh-duh-KOI-lee-uhs ver-JIN-ee-an-nuhs

Okapia johnstoni oh-KAH-pee-uh JOHNS-ton-eye

Ondatra zibethicus ON-dat-ruh ZIB-eth-ih-kuhs

Onychogalea fraenata oh-nik-uh-GAL-ee-uh FREE-nah-tuh

Orcinus orca OR-sigh-nuhs OR-kuh

Ornithorhynchidae OR-nith-oh-RIN-kuh-dee

Ornithorynchus anatinus OR-nith-oh-RIN-kuhs an-AH-tin-uhs

Orycteropodidae or-ik-ter-uh-POD-uh-dee

Orycteropus afer or-ik-TER-uh-puhs AF-er

Otariidae oh-tar-EYE-uh-dee

Otolemur garnettii oh-tuh-LEE-mer GAR-net-ee-eye

Ovis canadensis OH-vis kan-uh-DEN-sis

Pagophilus groenlandicus pa-GO-fil-luhs GREEN-land-ih-cuhs

Pan troglodytes PAN trog-luh-DIE-teez

Panthera leo PAN-ther-uh LEE-oh

Panthera tigris PAN-ther-uh TIE-gris

Paucituberculata paw-see-too-ber-KYOO-lah-tuh

Pedetidae ped-ET-uh-dee

Peramelemorphia per-uh-mel-eh-MOR-fee-uh

Peramelidae per-uh-MEL-uh-dee

Perameles gunnii PER-uh-MEL-eez GUN-ee-eye

Perissodactyla peh-RISS-uh-DAK-til-uh

Perodicticus potto per-uh-DIK-tuh-kuhs POT-toh

Perognathus inornatus PER-ug-NAH-thuhs in-AWR-nah-tuhs

Peropteryx kappleri per-OP-ter-iks KAP-ler-eye

Peroryctidae per-uh-RIK-tuh-dee

Petauridae pet-OR-uh-dee

Petauroides volans pet-or-OY-deez VOH-lanz

Petaurus breviceps PET-or-uhs BREV-ih-seps

Petrogale penicillata pet-ROH-gah-lee pen-ih-SIL-lah-tuh

Petromuridae pet-roh-MUR-uh-dee

Petromus typicus PET-roh-muhs TIP-ih-kuhs

Phalanger gymnotis FAH-lan-jer jim-NOH-tis

Phalangeridae fah-lan-JER-uh-dee

Phascogale tapoatafa fas-KOH-gah-lee TAP-oh-uh-TAH-fuh

Phascolarctidae fas-koh-LARK-tuh-dee

Phascolarctos cinereus fas-KOH-lark-tuhs sin-EAR-ee-uhs

Phocidae FOE-suh-dee

Phocoena phocoena FOE-see-nuh FOE-see-nuh

Phocoena spinipinnis FOE-see-nuh SPY-nih-PIN-is

Phocoenidae foe-SEE-nuh-dee

Pholidota foe-lih-DOH-tuh

Phyllostomidae fill-uh-STOH-muh-dee

Physeter macrocephalus FY-se-ter ma-crow-SEFF-uh-luhs

Physeteridae fy-se-TER-uh-dee

Piliocolobus badius fill-ee-oh-KOH-loh-buhs BAD-ee-uhs

Pithecia pithecia pith-EEK-ee-uh pith-EEK-ee-uh

Pitheciidae pith-eek-EYE-uh-dee

Plantanista gangetica plan-TAN-is-tuh gan-JET-ik-uh

Platanistidae plan-tan-IS-tuh-dee

Pongo pygmaeus PON-goh pig-MEE-uhs

Pontoporia blainvillei pon-toh-POR-ee-uh BLAIN-vill-ee-eye

Pontoporiidae PON-toh-por-EYE-uh-dee

Potoroidae pot-uh-ROY-dee

Primates PRY-maytes

Proboscidea proh-BOS-see-uh

Procavia capensis proh-CAVE-ee-uh KAP-en-sis

Procaviidae proh-kave-EYE-uh-dee

Procyon lotor proh-SIGH-on LOH-tor

Procyonidae proh-sigh-ON-uh-dee

Proechimys semispinosus proh-EK-ih-meez sem-ih-SPY-noh-suhs

Propithecus edwardsi proh-PITH-eek-uhs ED-werds-eye

Proteles cristatus PROH-tell-eez KRIS-tah-tuhs

Pseudocheiridae soo-doh-KY-ruh-dee

Pseudocheirus peregrinus soo-doh-KY-ruhs PEHR-eh-GRIN-uhs

Pteronotus parnellii ter-uh-NOH-tuhs PAR-nell-ee-eye

Pteropodidae ter-uh-POD-uh-dee

Pteropus giganteus ter-OH-puhs jy-GAN-tee-uhs

Pteropus mariannus ter-OH-puhs MARE-ih-an-uhs

Pudu pudu POO-doo POO-doo

Puma concolor PYOO-muh CON-kuh-luhr

Puripterus horrens PYOOR-ip-TER-uhs HOR-renz

Pygathrix nemaeus PIG-uh-thriks neh-MEE-uhs

Rangifer tarandus RAN-jih-fer TAR-an-duhs

Rhinoceros unicornis rye-NOS-er-uhs YOO-nih-KORN-is

Rhinocerotidae rye-NOS-er-UH-tuh-dee

Rhinolophidae rye-noh-LOH-fuh-dee

Rhinolophus capensis rye-noh-LOH-fuhs KAP-en-sis

Rhinolophus ferrumequinum rye-noh-LOH-fuhs FEHR-rum-EK-wy-num

Rhinopoma hardwickei rye-noh-POH-muh HARD-wik-eye

Rhinopomatidae rye-noh-poh-MAT-uh-dee

Rhynchocyon cirnei rin-koh-SIGH-on SIR-neye

Rodentia roh-DEN-she-uh

Rousettus aegyptiacus ROO-set-tuhs ee-JIP-tih-kuhs

Saccopteryx bilineata sak-OP -ter-iks BY-lin-EE-ah-tuh

Saguinus oedipus SAG-win-uhs ED-uh-puhs

Saimiri sciureus SAY-meer-eye sigh-OOR-ee-uhs

Sarcophilus laniarius SAR-kuh-FIL-uhs lan-ee-AIR-ee-uhs

Scalopus aquaticus SKA-loh-puhs uh-KWAT-ik-uhs

Scandentia skan-DEN-she-uh

Sciuridae sigh-OOR-uh-dee

Sciurus carolinensis SIGH-oor-uhs kar-uh-LINE-en-sis

Sigmodon hispidus SIG-muh-don HISS-pid-uhs

Sirenia sy-REEN-ee-uh

Solenodon paradoxus so-LEN-uh-don PAR-uh-DOCKS-uhs

Solenodontidae so-len-uh-DON-shuh-dee

Sorex palustris SOR-eks PAL-us-tris

Soricidae sor-IS-uh-dee

Stenella longirostris steh-NELL-uh LAWN-juh-ROS-tris

Suidae SOO-uh-dee

Sus scrofa SOOS SKRO-fuh

Sylvilagus audubonii SILL-vih-LAG-uhs AW-duh-BON-ee-eye

Symphalangus syndactylus SIM-fuh-LAN-guhs sin-DAK-til-uhs

Tachyglossidae TAK-ih-GLOS-suh-dee

Tachyglossus aculeatus TAK-ih-GLOS-suhs ak-YOOL-ee-ah-tuhs

Tadarida brasiliensis ta-DARE-ih-dah bra-ZILL-ee-en-sis

Talpidae TAL-puh-dee

Tamias striatus TAM-ee-uhs stry-AH-tuhs

Tapiridae tay-PUR-uh-dee

Tapirus indicus TAY-pur-uhs IN-dih-kuhs

Tapirus terrestris TAY-pur-uhs TER-rehs-tris

Tarsiidae tar-SIGH-uh-dee

Tarsipedidae tar-sih-PED-uh-dee

Tarsipes rostratus TAR-si-peez ROS-trah-tuhs

Tarsius bancanus TAR-see-uhs BAN-kan-uhs

Tarsius syrichta TAR-see-uhs STRIK-tuh

Tasmacetus shepherdi taz-muh-SEE-tuhs SHEP-erd-eye

Tayassu tajacu TAY-yuh-soo TAY-jah-soo

Tayassuidae tay-yuh-SOO-uh-dee

Tenrec ecaudatus TEN-rek ee-KAW-dah-tuhs

Tenrecidae ten-REK-uh-dee

Thomomys bottae TOM-oh-meez BOTT-ee

Thryonomyidae thry-oh-noh-MY-uh-dee

Thryonomys swinderianus THRY-oh-NOH-meez SWIN-der-
EE-an-uhs

Thylacinidae thy-luh-SEEN-uh-dee

Thylacinus cynocephalus THY-luh-SEEN-uhs sigh-nuh-SEFF-
uh-luhs

Thyroptera tricolor thy-ROP-ter-uh TRY-kuh-luhr
Thyropteridae thy-rop-TER-uh-dee
Tragulidae tray-GOO-luh-dee
Tragulus javanicus TRAY-goo-luhs jah-VAHN-ih-kuhs
Trichechidae trik-EK-uh-dee
Trichechus manatus TRIK-ek-uhs MAN-uh-tuhs
Trichosurus vulpecula TRIK-uh-SOOR-uhs vul-PEK-yoo-luh
Tubulidentata toob-yool-ih-DEN-tah-tuh
Tupaia glis too-PUH-ee-uh GLIS
Tupaiidae too-puh-EYE-uh-dee
Tursiops truncatus tur-SEE-ops TRUN-kah-tuhs
Uncia uncia UN-see-uh UN-see-uh
Ursidae UR-suh-dee
Ursus americanus UR-suhs uh-mer-uh-KAN-uhs
Ursus maritimus UR-suhs mar-ih-TIME-uhs
Vespertilionidae ves-puhr-TEEL-ee-UHN-uh-dee
Viverridae vy-VER-ruh-dee
Vombatidae vom-BAT-uh-dee
Vombatus ursinus VOM-bat-uhs ur-SIGH-nuhs
Vulpes vulpes VUHL-peez VUHL-peez
Xenarthra ZEN-areth-ruh
Yerbua capensis YER-byoo-uh KAP-en-sis
Zalophus californianus ZA-loh-fuhs kal-uh-FORN-uh-kuhs
Zalophus wollebaeki ZA-loh-fuhs VOLL-back-eye
Ziphiidae ziff-EYE-uh-dee

Words to Know

A

Aborigine: Earliest-known inhabitant of an area; often referring to a native person of Australia.

Adaptation: Any structural, physiological, or behavioral trait that aids an organism's survival and ability to reproduce in its existing environment.

Algae: Tiny plants or plantlike organisms that grow in water and in damp places.

Anaconda: A large snake of South America; one of the largest snakes in the world.

Aphrodisiac: Anything that intensifies or arouses sexual desires.

Aquatic: Living in the water.

Arboreal: Living primarily or entirely in trees and bushes.

Arid: Extremely dry climate, with less than 10 inches (25 centimeters) of rain each year.

Arthropod: A member of the largest single animal phylum, consisting of organisms with segmented bodies, jointed legs or wings, and exoskeletons.

B

Baleen: A flexible, horny substance making up two rows of plates that hang from the upper jaws of baleen whales.

Biogeography: The study of the distribution and dispersal of plants and animals throughout the world.

Bipedal: Walking on two feet.

Blowhole: The nostril on a whale, dolphin, or porpoise.

Blubber: A layer of fat under the skin of sea mammals that protects them from heat loss and stores energy.

Brachiation: A type of locomotion in which an animal travels through the forest by swinging below branches using its arms.

Brackish water: Water that is a mix of freshwater and saltwater.

Burrow: Tunnel or hole that an animal digs in the ground to use as a home.

C

Cache: A hidden supply area.

Camouflage: Device used by an animal, such as coloration, allowing it to blend in with the surroundings to avoid being seen by prey and predators.

Canine teeth: The four pointed teeth (two in each jaw) between the incisors and bicuspids in mammals; designed for stabbing and holding prey.

Canopy: The uppermost layer of a forest formed naturally by the leaves and branches of trees and plants.

Carnivore: Meat-eating organism.

Carrion: Dead and decaying animal flesh.

Cecum: A specialized part of the large intestine that acts as a fermentation chamber to aid in digestion of grasses.

Cervical vertebrae: The seven neck bones that make up the top of the spinal column.

Clan: A group of animals of the same species that live together, such as badgers or hyenas.

Cloud forest: A tropical forest where clouds are overhead most of the year.

Colony: A group of animals of the same type living together.

Coniferous: Refers to evergreen trees, such as pines and firs, that bear cones and have needle-like leaves that are not shed all at once.

Coniferous forest: An evergreen forest where plants stay green all year.

Continental shelf: A gently sloping ledge of a continent that is submerged in the ocean.

Convergence: In adaptive evolution, a process by which unrelated or only distantly related living things come to resemble one another in adapting to similar environments.

Coprophagous: Eating dung. Some animals do this to extract nutrients that have passed through their system.

Crepuscular: Most active at dawn and dusk.

Critically Endangered: A term used by the IUCN in reference to a species that is at an extremely high risk of extinction in the wild.

D

Data Deficient: An IUCN category referring to a species that is not assigned another category because there is not enough information about the species' population.

Deciduous: Shedding leaves at the end of the growing season.

Deciduous forest: A forest with four seasons in which trees drop their leaves in the fall.

Deforestation: Those practices or processes that result in the change of forested lands to non-forest uses, such as human settlement or farming. This is often cited as one of the major causes of the enhanced greenhouse effect.

Delayed implantation: A process by which the fertilized egg formed after mating develops for a short time, then remains inactive until later when it attaches to the uterus for further development, so that birth coincides with a better food supply or environmental conditions.

Den: The shelter of an animal, such as an underground hole or a hollow log.

Dentin: A calcareous material harder than bone found in teeth.

Desert: A land area so dry that little or no plant or animal life can survive.

Digit: Division where limbs terminate; in humans this refers to a finger or toe.

Digitigrade: A manner of walking on the toes, as cats and dogs do, as opposed to walking on the ball of the feet, as humans do.

Dingo: A wild Australian dog.

Diurnal: Refers to animals that are active during the day.

Domesticated: Tamed.

Dominant: The top male or female of a social group, sometimes called the alpha male or alpha female.

Dorsal: Located in the back.

Dung: Feces, or solid waste from an animal.

E

Echolocation: A method of detecting objects by using sound waves.

Ecotourist: A person who visits a place in order to observe the plants and animals in the area while making minimal human impact on the natural environment.

Electroreception: The sensory detection of small amounts of natural electricity by an animal (usually underwater), by means of specialized nerve endings.

Elevation: The height of land when measured from sea level.

Endangered: A term used by the U. S. Endangered Species Act of 1973 and by the IUCN in reference to a species that is facing a very high risk of extinction from all or a significant portion of its natural home.

Endangered Species Act: A U. S. law that grants legal protection to listed endangered and threatened species.

Endemic: Native to or occurring only in a particular place.

Erupt: In teeth, to break through the skin and become visible.

Estivation: State of inactivity during the hot, dry months of summer.

Estuary: Lower end of a river where ocean tides meet the river's current.

Eutherian mammal: Mammals that have a well-developed placenta and give birth to fully formed live young.

Evergreen: In botany, bearing green leaves through the winter and/or a plant having foliage that persists throughout the year.

Evolve: To change slowly over time.

Extinct: A species without living members.

Extinction: The total disappearance of a species or the disappearance of a species from a given area.

F

Family: A grouping of genera that share certain characteristics and appear to have evolved from the same ancestors.

Feces: Solid body waste.

Fermentation: Chemical reaction in which enzymes break down complex organic compounds into simpler ones. This can make digestion easier.

Forage: To search for food.

Forb: Any broad-leaved herbaceous plant that is not a grass; one that grows in a prairie or meadow, such as sunflower, goldenrod, or clover.

Fragment: To divide or separate individuals of the same species into small groups that are unable to mingle with each other.

Frugivore: Animal that primarily eats fruit. Many bats and birds are frugivores.

Fuse: To become joined together as one unit.

G

Genera: Plural of genus.

Genus (pl. genera): A category of classification made up of species sharing similar characteristics.

Gestation: The period of carrying young in the uterus before birth.

Gland: A specialized body part that produces, holds, and releases one or more substances (such as scent or sweat) for use by the body.

Gleaning: Gathering food from surfaces.

Grassland: Region in which the climate is dry for long periods of the summer, and freezes in the winter. Grasslands are characterized by grasses and other erect herbs, usually without trees or shrubs, and occur in the dry temperate interiors of continents.

Grooming: An activity during which primates look through each other's fur to remove parasites and dirt.

Guano: The droppings of birds or bats, sometimes used as fertilizer.

Guard hairs: Long, stiff, waterproof hairs that form the outer fur and protect the underfur of certain mammals.

Gum: A substance found in some plants that oozes out in response to a puncture, as plant sap, and generally hardens after exposure to air.

H

Habitat: The area or region where a particular type of plant or animal lives and grows.

Habitat degradation: The diminishment of the quality of a habitat and its ability to support animal and plant communities.

Hallux: The big toe, or first digit, on the part of the foot facing inwards.

Harem: A group of two or more adult females, plus their young, with only one adult male present.

Haul out: To pull one's body out of the water onto land, as when seals come out of the water to go ashore.

Herbivore: Plant-eating organism.

Hibernation: State of rest or inactivity during the cold winter months.

Hierarchy: A structured order of rank or social superiority.

Home range: A specific area that an animal roams while performing its activities.

I

Ice floe: A large sheet of floating ice.

Incisor: One of the chisel-shaped teeth at the front of the mouth (between the canines), used for cutting and tearing food.

Indigenous: Originating in a region or country.

Insectivore: An animal that eats primarily insects.

Insulate: To prevent the escape of heat by surrounding with something; in an animal, a substance such as fur or body fat serves to retain heat in its body.

Invertebrate: Animal lacking a spinal column (backbone).

IUCN: Abbreviation for the International Union for Conservation of Nature and Natural Resources, now the World Conservation Union. A conservation organization of government agencies and nongovernmental organizations best known for its Red Lists of threatened and endangered species.

K

Keratin: Protein found in hair, nails, and skin.

Krill: Tiny shrimp-like animals that are the main food of baleen whales and are also eaten by seals and other marine mammals.

L

Lactate: To produce milk in the female body, an activity associated with mammals.

Larva (pl. larvae): Immature form (wormlike in insects; fishlike in amphibians) of an organism capable of surviving on its own. A larva does not resemble the parent and must go through metamorphosis, or change, to reach its adult stage.

Leprosy: A disease of the skin and flesh characterized by scaly scabs and open sores.

Lichen: A complex of algae and fungi found growing on trees, rocks, or other solid surfaces.

Litter: A group of young animals, such as pigs or kittens, born at the same time from the same mother. Or, a layer of dead vegetation and other material covering the ground.

M

Malaria: A serious disease common in tropical countries, spread by the bites of female mosquitoes, that causes complications affecting the brain, blood, liver, and kidneys and can cause death.

Mammae: Milk-secreting organs of female mammals used to nurse young.

Mammals: Animals that feed their young on breast milk, are warm-blooded, and breathe air through their lungs.

Mangrove: Tropical coastal trees or shrubs that produce many supporting roots and that provide dense vegetation.

Marsupial: A type of mammal that does not have a well-developed placenta and gives birth to immature and underdeveloped young after a short gestation period. It continues to nurture the young, often in a pouch, until they are able to fend for themselves.

Matriarchal: Headed by a dominant female or females; said of animal societies.

Mechanoreceptor: Sensory nerve receptor modified to detect physical changes in the immediate environment, often having to do with touch and change of pressure or turbulence in water or air. In the platypus, mechanoreceptors in its bill may detect prey and obstacles.

Megachiroptera: One of the two groups of bats; these bats are usually larger than the microchiroptera.

Melon: The fatty forehead of a whale or dolphin.

Membrane: A thin, flexible layer of plant or animal tissue that covers, lines, separates or holds together, or connects parts of an organism.

Microchiroptera: One of two categories of bats; these make up most of the bats in the world and are generally smaller than the megachiroptera.

Migrate: To move from one area or climate to another as the seasons change, usually to find food or to mate.

Migratory pattern: The direction or path taken while moving seasonally from one region to another.

Molar: A broad tooth located near the back of the jaw with a flat, rough surface for grinding.

Mollusk: A group of animals without backbones that includes snails, clams, oysters, and similar hard-shelled animals.

Molt: The process by which an organism sheds its outermost layer of feathers, fur, skin, or exoskeleton.

Monogamous: Refers to a breeding system in which a male and a female mate only with each other during a breeding season or lifetime.

Muzzle: The projecting part of the head that includes jaws, chin, mouth, and nose.

Myxomatosis: A highly infectious disease of rabbits caused by a pox virus.

N

Near Threatened: A category defined by the IUCN suggesting that a species could become threatened with extinction in the future.

Nectar: Sweet liquid secreted by the flowers of various plants to attract pollinators (animals that pollinate, or fertilize, the flowers).

Neotropical: Relating to a geographic area of plant and animal life east, south, and west of Mexico's central plateau that includes Central and South America and the West Indies.

New World: Made up of North America, Central America, and South America; the western half of the world.

Nocturnal: Occurring or active at night.

Non-prehensile: Incapable of grasping; used to describe an animal's tail that cannot wrap around tree branches.

Noseleaf: Horseshoe-shaped flap of skin around the nose.

Nurse: To feed on mother's milk.

O

Old World: Australia, Africa, Asia, and Europe; in the eastern half of the world.

Omnivore: Plant- and meat-eating animal.

Opportunistic feeder: An animal that eats whatever food is available, either prey they have killed, other animals' kills, plants, or human food and garbage.

P

Pack ice: Large pieces of ice frozen together.

Patagium: The flap of skin that extends between the front and hind limbs. In bats, it stretches between the hind legs and helps the animal in flight; in colugos this stretches from the side of the neck to the tips of its fingers, toes, and tail.

Phylogenetics: Field of biology that deals with the relationships between organisms. It includes the discovery of these relationships, and the study of the causes behind this pattern.

Pinnipeds: Marine mammals, including three families of the order Carnivora, namely Otariidae (sea lions and fur seals), Phocidae (true seals), and Odobenidae (walrus).

Placenta: An organ that grows in the mother's uterus and lets the mother and developing offspring share food and oxygen through the blood.

Placental mammal: Any species of mammal that carries embryonic and fetal young in the womb through a long gestation period, made possible via the placenta, a filtering organ passing nutrients, wastes, and gases between mother and young.

Plantigrade: Walking on the heel and sole of the foot, instead of on the toes. Plantigrade species include bears and humans.

Plate tectonics: Geological theory holding that Earth's surface is composed of rigid plates or sections that move about the surface in response to internal pressure, creating the major geographical features such as mountains.

Poach: To hunt animals illegally.

Pod: In animal behavioral science (and in some zoology uses) the term pod is used to represent a group of whales, seals, or dolphins.

Pollen: Dust-like grains or particles produced by a plant that contain male sex cells.

Pollination: Transfer of pollen from the male reproductive organs to the female reproductive organs of plants.

Pollinator: Animal which carries pollen from one seed plant to another, unwittingly aiding the plant in its reproduction. Common pollinators include insects, especially bees, butterflies, and moths; birds; and bats.

Polyandry: A mating system in which a single female mates with multiple males.

Polyestrous: A female animal having more than one estrous cycle (mating period) within a year.

Polygamy: A mating system in which males and females mate with multiple partners.

Polygyny: A mating system in which a single male mates with multiple females.

Predator: An animal that eats other animals.

Prehensile: Able to control and use to grasp objects, characteristically associated with tails. Prehensile tails have evolved independently many times, for instance, in marsupials, rodents, primates, porcupines, and chameleons.

Prey: Organism hunted and eaten by a predator.

Primary forest: A forest characterized by a full-ceiling canopy formed by the branches of tall trees and several layers of smaller trees. This type of forest lacks ground vegetation because sunlight cannot penetrate through the canopy.

Promiscuity: Mating in which individuals mate with as many other individuals as they can or want to.

Puberty: The age of sexual maturity.

Q

Quadruped: Walking or running on four limbs.

R

Rabies: A viral infection spread through the bite of certain warm-blooded animals; it attacks the nervous system and can be fatal if untreated.

Rainforest: An evergreen woodland of the tropics distinguished by a continuous leaf canopy and an average rainfall of about 100 inches (250 centimeters) per year.

Regurgitate: Eject the contents of the stomach through the mouth; to vomit.

Rookery: A site on land where seals congregate to mate and raise the young.

Roost: A place where animals, such as bats, sit or rest on a perch, branch, etc.

S

Savanna: A biome characterized by an extensive cover of grasses with scattered trees, usually transitioning between areas dominated by forests and those dominated by grasses and having alternating seasonal climates of precipitation and drought.

Scavenger: An animal that eats carrion, dead animals.

Scent gland: Formed from modified, or changed, sweat glands, these glands produce and/or give off strong-smelling chemicals that give information, such as marking territory, to other animals.

Scent mark: To leave an odor, such as of urine or scent gland secretions, to mark a territory or as a means of communication.

Scrotum: The external pouch containing the testicles.

Scrub forest: A forest with short trees and shrubs.

Scrubland: An area similar to grassland but which includes scrub (low-growing plants and trees) vegetation.

Seamount: An underwater mountain that does not rise above the surface of the ocean.

Seashore: When referring to a biome, formed where the land meets the ocean.

Secondary forest: A forest characterized by a less-developed canopy, smaller trees, and a dense ground vegetation found on the edges of forests and along rivers and streams. The immature vegetation may also result from the removal of trees by logging and/or fires.

Semiaquatic: Partially aquatic; living or growing partly on land and partly in water.

Semiarid: Very little rainfall each year, between 10 and 20 inches (25 to 51 centimeters).

Sexually mature: Capable of reproducing.

Solitary: Living alone or avoiding the company of others.

Species: A group of living things that share certain distinctive characteristics and can breed together in the wild.

Spermaceti: A waxy substance found in the head cavity of some whales.

Steppe: Wide expanse of semiarid relatively level plains, found in cool climates and characterized by shrubs, grasses, and few trees.

Streamline: To smooth out.

Succulent: A plant that has fleshy leaves to conserve moisture.

Suckle: To nurse or suck on a mother's nipple to get milk.

Syndactyly: A condition in which two bones (or digits) fuse together to become a single bone.

T

Tactile: Having to do with the sense of touch.

Talon: A sharp hooked claw.

Taxonomy: The science dealing with the identification, naming, and classification of plants and animals.

Teat: A projection through which milk passes from the mother to the nursing young; a nipple.

Temperate: Areas with moderate temperatures in which the climate undergoes seasonal change in temperature and moisture. Temperate regions of the earth lie primarily between 30 and 60° latitude in both hemispheres.

Terrestrial: Relating to the land or living primarily on land.

Territorial: A pattern of behavior that causes an animal to stay in a limited area and/or to keep certain other animals of the same species (other than its mate, herd, or family group) out of the area.

Thicket: An area represented by a thick, or dense, growth of shrubs, underbrush, or small trees.

Threatened: Describes a species that is threatened with extinction.

Torpor: A short period of inactivity characterized by an energy-saving, deep sleep-like state in which heart rate, respiratory rate and body temperature drop.

Traction: Resistance to a surface to keep from slipping.

Tragus: A flap of skin near the base of the external ear.

Tributary: A small stream that feeds into a larger one.

Tropical: The area between 23.5° north and south of the equator. This region has small daily and seasonal changes in temperature, but great seasonal changes in precipitation. Generally, a hot and humid climate that is completely or almost free of frost.

Tundra: A type of ecosystem dominated by lichens, mosses, grasses, and woody plants. It is found at high latitudes (arctic tundra) and high altitudes (alpine tundra). Arctic tundra is underlain by permafrost and usually very wet.

Turbulent: An irregular, disorderly mode of flow.

U

Underfur: Thick soft fur lying beneath the longer and coarser guard hair.

Understory: The trees and shrubs between the forest canopy and the ground cover.

Ungulates: Hoofed animals, such as deer and elk.

Urine washing: A monkey behavior in which it soaks its hands with urine, then rubs the liquid on its fur and feet so as to leave the scent throughout its forest routes.

Uterus: A pear-shaped, hollow muscular organ in which a fetus develops during pregnancy.

V

Vertebra (pl. vertebrae): A component of the vertebral column, or backbone, found in vertebrates.

Vertebrate: An animal having a spinal column (backbone).

Vertical: Being at a right angle to the horizon. Up and down movements or supports.

Vestigial: A degenerate or imperfectly developed biological structure that once performed a useful function at an earlier stage of the evolution of the species.

Vibrissae: Stiff sensory hairs that can be found near the nostrils or other parts of the face in many mammals and the snouts, tails, ears, and sometimes feet of many insectivores.

Vocalization: Sound made by vibration of the vocal tract.

Vulnerable: An IUCN category referring to a species that faces a high risk of extinction.

W

Wallaby: An Australian marsupial similar to a kangaroo but smaller.

Wean: When a young animal no longer feeds on its mother's milk and instead begins to eat adult food.

Wetlands: Areas that are wet or covered with water for at least part of the year and support aquatic plants, such as marshes, swamps, and bogs.

Woodlands: An area with a lot of trees and shrubs.

Y

Yolk-sac placenta: A thin membrane that develops in the uterus of marsupials that does not fuse with the mother's uterus and results in short pregnancies with the young being born with poorly developed organs.

Getting to Know Mammals

MAMMALS

Mammals are found on all continents and in all seas. It isn't easy to tell that an animal is a mammal. A combination of special features separates mammals from other animals.

Mammal milk

Only mammals can feed their young with milk produced by their body. This milk comes from special glands called mammae. A female may have two mammary glands or as many as a dozen or more. Mammal milk is very healthy for infants and immediately available.

Body temperature

Mammals are warm-blooded, meaning they keep a constant body temperature. To keep their temperature fairly constant, a mammal needs some protective covering. Hair, made of a protein called keratin, serves several functions. One function is insulation, controlling the amount of body heat that escapes into the mammal's environment through the skin.

Mammal hair

All mammals have hair at some time of their life. Some have a lot, such as gorillas, and some have very little, such as the naked mole rats. There are three types of hair: a coarse long topcoat, a fine undercoat, and special sensory hairs, or whiskers.

In some mammals, hair has unusual forms. Porcupines have stiff, sharp, and thickened hairs called quills. Anteaters have

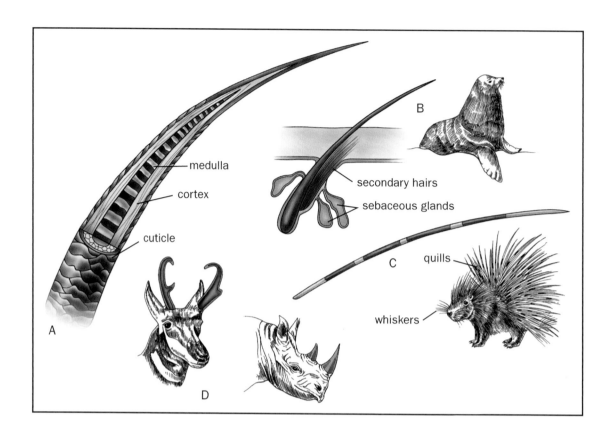

sharp-edged scales made of modified hairs. These modified, or changed, hairs are protective against predators.

Mammals that live all or most of their lives in water, such as sea otters, may have a lot of dense, long hair, or fur. Others have much less hair, but a very thick hide, or skin, plus a thick layer of fat or blubber underneath the hide.

Hair color and pattern may vary. Males and females may have different fur colors. Special color patterns, such as a skunk's black and white fur, act as warnings. Hair color can also serve as camouflage, enabling the mammal to blend into its background.

Some mammals have fur color changes in summer and winter. Colors can be entirely different. Snowshoe rabbits and weasels can be brownish in summer, and almost pure white in winter. But this only happens if there is snow where they live. If it seldom snows, weasels and snowshoe rabbits stay brown.

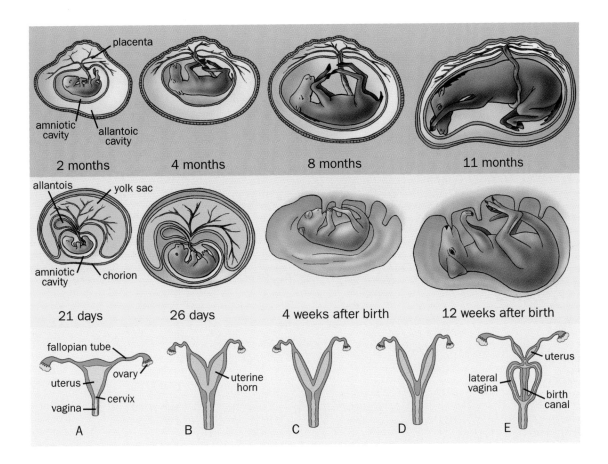

Top: Placental mammal development. Middle row: Marsupial mammal development. Types of uterus: A. Simplex; B. Bipartite; C. Bicornuate; D. Duplex; E. Marsupial. (Illustration by Patricia Ferrer. Reproduced by permission.)

Reproduction

Mammals have two genetic sexes, male and female. Ninety percent of mammals are placental (pluh-SENT-ul). In placental mammals, the baby develops, or grows, within the mother's body before it enters the world. What about the other 10 percent? These mammals lay eggs. There are only three egg-laying mammals alive today.:

Other mammal features

Other bodily mammal features include their ability to breathe air through their lungs. Water-dwelling mammals, such as the whale and porpoise, do this too. Mammals have jaws, usually with teeth. Mammals usually have four limbs. Mammals have a four-chambered heart. Mammals have vertebrae, or back bones, unlike invertebrates such as insects, in which there is an outside shell or structure called an exoskeleton.

This life-sized woolly mammoth model is kept in the Royal British Columbia Museum. Woolly mammoths were as tall as 10 feet (3 meters). (© Jonathan Blair/Corbis. Reproduced by permission.)

FOSSIL MAMMALS

Fossils are body parts of animals that lived very long ago. Not many long-ago mammals are preserved as fossils. But some entire mammal fossils have been discovered, such as a 10-foot (3-meter) woolly mammoth preserved in Siberian frozen ground, and an Ice Age woolly rhinoceros discovered in Poland, preserved in asphalt.

Many long-ago mammals lived in a warm, wet world. They ate soft, leafy plants. The earliest known mammals were possibly shrew-like creatures living about 190 million years ago. Later larger mammals occurred, then disappeared, or became extinct. These include the mesohippus, a three-toed horse only 24 inches (60 centimeters) high; a giant pig with a head that was 4 feet (1.22 meters) in length; and the smilodon, a huge saber-toothed cat with canine teeth that were 8 inches (20.3

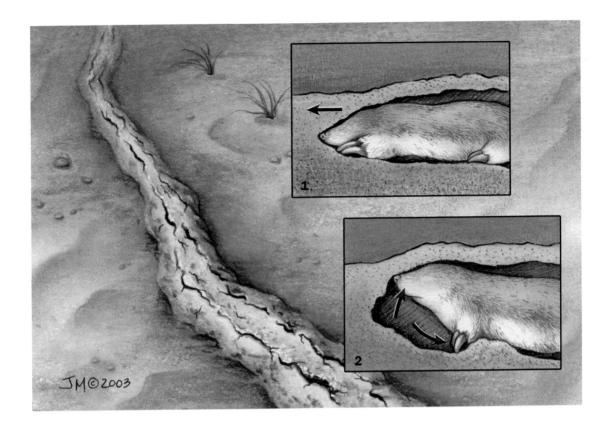

centimeters) in length. By about 15,000 years ago, long-ago people were hunting mammals with stone-pointed spears. Most of the animals they hunted are extinct for various reasons, some known, and some unknown.

WHERE MAMMALS LIVE

Underground mammals

Some small mammals spend all or most of their lives living underground. These include many species of prairie dogs, chipmunks, moles, groundhogs, Greenland collared lemmings, and Peruvian tuco-tucos. Each of these mammals has a special body design enabling it to survive underground.

Moles have large, powerful shoulders and short, very powerful forelimbs. Spade-like feet have claws, enabling quick digging. Hind feet have webbed toes, enabling the mole to kick soil backwards effectively. Velvety-type fur enables a mole to slip easily through its tunnels. And, although moles

The Grant's desert mole uses its powerful forelimbs to burrow through the sands of the Namib Desert in southern Africa. The golden mole moves forward (1), and enlarges the tunnel by pushing dirt up with its head and back with its claws (2). (Illustration by Jacqueline Mahannah. Reproduced by permission.)

A RECENT DISCOVERY

A bright orange, mouse-like mammal, weighing 0.5 ounces (15 grams) and measuring 3.12 inches (8 centimeters) plus a long tail, has recently been discovered in the Philippines. It has whiskers five times longer than its head. It can open and eat very hard tree nuts that no other mammal in the area can eat.

have almost no eyes, they can rely on touch, smell, and sensitivity to vibration to find underground insects and earthworms.

Sea mammals

Some mammals live in the sea, including manatees, whales, seals, and dolphins. While some need air every few minutes, a sperm whale can remain underwater for an hour and a half. How is this possible? Some sea mammals have a very low metabolism. They don't use up the their oxygen quickly and can store large amounts of oxygen in their bodies.

Tree mammals

Some mammals spend all or most of their lives in trees. Tree-dwelling mammals are often hidden from sight by leaves, vines, and branches. Tree-dwelling mammals include the Eastern pygmy possum, which nests in small tree hollows; the koala; Lumholtz's tree kangaroo, which leaps from branch to branch; the three-toed sloth; and the clouded leopard.

Flying mammals

The only truly flying mammals are bats. The sound of bat wings was first heard about 50 million years ago. Some bats are large, with a wingspan almost 7 feet (21.3 meters) wide. Some are small, as the Philippine bamboo bat, whose body is just 2 inches (5.08 centimeters) long.

Other mammals only appear to fly, such as the southern flying squirrel and the colugo, or Malayan flying lemur. These mammals have gliding membranes, skin folds from body front to legs, that, when spread out, act almost like a parachute. For example, the feathertail glider, a tiny possum, crawls along narrow branches. At branch end, it leaps out and slightly downward. Spreading its gliding membranes, it speeds through the air, landing on a nearby tree.

Mountain mammals

Some mammals spend most of their lives on mountain peaks. These include Asian corkscrew-horned markhor goats, North

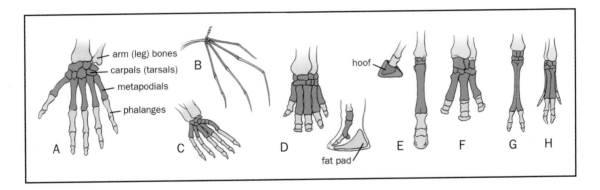

American Rocky Mountain bighorn sheep, and Siberian ibex. Siberian ibex can stand anyplace on any pinnacle with just enough room for its four feet. North American mountain goats can climb up a mountain peak, almost going straight up. Specially shaped hooves help.

Other high mountain dwelling mammals include snow leopards and Asian pikas that can survive at 19,685 feet (6,000 meters). Gunnison's prairie dogs do well up to 11,500 feet (3,505 meters).

Desert mammals

Some mammals spend most of their lives in arid, or very dry areas. Not all deserts are sandy like Death Valley or the Sahara. Some are rocky. Other arid areas are mountainous. Desert dwelling mammals include the North African elephant shrew, white-tailed antelope squirrel, and the desert kangaroo rat. No mammal can live without water. Desert rodents have a way to extract, or get, water from their own body functions. Rodents may also get water by eating plants, seeds, roots, and insects that contain water.

Larger mammals live in arid regions too. The striped hyena can survive in stony desert as long as it is within 6 miles (9.7 kilometers) of water. Fennecs, a very small fox living near sand dunes, can go a long time without drinking. Camels can use body fluids when no water is available.

WHAT DO MAMMALS EAT?

Insect-eaters

Some mammals have mostly insect meals. Insect-eating mammals include the moles, aye-ayes and aardvarks. The aardvark

Mammals' hands and feet differ depending on where the animal lives and how it gets around. A. A hominid hand is used for grasping objects; B. A bat's wing is used for flight; C. A pinniped's flipper helps move it through the water. Hoofed animals move around on all fours: D. Elephant foot; E. Equid (horse family) foot; F. Odd-toed hoofed foot; G. Two-toed hoofed foot; H. Four-toed hoofed foot. (Illustration by Patricia Ferrer. Reproduced by permission.)

has a sticky tongue that can reach out as long as 1 foot (0.3 meters) to capture its ant and termite meals.

Plant eaters

Some mammals eat nothing but plants. Plant eaters include pandas, the West Indian manatee, and the red-bellied wallaby. Some mammals have a single stomach that breaks the plant food down into small pieces. Other mammals, such as cows and camels, have a large stomach made of several parts. Each part does a separate job of breaking down difficult-to-digest plants.

Some mammals eat both plants and fruit. These include the 14-ounce (400-gram) Eurasian harvest mouse, the 100-pound (45-kilogram) South American capybara, and the African elephant. An elephant can eat up to 500 pounds (227 kilograms) of grass, plants, and fruit per day.

Meat eaters

Mammals eating mostly meat or fish are carnivorous. Carnivorous mammals have long, pointed, and very strong incisor teeth. Carnivores include polar bears, hyenas, walruses, and Eu-

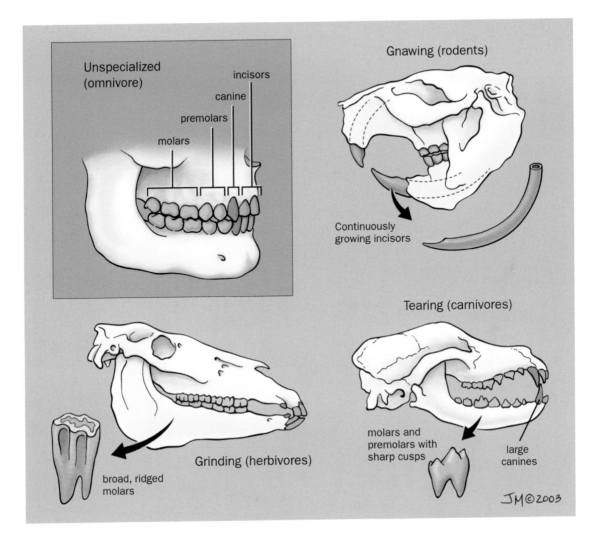

Unspecialized (omnivore)

incisors
canine
premolars
molars

Gnawing (rodents)

Continuously growing incisors

Tearing (carnivores)

molars and premolars with sharp cusps

large canines

Grinding (herbivores)

broad, ridged molars

JM©2003

ropean wild cats. The European wild cat may be an ancestor of our house cats.

Omnivores

Some mammals eat just about anything. They are omnivorous. Omnivorous mammals include wolverines, raccoons, and wild pigs. Wild pigs are the ancestors of our domestic pigs.

MAMMAL SLEEPING HABITS

Day or night

Some mammals sleep during the night, others sleep during the day. The night sleepers are diurnal, active during the day.

Mammals have different tooth shapes for different functions. Herbivores typically have large, flattened teeth for chewing plants. Rodents' ever-growing incisors are used for gnawing. Carnivores have teeth for holding and efficiently dismembering their prey. (Illustration by Jacqueline Mahannah. Reproduced by permission.)

THE BIGGEST, THE TALLEST, AND THE SMALLEST

The largest and heaviest mammal alive today is the blue whale. One adult female measured 110.2 feet (33.6 meters). Blue whale weight can reach 268,400 pounds (121,853 kilograms).

The largest living land animal is the African bush elephant. From trunk tip to tail tip, a male has measured 33 feet (10 meters). Body weight was 24,000 pounds (10,886 kilograms).

The smallest non-flying mammal is the Savi's white-toothed pygmy shrew. An adult's head and body together measure only 2 inches (5.1 centimeters) long. Maximum weight is 0.09 ounces (2.5 grams).

How small is this? This pygmy shrew can travel through tunnels left by large earthworms!

The smallest flying mammal is the rare Kitti's hog-nosed bat, or "bumblebee bat," from Thailand. Head and body length is just 1.14 to 1.29 inches (29 to 33 millimeters). Weight is just 0.06 to 0.07 ounces (1.75 to 2 grams). This tiny bat was only discovered in 1973.

The tallest living animal is the giraffe. The average adult male, or bull, is 16 feet (4.9 meters) high, from front hoof to head horn tip. This size male weighs 2,376 to 2,800 pounds (1,078 to 1,270 kilograms).

The day sleepers are nocturnal, active at night. They may have special night vision. Many desert animals are nocturnal, moving about when it is cooler.

Hibernation

Some bat species hibernate through an entire winter. Hibernation is like a very long deep sleep. When a mammal hibernates, it uses up body fat that has accumulated from food eaten in good weather. Hibernators include the North African jird, groundhogs or woodchucks, and several dormice species. Dormice enter a tree hollow or ground burrow in autumn, and don't come out until springtime.

Bears don't truly hibernate. Their sleep isn't deep. They slow down quite a bit, and nap a lot, but do not sleep through an entire winter.

A new hibernating pattern has just been discovered. Madagascar fat-tailed lemurs hibernate in tree holes when winter daytime temperatures rise above 86° Fahrenheit (30° Celsius). They sleep for seven months. Scientists belief these dwarf lemurs find less food in what is the dry season in Madagascar, so they go to into deep sleep to preserve energy until a better food supply appears.

REPRODUCTION

Mating

Some mammals mate for life, such as wolves and sometimes coyotes. More commonly, a male may mate with several females each breeding period. Or a female may mate with several males.

Some mammals have one litter each year. Others have a litter only every two or three years. But the North American meadow mouse can have seventeen litters per year. That's a group of babies about every three weeks!

There may be one or more infants in a litter. Bats, giraffes, and two-toed sloths have just one baby per year. However, the Madagascar tenrec can produce thirty-two babies in just one litter.

Opossums are marsupial animals. The mother has a pouch in which the young continue to develop after they're born. (© Mary Ann McDonald/Corbis. Reproduced by permission.)

Child care

All mammal infants need protection. They are very small compared to their parents. They may be blind and hairless. Usually females provide care. However, in a few mammal species, such as the golden lion marmoset, the male does most of the care.

Female marsupial mammals, such as opossums, koalas, and kangaroos, have a pouch, like a pocket, on the front or under the body. Their tiny babies are incompletely developed when they are born. At birth, an opossum baby is about the size of a dime. It crawls immediately into its mother's pouch and stays there until ready to survive outside. The pouch contains mammary glands so babies can feed.

SOCIAL LIFE

Solitary mammals

Some mammals are solitary. They keep company with another of the same kind only when mating or when raising young. Solitary mammals include the giant anteaters, European bison, and right whales.

Japanese macaques are social animals, and groom each other regularly. (© Herbert Kehrer/OKAPIA/Photo Researchers, Inc. Reproduced by permission.)

Group living

Many mammals live in groups. In large groups, some eat, some rest, and some keep guard. Baboons, for example, may have from twenty to 300 animals in a group. One or more adult males lead each group. If a predator, such as a leopard, approaches, the males take action against it, while the females and young escape.

Some mammals travel in herds. Musk oxen travel in closely packed herds of fifteen to 100 individuals. These herds include males and females. Bighorn sheep females travel in herds of five to fifteen, with a dominant ewe, or female, as the leader.

Pack mammals get their food by cooperation. They work together to bring down much larger prey. Dingoes, killer whales, and lions hunt in packs.

MAMMALS AND PEOPLE

Domesticated mammals

About 14,000 years ago, humans began controlling, or domesticating, certain animals. This made humans' lives easier.

Horses have been domesticated for practical uses, such as transportation, and for entertainment, such as horse riding and racing. (© Kevin R. Morris/Corbis. Reproduced by permission.)

The earliest domesticated mammal was probably the dog. Some scientists think hunters adopted wolf cubs and trained them to smell out game, animals they hunted for food.

People use mammals for many purposes. Cows provide meat, milk, cheese, butter, and hide. Camels, yaks, and Indian elephants carry or pull heavy items. Water buffaloes do hauling and can provide milk. Horses provide transportation and racing activities. Other domesticated animals include rabbits, pigs, goats, sheep, cavies, and capybaras.

People keep animals as pets. Common mammal pets are dogs, cats, guinea pigs, and hamsters.

Pest mammals

Some mammals are considered pests. These include rats, mice, and, depending where they live, gophers, rabbits, and ground squirrels. Rats can transmit disease-carrying fleas. Rabbits and gophers eat garden and food plants.

ENDANGERED MAMMALS

Mammals in danger

Of about 5,000 mammal species currently existing, over 1,000 are seriously endangered. Few wild mammals can live outside their natural habitat. When land is cleared for farming or housing, animals making homes there must leave, if there is any place for them to go. If not, they die from starvation or (because they are easily seen) from predators. Slowly, or quickly, the mammal species disappears.

Many human habits lead to endangerment. Hunting for amusement, killing for fur or body parts, native and commercial killing for food, fishing gear entrapment, land-destructive wars, and the illegal pet trade all take their toll. So do chemicals.

Some mammals are probably on the way to extinction, or total elimination. There are only about sixty Java rhinoceros left in the world. The Seychelles sheath-tailed bat has only about fifty individuals remaining. Yellow-tailed woolly monkeys number no more than 250 individuals. Mediterranean monk seals may be killed by scuba divers, and number only 600 individuals.

Saving endangered animals

Today many people are trying to save endangered animals. Methods include zoo breeding, establishing forest reserves, and training native populations that animals can be an economic benefit. Ecotourism, people visiting a country to see its animals in their natural habitat, is increasing. There are laws against importing and exporting endangered species. And, in some parts of the world, there are laws against land destruction.

Some mammals have possibly been rescued from immediate extinction. The American bison once roamed the North American prairies, numbering about 50 million. After slaughter by soldiers and settlers for food and sport, by 1889 only 541 remained alive. Now, in the United States, there are about 35,000 in protected areas. California northern elephant seals were once reduced to fewer than 100 members due to hunting. Today, protected, there are about 50,000. The ibex was once hunted for supposedly curative body parts and few were left. But in 1922, a National Park was established in the Italian Alps, where several thousand now live. The Mongolian wild horse, once thought to be extinct, now has a special reserve in Mongolia.

Too late to save

Some mammals became extinct only recently. Recently extinct animals include Steller's sea cows, which became extinct in about 1768. The Tasmanian wolf was last seen in 1933, eliminated by bounty hunters. The African bluebuck disappeared from Earth in 1880. The quagga, from southern Asia, was hunted for hides and meat. The last known quagga, a relative of the zebra, died in a Dutch zoo in 1883.

FOR MORE INFORMATION

Books

Boitani, Luigi, and Stefania Bartoli. *Guide to Mammals*. New York: Simon and Schuster, 1982.

Booth, Ernest S. *How to Know the Mammals*. Dubuque, IA: Wm. C. Brown Company Publishers, 1982.

Embery, Joan, and Edward Lucaire. *Joan Embery's Collection of Amazing Animal Facts*. New York: Dell Publishing, 1983.

Jones, J. Knox Jr., and David M. Armstrong. *Guide to Mammals of the Plains States*. Lincoln, NE: University of Nebraska Press, 1985.

Kite, L. Patricia. *Raccoons*. Minneapolis: Lerner Publications Company, 2004.

Kite, L. Patricia. *Blood-Feeding Bugs and Beasts*. Brookfield, CT: Millbrook Press, 1996.

Line, Les, and Edward Ricciuti. *National Audubon Society Book of Wild Animals*. New York: H. L. Abrams, 1996.

Nowak, Ronald M., and John L. Paradiso. *Walker's Mammals of the World*. Baltimore and London: The Johns Hopkins University Press, 1983.

Vogel, Julia, and John F. McGee. *Dolphins (Our Wild World*. Minnetonka, MN: Northword Press, 2001.

Walters, Martin. *Young Readers Book of Animals*. New York, London, Toronto, Sydney, and Tokyo: Simon & Schuster Books for Young Readers, 1990.

Whitaker, John O. Jr. *National Audubon Society Field Guide to North American Mammals*. New York: Alfred A. Knopf, 2000.

Wilson, D. E., and D. M. Reeder. *Mammal Species of the World*. Washington, DC: Smithsonian Institution Press, 1993.

Wood, Gerald L. *Animal Facts and Feats*. New York: Sterling Publishing, 1977.

Woods, Samuel G., and Jeff Cline. *Amazing Book of Mammal Records: The Largest, the Smallest, the Fastest, and Many More!* Woodbridge, CT: Blackbirch Press, 2000.

Periodicals

Allen, Leslie. "Return of the Pandas." *Smithsonian Magazine* (April 2001): 44–55.

Chadwick, Douglas H. "A Mine of Its Own." *Smithsonian Magazine* (May 2004): 26–27.

Cheater, Mark. "Three Decades of the Endangered Species Act." *Defenders* (Fall 2003): 8–13.

Conover, Adele. "The Object at Hand." *Smithsonian Magazine* (October 1996).

Gore, Rick. "The Rise of Mammals." *National Geographic* (April 2003): 2–37.

Mitchell, Meghan. "Securing Madagascar's Rare Wildlife." *Science News* (November 1, 1997): 287.

Pittman, Craig. "Fury Over a Gentle Giant." *Smithsonian Magazine* (February 2004): 54–59.

"Prehistoric Mammals." *Ranger Rick* (October 2000): 16.

Sherwonit, Bill. "Protecting the Wolves of Denali." *National Parks Magazine* (September/October 2003): 21–25.

Sunquist, Fiona. "Discover Rare Mystery Mammals." *National Geographic* (January 1999): 22–29.

Weidensaul, Scott. "The Rarest of the Rare." *Smithsonian Magazine* (November 2000): 118–128.

"Wildlife of Tropical Rain Forests." *National Geographic World* (January 2000): 22–25.

Web sites

Animal Info. http://www.animalinfo.org/ (accessed on June 6, 2004).

"Class Mammalia." Animal Diversity Web. http://animaldiversity.ummz.umich.edu/site/accounts/information/Mammalia004 (accessed on June 5, 2004).

"Hibernating Primate Found in Tropics." CNN Science & Space. http://www.cnn.com/2004/TECH/science/06/24/science.hibernation.reuit/inex.html (accessed on June 24, 2004).

"Ice Age Mammals." National Museum of Natural History. http://www.mnh.si.edu/museum/VirtualTour/Tour/First/IceAge/index.html (accessed on June 6, 2004).

"Mammary Glands." Animal Diversity Web. http://animaldiversity.ummz.umich.edu/site/topics/mammal_anatomy/mammary_glands.html (accessed on June 6, 2004).

WHALES, DOLPHINS, AND PORPOISES

Cetacea

Class: Mammalia

Order: Cetacea

Number of families: 14 families

PHYSICAL CHARACTERISTICS

Cetaceans (sih-TAY-shunz) are whales, dolphins, and porpoises. These mammals live, eat, reproduce, and rest in the water. They range in size from that of a small human—5 feet (1.5 meters) and 110 pounds (50 kilograms)—to huge, building-sized animals of 110 feet (33 meters) and 400,000 pounds (180,000 kilograms). Their ancestors were land mammals. More than fifty million years ago, these ancestors evolved physical characteristics that allowed them to live successfully in the water. Today scientists believe that the closest living land-based relative of whales, dolphins, and porpoises is the hippopotamus.

All cetaceans share certain physical characteristics that allow them to live their entire life in the water. Most notably, they all have streamlined, smooth, bodies to cut down on friction and turbulence as they move through the water. This streamlining has come about because the bones in their front legs are shortened and compressed to form paddles called flippers that have no fingers or claws. In addition, their back legs are so reduced that all that remains are a few internal pelvic bones. Likewise, they have no external reproductive organs. Male cetaceans have a retractable penis, which means that they can draw it up inside their body. The nipples of the female are also hidden in a slit within their belly.

The need to be streamlined has affected the shape of the skull and the sense organs found it in. The bones of the skull and the jawbones have become elongated, stretched out. The nostrils, usually on the front of the face in land mammals, have

phylum

class

subclass

● **order**

monotypic order

suborder

family

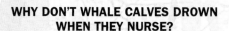

WHY DON'T WHALE CALVES DROWN WHEN THEY NURSE?

Whale calves must nurse from their mothers while in the water. How can the baby suckle and not suck huge amounts of water into its lungs when it breathes? The answer lies in an adaptation to aquatic life. Unlike land mammals where air and food share a single passage into the body, the digestive system and the breathing passage of the whale are separate. The whale's blowhole leads directly to the lungs, while the mouth and esophagus, throat, lead only to the stomach. This allows the whale calf to eat and breathe at the same time.

moved to the top of the head and are called blowholes. There can be one or two blowholes, depending on species, or a single slit on the top of the head. Blowholes are connected to the lungs and can be closed to keep out water when the animal dives.

Cetaceans have no external, outside, ears, although they have very good hearing. Sound is transmitted to the internal ear through bones. Most members of this order have good eyesight, although some species that live in cloudy water have lost most of the ability to see. Cetaceans use a complex system of communication and are thought to be highly intelligent. They have large brains in proportion to their body size.

All members of this order are hairless, they may have a few hairs at birth, but have a thick layer of oil and fat called blubber under the skin. They are warm-blooded; their core body temperature stays about the same as that of a human, even in cold Arctic waters. Cetaceans have no sweat glands. They regulate their temperature by controlling the amount of blood flowing through their flippers and fins, which are not covered with blubber.

Members of this order are known for their ability to make deep dives and remain underwater for long periods. Sperm whales have been known to dive more than 6,080 feet (1,853 meters). They have an efficient circulatory system that allows them to store and retrieve large amounts of oxygen in their blood and muscle tissue. In addition, when they dive, they reduce blood flow to their skeletal muscles, decreasing oxygen use in the muscles while keeping blood flow to the brain. Finally, when they dive, they expel, push out, the air in their lungs. Reducing the amount of air in the lungs helps them withstand the high pressure that occurs when they dive deeply.

Although all cetaceans have common characteristics that suit them to life in the water, different species have evolved physical and behavioral features that allow them to eat certain foods or inhabit specific zones. There are two suborders of whales, each with identifying physically characteristics. Mysticeti are the baleen (buh-LEEN or BAY-leen) whales. These whales have no teeth. To feed, they filter large amounts of water through flexible plates in their mouth called baleen. The baleen strains out krill, small shrimp and plankton, which they collect with their tongue and swallow. This suborder includes the largest whales on Earth.

Odontoceti, the other suborder of whales, all have teeth that they use to catch fish, squid, octopus, and marine mammals such as seals, dolphins, and other whales. They are often referred to as toothed whales to distinguish them from baleen whales. These whales use echolocation (eck-oh-loh-KAY-shun) to navigate and find prey. Echolocation involves making sounds that bounce off objects. Sense organs pick up the echo or reflected sound and use the timing, direction, and strength of the echo in order to locate objects. In some species, echolocation is so sensitive that it can locate an object less than 0.5 inches across (1.25 centimeters) at a distance of 50 feet (15 meters). Unlike toothed whales, baleen whales do not have a highly developed sense of echolocation.

This order also contains porpoises and dolphins. These animals are smaller than most whales, and some dolphins and porpoises live in fresh water rivers rather than in salt water. Strictly speaking, porpoises belong to only one family and are distinguished by their spade-shaped teeth. However, casual language makes little distinction between the terms porpoise and dolphin.

GEOGRAPHIC RANGE

Cetaceans are found in all oceans of the world. In the Arctic and Antarctic they avoid ice-covered water, since they must rise to the surface to breathe. Dolphins live in the ocean, but are also found in several freshwater rivers in Asia and South America.

HABITAT

The ocean is divided into different zones or regions based on depth, closeness to land, and underwater features. Cetaceans inhabit virtually all ocean zones, including zones in semi-enclosed water such as the Red and Black Seas. Cetaceans that live in freshwater rivers inhabit clear, rapidly flowing water and dark muddy water.

DIET

Members of this order are primarily carnivores, meat eaters. Baleen whales have evolved special filter-like structures to gather small shrimp, small fish, squid, and plankton. Other cetaceans actively hunt prey, either alone or in cooperative groups. Typically they eat whatever fish are found in the oceanic zone that they inhabit. Many also eat squid, octopus, shrimp, and crabs. A few species, especially the killer whale, hunt other whales, seals, sea lions, sea turtles, and sea birds.

BEHAVIOR AND REPRODUCTION

Cetaceans generally have pregnancies that last ten to sixteen months. Like all mammals, they nurse their young. The young tend to stay with their mothers for at least a year and often much longer. Many cetaceans give birth only every two to five years. These animals do not become capable of reproducing for about three to ten years. Large whales may live for close to 100 years and are slow to mature.

Cetaceans have evolved a wide spectrum of behaviors. Some species such as the spinner dolphin are known for the way they leap out of the water, while other species, like almost all porpoises, rarely jump when they come to the surface. Some members of this order live in groups of up to one thousand, while others live in groups of ten or fewer animals. Some groups show great social stability and communication. Killer whales, for example, are known to hunt in packs. Other social groups are simply casual associations, with members coming and leaving at will. Communication seems to involves several different types of sounds combined with echolocation.

CETACEANS AND PEOPLE

People have been fascinated with cetaceans from the earliest times. These animals have figured in stories and mythology in many countries. Perhaps the best known example is the biblical story of Jonah being swallowed by a whale.

Whales have been hunted for their oil, meat, baleen, and bones for hundreds of years. As sailing and hunting technologies improved, increasing pressure was put on some whale species. Whaling, whale hunting, reached its peak in 1847 when about 700 American ships, along with ships from many other nations, took part in whale hunts. In 1935, the United States and several European countries entered into the first international agreement to protect certain species of whales. Since then, there have been other international agreements, all of which have loopholes that allow at least some whale hunting to continue. In 1972, the United States passed the Marine Mammal Protection Act. This legislation extended protection to all cetaceans as well as other marine mammals such as seals, sea lions, and sea otters. Today, whale hunting, along with regulation of other types of fishing, continues to be a source of international tension.

Other pressures on cetaceans include being trapped and exhibited, put on display, for entertainment. Many tourist destinations offer visitors the opportunity to swim with dolphins in confined areas, and businesses trap wild dolphins for this purpose. In addition, the United States Navy trains dolphins to retrieve potentially dangerous materials from under water.

CONSERVATION STATUS

Interest in protecting cetaceans is high, and several organizations such as the American Cetacean Society and the Whale and Dolphin Conservation Society in Great Britain work hard at promoting conservation awareness among the public. Public pressure has lead to the development of "dolphin-safe" fishing nets and "dolphin-free" tuna, but many cetaceans are still drowned when they accidentally become trapped in fishing gear. Estimates of populations of different species are difficult to make, but the population of many species appears to be declining. Some, such as the baiji, a Chinese river dolphin, are Critically Endangered, facing an extremely high risk of extinction.

FOR MORE INFORMATION

Books:

Carwadine, Mark, and Martin Camm. *Smithsonian Handbooks: Whales Dolphins and Porpoises.* New York: DK Publishing, 2002.

Gowell, Elizabeth T. *Whales and Dolphins: What They Have in Common.* New York: Franklin Watts, 2000.

Mead, James G., and Joy P. Gold. *Whales and Dolphins in Question: The Smithsonian Answer Book.* Washington, DC: Smithsonian Institution Press, 2002.

Nowak, Ronald. M. "Order Cetacea." In *Walker's Mammals of the World Online 5.1.* Baltimore: Johns Hopkins University Press, 1997. http://www.press.jhu.edu/books/walkers_mammals_of_the_world/cetacea/cetacea.html (accessed on July 8, 2004)

Other sources:

American Cetacean Society. P.O. Box 1391, San Pedro, CA 94536. Phone: (310) 548-6279. Fax: (310) 548-6950. E-mail: info@acsonline .org Web site: http://www.acsonline.org.

Whale and Dolphin Conservation Society. P.O. Box 232, Melksham, Wiltshire SN12 7SB United Kingdom. Phone: (44) (0) 1225 354333. Fax: (44) (0) 1225 791577. Web site: http://www.wdcs.org.

GANGES AND INDUS DOLPHIN
Platanistidae

Class: Mammalia

Order: Cetacea

Family: Platanistidae

One species: Ganges and Indus dolphin (*Plantanista gangetica*)

PHYSICAL CHARACTERISTICS

The single member of this family is a dolphin that lives in freshwater rivers on the Indian subcontinent. At one time, scientists thought that there were two species in this family, the Indus river dolphin and the Ganges river dolphin. However, recent genetic testing shows that even though these groups are separated geographically, they are the same species. Native people call these dolphins "susu," which sounds like the noise they make when they breathe.

Ganges and Indus river dolphins are small, gray-brown dolphins. Adults measure between 5 and 8 feet (1.5 to 2.5 meters) and weigh between 150 and 200 pounds (70 to 90 kilograms). These dolphins have a long beak, or snout, and when they close their mouth, their sharp front teeth are still visible. They use these teeth to catch their prey, animals they hunt for food, mainly fish. Ganges and Indus river dolphins have a small hump behind the center of their back instead of a dorsal (back) fin. Their flippers are broad and paddle-shaped, and their blowhole is a single slit, set off-center on the top of their head. Unlike other dolphins, the opening to their ear is below their eyes.

Ganges and Indus river dolphins have poorly developed eyes. They are able to see only light and dark patterns, which is why they are sometimes called blind river dolphins. Instead of relying on sight to find food, they use a system called echolocation (eck-oh-loh-KAY-shun). Dolphins make sounds (scientists disagree about how this is done) that seem to be focused through the melon, a lump of fatty tissue in the dolphin's

phylum

class

subclass

order

monotypic order

suborder

▲ **family**

LOW WATER

Ganges and Indus river dolphins have developed an unusual method of swimming on their side with their tail held slightly higher than their head. As they swim, they drag one flipper along the bottom to stir up food. Scientists believe that this is an adaptation that allows them to live in water as shallow as 3 feet (1 meter) deep. While swimming like this, these dolphins sometimes carry their young on their back.

forehead, and skull and then sent out into the environment. When the sounds bounce back, the echo is passed through special tissue in the lower jaw to the inner ear. From the time it takes to collect the echoes, their strength, and their direction, dolphins construct a "sound picture" of their environment. This process is so sensitive, that they can "see" an object the size of a kernel of corn at a distance of 50 feet (15 meters), and can find their way around muddy waters as well as clear waters. Ganges and Indus river dolphins also use sound to communicate with each other.

GEOGRAPHIC RANGE

The Ganges and Indus river dolphin is found only on the Indian subcontinent. Indus river dolphins live in about a 100-mile (160-kilometer) stretch of the Indus River where it flows through the Sind and Punjab provinces of Pakistan. Their distribution is limited by two dams built in the 1930s.

Ganges river dolphins live in the Ganges, Meghna, Brahmaputra, and Karnaphuli Rivers, and their tributaries (streams that flow into these rivers). These rivers flow through western India, Nepal, Bhutan, and Bangladesh. The dolphins' range has been reduced, and populations have been fragmented or separated from each other by the construction of dams and water control projects, especially along the Ganges River.

HABITAT

These dolphins live in freshwater rivers from sea level to an elevation of 820 feet (250 meters). They can be found in clear, swift-moving water or muddy, cloudy water. They are often found where streams feed into the main river or where there are eddies, which are currents in the water that run opposite the main current. These river dolphins prefer living in water 10 to 30 feet deep (3 to 9 meters), but they are able to live in water as shallow as 3 feet (1 meter). They can survive a wide range of water temperatures, from about 46 to 91°F (8 to 33°C).

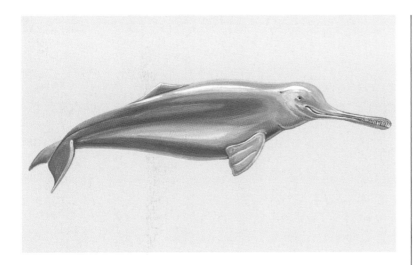

DIET

Ganges and Indus river dolphins eat bottom-dwelling fish such as carp and catfish, and occasionally shrimp and clams. In captivity they eat from 1 to 3.3 pounds (0.5 to 1.5 kilograms) of fish daily.

BEHAVIOR AND REPRODUCTION

Unlike some social dolphins, Ganges and Indus river dolphins swim alone or with one or two other dolphins. Adults rarely leap out of the water or expose much more of their body than their beak (snout) and melon. Compared to other dolphins, they swim slowly, although they are capable of short bursts of speed. Ganges and Indus river dolphins use echolocation to find their food and navigate around objects in the river. They also communicate with each other frequently through pulses of sound.

Not much is known about the reproductive behavior of these dolphins. Pregnancy is believed to last eight to eleven months. Newborns are about 3 feet (1 meter) long when they are born, and weigh about 17 pounds (7.5 kilograms). It appears that births occur throughout the year. Scientists are not certain, but they think the young nurse anywhere from two months to one year. These dolphins are capable of living long lives and do not become sexually mature (able to reproduce) until they are about ten years old.

GANGES AND INDUS RIVER DOLPHINS AND PEOPLE

River dolphins live in rivers that run through heavily populated and extremely poor areas. These dolphins are sometimes

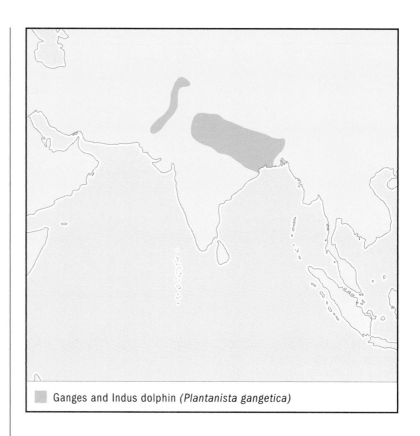

Ganges and Indus dolphin (*Plantanista gangetica*)

hunted for their oil, which is used in folk medicines for humans and livestock. Occasionally dolphin meat is eaten, and it is often used as bait to attract other fish. Dolphins are also accidentally trapped and drowned in fishing nets. Human development, such as dam building, water control projects, and pollution have all decreased the river dolphin population.

CONSERVATION STATUS

River dolphins are Endangered, facing a very high risk of extinction. There may be fewer than one thousand individuals remaining in the Indus River, while the outlook is equally grim in other river systems, including the Ganges River.

River dolphins are threatened mainly by human development. Dam building, begun in the 1920s, still continues today. Not only do dams isolate groups of dolphins, they interfere with migration and water flow. Heavy fishing, reducing water flow, and preventing flooding all decrease the population of fish that are the main source of food for these animals. In addition, pollution puts a strain on their health and may shorten their lives. Hunting and "accidental intentional" killing of dolphins in fishnets also are threats to their survival.

To combat the decline in population, the Whale and Dolphin Conservation Society recommends establishing protected habitats, training local people to manage river dolphins as a protected resource, educating the public to substitute other oils for dolphin oil, and enforcing protection laws already in existence.

FOR MORE INFORMATION

Books:

Carwadine, Mark, and Martin Camm. *Smithsonian Handbooks: Whales Dolphins and Porpoises.* New York: DK Publishing, 2002.

Gowell, Elizabeth T. *Whales and Dolphins: What They Have in Common.* New York: Franklin Watts, 2000.

Mead, James G., and Joy P. Gold. *Whales and Dolphins in Question: The Smithsonian Answer Book.* Washington, DC: Smithsonian Institution Press, 2002.

Smith, Alison M., and Brian D. Smith. "Review Status and Threats to River Dolphins and Recommendations for Their Conservation." In *Environmental Reviews.* Vol 6, edited by T. C. Hutchinson. Ottawa, Canada: NRC Research Press, 1998, 189-206.

Web sites:

American Cetacean Society. http://www.acsonline.org (accessed on July 8, 2004).

Whale and Dolphin Conservation Society. http://www.wdcs.org (accessed on July 8, 2004).

BAIJI
Lipotidae

Class: Mammalia
Order: Cetacea
Family: Lipotidae
One species: Baiji (*Lipotes vexillifer*)

family
CHAPTER

phylum
class
subclass
order
monotypic order
suborder
family

PHYSICAL CHARACTERISTICS

The baiji is a freshwater river dolphin that lives in the Yangtze (yang-see) River in eastern China. It has a long, narrow beak (snout), which curves slightly upward and grows longer with age. It has a steeply sloped forehead and tiny eyes that are set high on the sides of the head. These eyes are only slightly functional and leave the dolphin almost completely blind. This is why baijis use echolocation (eck-oh-loh-KAY-shun) to navigate and find food. Baijis have about 130 teeth, which are all alike in size and shape. The cone-shaped teeth are made for catching fish, not chewing.

The baiji has short, round flippers and a low, triangular shaped dorsal (back) fin. It has a very distinctive notch in the middle of its fluke, or tail. The body is a bluish gray, fading into white on its stomach. The average length for a baiji is between 6.5 and 8 feet (2 and 2.4 meters). Females grow to be larger than males. They weigh between 220 and 355 pounds (100 and 160 kilograms).

GEOGRAPHIC RANGE

The baiji lives along the 1,056 miles (1,700 kilometers) of the Yangtze River in eastern China. During the late spring and early summer, this freshwater dolphin moves to smaller streams and lakes if the water is high enough. At one time the lakes of Dongting and Poyang were home to the baiji year-round, but with the drop in water level these lakes can no longer support its presence.

HABITAT

The baiji is often found at places where tributaries (smaller streams) enter the river or along sandbars and dikes. When resting, it spends a lot of its time where the river is wide and slow moving. The baiji comes closer to shore to feed. During this time, it uses its long beak or snout to probe through the mud on the river's bottom.

DIET

Baijis, like many dolphins, are carnivores and have a diet consisting only of fish. A wide variety of species is consumed, limited only by the size of fish that can fit down its throat. Most of the fish are less than 2.6 inches (6.5 cm) long and weigh less than 9 ounces (250 grams). The baiji does not chew its food. It eats the whole fish at once, head first.

THE LEGEND OF THE BAIJI

There is a legend about the baiji that says there was once a young girl who was beaten by her stepfather. One day while they were out in a boat, the boat capsized and both the girl and her stepfather were thrown into the water. It is said that the girl emerged as a baiji while the stepfather emerged as a black finless porpoise.

BEHAVIOR AND REPRODUCTION

Little is known about the baiji because so few of them are left in the world. In the wild they are extremely shy, easily frightened, and difficult to approach. The baiji are thought to live in groups of two to seven individuals, but groups as large as sixteen have been observed. They do not leap out of the water the way some other dolphins do, but only expose their head and beak when they come to surface after dives.

The baiji's dives are often short, only lasting ten to twenty seconds, but they can be as long as two minutes. While underwater, they emit a wide range of sounds. These includes a whistle sound used to communicate and a variation of clicks used in echolocation.

Echolocation involves making sounds that bounce off objects. Sense organs pick up the echo or reflected sound and use that information to locate objects. The forehead of a dolphin is a lump of fatty tissue called the melon. The dolphin makes sounds (scientists disagree about how this is done) that seem to be focused through the melon and skull and then sent out into the environment. When the sounds bounce back, the echo is passed through special tissue in the lower jaw to the inner ear. From the time it

There may be only a few dozen baijis left in the world. (© Roland Seitre/Seapics.com. Reproduced by permission.)

takes to collect the echoes, their strength, and their direction, dolphins construct a "sound picture" of their environment. This process is so sensitive that they can "see" an object less than one-half inch (1.25 centimeters) across at a distance of 50 feet (15 meters).

The baiji is a very fast and strong swimmer and has been seen swimming over 60 miles (100 kilometers) in three days going against the current. While resting, the baiji stays in areas of very slow current.

Little is known about how this animal reproduces, because there have been no studies conducted on baiji reproduction. It is thought that males become mature at four years of age, while females mature at the age of six. A single calf is born in the spring, after a pregnancy of ten to eleven months. These calves are about 3 feet (91 centimeters) long and weigh between 6 and 11 pounds (2.5 and 4.8 kilograms). The baiji can live up to twenty-five years in the wild.

BAIJI AND PEOPLE

The baiji is very shy and has little interaction with humans. The presence of humans has made a major disturbance in the life of baijis. Chemical pollution, accidents, hunting, and habitat loss are all reasons for the decline in its numbers. Another large problem is the number of dams located along the Yangtze River. These dams alter the water level and flow of the current along the river and block fish migration. They also separate and isolate groups of baiji.

Propellers interfere with the dolphin's use of echolocation. Baijis often get confused and run into boats, hurting themselves. They can also be accidentally hooked or netted by fishermen. Many scientists believe that there are only a few dozen of these animals left in the world today. The baiji is the world's most endangered cetacean. There are no baijis held in captivity. Both a male and female who had been hurt and taken into captivity in different locations died.

CONSERVATION STATUS

Hope of saving the baijis is dim. Although it was declared a National Treasure of China and has been protected from hunting

Baiji *(Lipotes vexillifer)*

since 1975, the population continues to decline. Human use of the Yangtze River may be too intense for the baiji to survive.

There have been many ideas about how to help this dolphin survive, including capturing animals for breeding, developing "semi-natural reserves," and conducting population surveys. One idea even involved cloning the dolphin to help its population grow. In order to clone one of these dolphins at least three would need to be caught, which is a next to impossible task considering that fewer than ten are seen each year. Many successful breeding techniques have been developed for other dolphin species, including the bottlenosed dolphin. However, the baiji has not had the same luck as the bottlenosed, and every attempt to breed a baiji in captivity has failed. Now the idea of starting a breeding program seems even more unlikely because the only male who had ever been in captivity died in 2002 after living alone in a tank for twenty-three years. Sadly, despite what is being done to protect the baiji, it seems that they are doomed to extinction.

FOR MORE INFORMATION

Books:

Carwadine, Mark, and Martin Camm. *Smithsonian Handbooks: Whales Dolphins and Porpoises.* New York: DK Publishing, 2002.

Ellis, Richard. *Dolphins and Porpoises.* New York: Knopf, 1989.

Gowell, Elizabeth T. *Whales and Dolphins: What They Have in Common.* New York: Franklin Watts, 2000.

Mead, James G., and Joy P. Gold. *Whales and Dolphins in Question: The Smithsonian Answer Book.* Washington, DC: Smithsonian Institution Press, 2002.

Nowak, Ronald. M. *Walker's Mammals of the World.* Baltimore: Johns Hopkins University Press, 1995.

Smith, Alison M., and Brian D. Smith. "Review Status and Threats to River Dolphins and Recommendations for Their Conservation." In *Environmental Reviews.* Vol. 6, edited by T. C. Hutchinson. Ottawa, Canada: NRC Research Press, 1998.

Web sites:

American Cetacean Society. http://www.acsonline.org (accessed on July 8, 2004).

Whale and Dolphin Conservation Society. http://www.wdcs.org (accessed on July 8, 2004).

FRANCISCANA DOLPHIN
Pontoporiidae

Class: Mammalia
Order: Cetacea
Family: Pontoporiidae
One species: Franciscana dolphin
(*Pontoporia blainvillei*)

family
C H A P T E R

phylum

class

subclass

order

monotypic order

suborder

▲ **family**

PHYSICAL CHARACTERISTICS

Franciscana dolphins are also called La Plata dolphins, because the first described specimen, or animal, came from the mouth of La Plata River, Uruguay, in 1884. These dolphins are considered river dolphins, even though they live in the ocean near the shoreline. Originally scientists thought that the franciscana dolphin moved from fresh water to salt water during its lifetime, but now they know that it spends its entire life in the ocean. In the past, franciscana dolphins have been classified in several different dolphin families, but they are currently classified in a family of their own.

The franciscana dolphin is one of the smallest members of the cetacean order. They measure between 4.4 and 5.7 feet (1.3 and 1.7 meters) and weigh between 75 and 115 pounds (34 and 53 kilograms). Females are larger than males. Franciscana dolphins are gray-brown on their back and lighter underneath. Young franciscana dolphins are darker than older animals. Very old animals can appear almost white.

The most notable feature of the franciscana dolphin is its long, slender beak, or snout. They have the longest beak of any dolphin. Their beak may be 15 percent of their body length. Franciscana dolphins have triangular dorsal, or back, fins with rounded tips. Their flippers are broad and short. This dolphin has between 208 and 242 teeth small teeth. The blowhole, or nostril, is a crescent-shaped slit. Unlike the Ganges and Indus river dolphins, franciscana dolphins have good eyesight.

HOW DO DOLPHINS SLEEP?

Dolphins must rise to the surface to breathe every few minutes. How can they do this and still sleep? The answer is found in the way their brain functions. One half or hemisphere of the brain rests, while the other stays alert and makes sure the dolphin surfaces and breathes. When one half of the brain is rested, it takes over and the other half sleeps.

Even though franciscana dolphins can see well, they use echolocation (eck-oh-loh-KAY-shun) to find food and navigate through their environment. The forehead of a dolphin is a lump of fatty tissue called the melon. Echolocation is a sensory system in which dolphins make sounds that seem to be focused through the melon and then sent out into the environment. When the sounds bounce back, the echo is passed through special tissue in the lower jaw to the inner ear. From the time it takes to collect the echoes, their strength, and their direction, dolphins construct a "sound picture" of their environment. This system is extremely sensitive and allows the animal to locate very small objects. Scientists disagree about just how the dolphins actually make the sounds.

GEOGRAPHIC RANGE

Franciscana dolphins are found in the Atlantic Ocean along the coasts of Brazil, Uruguay, and Argentina in South America. Their northern boundary is near Rio de Janeiro, Brazil, and their southern boundary is the Valdes Peninsula in Argentina. Their distribution within this range is uneven. In some places they are rare or absent, and in others they are more common.

HABITAT

Franciscana dolphins are usually found within 33 miles (53 kilometers) of shore in waters no more than 30 feet (10 meters) deep. Often they are found in muddy, murky water with poor visibility. They seem to prefer estuaries, which are places where rivers empty into the ocean and fresh water mixes with salt water.

DIET

Franciscana dolphins eat a wide variety of small bottom-dwelling fish, squid, octopus, and shrimp. Most of the fish they feed on are less than 4 inches (10 centimeters) long.

BEHAVIOR AND REPRODUCTION

Franciscana dolphins usually swim alone or in small groups. Several dolphins may cooperate when feeding. They will swim

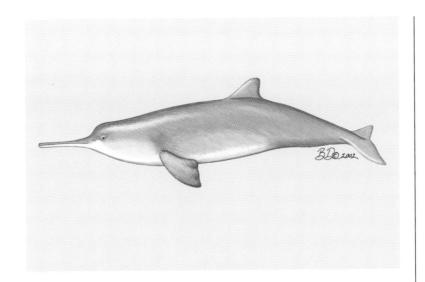

in a tight circle, surrounding the fish and pushing them together.

Franciscana dolphins are very quiet and shy at the surface. They rarely jump and often only raise their heads out of the water enough to breathe. They are preyed upon by sevengill sharks, hammerhead sharks, and possibly killer whales.

Female franciscana dolphins give birth to one calf after an eleven-month pregnancy. Most calves are born between October and January, spring in the Southern Hemisphere. Newborns are about 28 inches (71 centimeters) long and weigh 16 to 19 pounds (7 to 8.5 kilograms). They nurse, feed on their mother's milk, for about three months. After that, they continue to nurse, but also eat fish until they are completely weaned and not dependent on their mother's milk at about nine months. There is some disagreement about when these dolphins become sexually mature and able to reproduce. Estimates range from two to four-and-a-half years. Their average natural lifespan is about fifteen years.

Franciscana dolphins do not strictly migrate. However, it appears that in areas off the coast of Argentina where there is noticeable seasonal variation in water temperature, they may change their range. This movement does not seem to happen off the coast of Brazil, where water temperatures remain more constant throughout the year.

Franciscana dolphin (*Pontoporia blainvillei*)

FRANCISCANA DOLPHINS AND PEOPLE

Franciscana dolphins are shy and rarely intentionally interact with people. However, these dolphins are sometimes caught in fishing nets. In these cases, their oil is used in tanning leather, and their flesh is used as pig feed or shark bait.

CONSERVATION STATUS

The wild population of franciscana dolphins is unknown. Because of this, they are given a Data Deficient conservation status. However, it is estimated that up to 1,500 of these animals are drowned every year by becoming tangled in gillnets and other fishing gear. Scientists believe that as a result, the wild population is decreasing. In addition, because these dolphins live close to shore, they are more at risk for habitat pollution than dolphins that live in the open ocean.

FOR MORE INFORMATION

Books:

Carwadine, Mark, and Martin Camm. *Smithsonian Handbooks: Whales Dolphins and Porpoises.* New York: DK Publishing, 2002.

Gowell, Elizabeth T. *Whales and Dolphins: What They Have in Common.* New York: Franklin Watts, 2000.

Mead, James G., and Joy P. Gold. *Whales and Dolphins in Question: The Smithsonian Answer Book.* Washington, DC: Smithsonian Institution Press, 2002.

Nowak, Ronald. M. "Franciscana, or La Plata Dolphin." *Walker's Mammals of the World Online 5.1.* Baltimore: Johns Hopkins University Press, 1997. http://www.press.jhu.edu/books/walkers_mammals_of_the_world / cetacea/cetacea.pontoporiidae.pontoporia.html (accessed on July 8, 2004).

Web sites:

American Cetacean Society. http://www.acsonline.org (accessed on July 8, 2004).

Whale and Dolphin Conservation Society. http://www.wdcs.org (accessed on July 8, 2004).

BOTO
Iniidae

Class: Mammalia
Order: Cetacea
Family: Iniidae
One species: Boto (*Inia geoffrensis*)

family
CHAPTER

PHYSICAL CHARACTERISTICS

Botos, also called Amazon river dolphins or pink river dolphins, live only in fresh water rivers in South America. They are the largest and most abundant of the river dolphins. Adult botos range in length from 6.6 to 8.5 feet (2 to 2.5 meters) and in weight from about 185 to 400 pounds (85 to 180 kilograms). Males are larger than females. Young animals are usually dark gray. As they mature, their color changes and they become pink. However, individuals that live in dark, muddy water tend to remain darker than those that live in clear water.

Botos have thick bodies and a large slender beak (snout) that contains about 140 teeth. Instead of a distinct dorsal (back) fin, they have a small triangular peaked ridge along their back. Their flippers are large and pointed. Botos are very flexible, allowing them to live in shallow, cluttered environments. One reason for their flexibility is that their cervical vertebrae, or neck bones, are not fused or joined, giving them the freedom to twist and turn their head easily.

Botos have good eyesight both above and under water. However, because they often live in dark, murky water, they usually rely on echolocation (eck-oh-loh-KAY-shun) to avoid objects and find food. The forehead of a dolphin is a lump of fatty tissue called the melon. Dolphins make sounds (scientists disagree about how this is done) that seem to be focused through the melon and skull. These sounds are then sent out into the environment. When the sounds bounce back, the echo is passed through special tissue in the lower jaw to the inner ear. From the time it takes to collect the echoes, their strength, and their direction, dolphins construct a "sound picture" of their environment. This system is extremely sensitive and allows the animal to locate objects very small objects.

GEOGRAPHIC RANGE

Botos are found in the Amazon and Orinoco River systems in Brazil, Bolivia, Colombia, Ecuador, Guyana, Peru, and Venezuela. They require fresh water and do not live in estuaries (EST-yoo-air-eez) where rivers meet the ocean.

HABITAT

Botos live mainly in dark, cloudy water. They seem to prefer areas where water currents meet and cause turbulence. Several studies have found that they are attracted to places where streams flow into the main river channel or to areas around sand bars or sharp bends in the river. Botos live in water with temperatures ranging from about 73 to 86°F (23 to 30°C). During the rainy season (November to May) when rivers flood, they move out of the main river channel into the shallow flooded forests. As the waters go down, they move back into the deeper main channels.

DIET

Botos eat a broad range of food, including up to fifty different species of fish. Most of the fish they eat are from 8 to 12 inches (20 to 30 centimeters) long, although they are able to eat fish as long as 31 inches (80 centimeters). During the rainy season, the forests flood, fish swim into the flooded areas to eat seeds and fruits, and botos follow the fish. They are able to move easily in this shallow water, because they are so flexible and they have a well-developed sense of echolocation. When the water level starts to fall, the fish and the botos return to the deeper main channel.

Botos also eat small turtles, mollusks (hard shelled animals like clams), freshwater shrimp, and crabs. Other species of dolphins have only sharp cone-shaped teeth. Botos have this type of tooth, but also have some teeth that are modified for grinding. This allows them to eat a wide variety of food.

SAVED BY BAD LUCK

Along the South American rivers where the botos live, the dolphin is associated with unhappiness. The boto is said to turn into a man at night, one who seduces young girls and impregnates them. The boto is also said to turn into a lovely girl who leads men into the river and takes them away forever. Seeing a boto is supposed to be bad luck and burning boto oil in a lamp is supposed to make people who look at the lamp go blind. The boto's connection to bad luck and unhappy events may have helped save it, since the boto has never been hunted for oil or food.

Boto (*Inia geoffrensis*)

BEHAVIOR AND REPRODUCTION

Botos usually swim alone or occasionally with one or two other botos. They communicate with each other using a series of "clicks" that are above the range of human hearing. These communication sounds are not well understood. Botos kept in captivity have been aggressive toward each other, suggesting that in the wild they need to keep a certain distance between themselves and other botos. They are occasionally observed in larger groups when feeding.

Botos swim slowly, sometimes on their backs. They come to the surface to breathe every thirty to sixty seconds, but rarely leap out of the water or even show much of their body above the surface. They are, however, playful and curious. Botos have been seen playing with floating logs or turtles and have been known to come up to boats and rub against them.

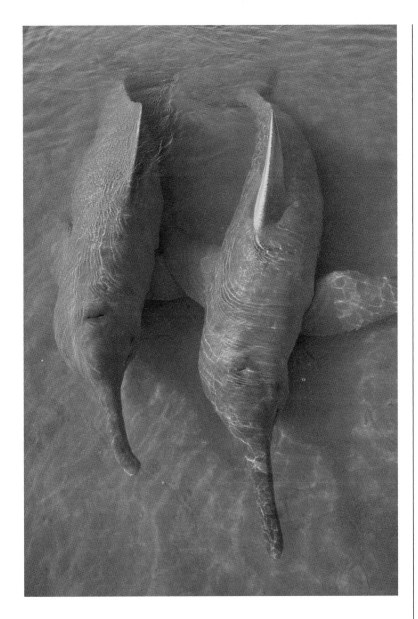

Female botos give birth to a single calf after an eleven-month pregnancy beginning when they are three to five years old. After that, they have a single calf every two to five years. Most births occur between May and August, newborns being about 30 inches long (75 centimeters) and weighing about 15 pounds (7 kilograms). They nurse, feed on their mother's milk, for more than a year. Natural lifespan is estimated at about thirty years. Botos do not appear to migrate.

BOTOS AND PEOPLE

Botos are not hunted, but are sometimes intentionally killed to prevent them from destroying fishing gear. Botos are associated in folklore with misfortune and bad luck.

CONSERVATION STATUS

Although the population of botos in the wild is not known, it is estimated to be in the tens of thousands. Botos are considered Vulnerable, facing a high risk of extinction. The biggest threat comes from human development. In 2000, there were ten dams on the Amazon River that fragmented, or separated, groups of botos and interfered with their free movement. More dams are planned on the rivers that botos inhabit. In addition, water control projects that prevent the forest from flooding during the rainy season reduce food available for fish. This causes the fish population to decrease, meaning the botos will also have less food. Other threats to the boto include mercury pollution from the mining of gold near the rivers, other types of pollution associated with human development, and accidental drowning in fishing gear. Although the boto is protected by law in some parts of its range, enforcement is difficult and not very effective.

FOR MORE INFORMATION

Books:

Carwadine, Mark, and Martin Camm. *Smithsonian Handbooks: Whales Dolphins and Porpoises.* New York: DK Publishing, 2002.

Gowell, Elizabeth T. *Whales and Dolphins: What They Have in Common.* New York: Franklin Watts, 2000.

Mead, James G., and Joy P. Gold. *Whales and Dolphins in Question: The Smithsonian Answer Book.* Washington, DC: Smithsonian Institution Press, 2002.

Nowak, Ronald. M. *Walker's Mammals of the World Online 5.1.* Baltimore: Johns Hopkins University Press, 1997. http://www.press.jhu.edu/books/walkers_mammals_of_the_world/ (accessed on July 8, 2004)

Web sites:

American Cetacean Society. http://www.acsonline.org (accessed July 8, 2004).

Convention on Migratory Species. http://www.cms.int/ (accessed July 8, 2004).

Whale and Dolphin Conservation Society. http://www.wdcs.org (accessed July 8, 2004).

PORPOISES
Phocoenidae

Class: Mammalia

Order: Cetacea

Family: Phocoenidae

Number of species: 6 species

family

CHAPTER

phylum

class

subclass

order

monotypic order

suborder

▲ **family**

PHYSICAL CHARACTERISTICS

Porpoises are mostly ocean-dwelling marine mammals, although some species can also live in freshwater rivers. They are often confused with dolphins. In casual conversation many people incorrectly use the terms dolphin and porpoise to mean the same thing. Both porpoises and dolphins came from a common ancestor, ancient relative, however they have been distinct families for about eleven million years.

Porpoises have a blunt snout, as opposed to the beak and elongated snout of dolphins. Their dorsal, back, fins are triangular. They have thick, stocky bodies that help them to conserve heat in cold waters. There are several differences between the skulls of porpoises and dolphins, but the most obvious is in the teeth. Porpoises have between sixty and 120 almost triangular, spade-shaped teeth, while dolphins have cone-shaped teeth. Most members of this family lack a melon. The melon is a fatty organ on the forehead. This gives their heads a tapered rather than a bulging look.

Porpoises range in weight from 90 to 485 pounds (40 to 220 kilograms) and in length from 4 to 7 feet (1.2 to 2.2 meters). The smallest porpoise is the vaquita (vah-KEE-tah), which lives in the Gulf of California in Mexico. Dall's porpoise and the spectacled porpoise are the two largest porpoises. In all species except the spectacled porpoise, females are larger than males.

Porpoises range in color from black to gray to tan. Generally, their backs are dark and their bellies are lighter. Some, such as the spectacled porpoise and Dall's porpoise, have quite distinctive black and white markings. Others, such as the finless porpoise, are a single dull color.

GEOGRAPHIC RANGE

Porpoises are found along the coasts of large parts of North and South America (except the tropics and subtropics), Europe, and in the Mediterranean and Black Sea. They are also found off the coast of Siberia and northern Japan.

HABITAT

Porpoises live in a variety of ocean habitats. The spectacled porpoise lives in cold, open ocean in the Southern Hemisphere. Another Southern Hemisphere porpoise, Burmeister's porpoise, lives in warmer, shallow waters along the coast of South America. This porpoise can also live in freshwater rivers. The finless porpoise and the vaquita also like shallow warm water. The harbor porpoise and Dall's porpoise both live in cold water habitats.

DIET

Porpoises are carnivores, meat eaters. They eat mainly fish. The type of fish they prefer depends on the habitat in which they live. They also eat squid and octopus. Some also eat shrimp and mollusks (hard shelled animals like clams). Many porpoises migrate seasonally in order to follow the fish they feed on. Their natural predators, animals that hunt them for food, are some sharks, killer whales, and bottlenosed dolphins.

Porpoises use echolocation (eck-oh-loh-KAY-shun) to help find food. They make sounds (scientists disagree about how this is done) that are sent out into the environment. When the sounds bounce back, the echo is passed through special tissue in the lower jaw to the inner ear. From the time it takes to collect the echoes, their strength, and their direction, the animal can construct a "sound picture" of its environment. This system is extremely sensitive and allows the animal to locate very small objects.

BEHAVIOR AND REPRODUCTION

Except for the finless porpoise on the Yangtze (yang-see; or Chang) River in China, which seems to have become used to heavy boat traffic, porpoises tend to avoid boats. This makes them difficult to study. They rise to the surface to breathe quietly without showing much of their bodies. Rarely do they leap above the surface of the water. Generally porpoises live in small groups of no more than ten individuals. When larger groups occasionally gather, it may be to feed or follow schools of fish.

Very little is known about the reproduction of vaquita and spectacled porpoises. Other porpoises become mature at three to five years, and have a single calf every year after that. Pregnancy lasts about eleven months and mothers nurse their young, feed them breast milk, for more than a year. Porpoises live about fifteen years.

PORPOISES AND PEOPLE

Because porpoises are shy and avoid boats, they have very few interactions with people. Until the mid 1940s, they were hunted for food and oil, but now intentional hunting occurs only occasionally in Greenland and in the Black Sea. They are, however, often caught and drowned in fishing gear.

CONSERVATION STATUS

The vaquita is the least abundant porpoise. There may be only a few hundred individuals remaining. The vaquita is considered Critically Endangered, facing an extremely high risk of extinction in the wild. It lives in northern Mexico in the Gulf of California where there is a lot of commercial fishing. The main threat to its survival is being accidentally killed by becoming entangled in fishing nets.

The harbor porpoise is listed as Vulnerable, facing a high risk of extinction. It is a protected species in the United States and Canada. Threats to its survival include pollution and accidental death in fishing gear. Little is known about the population levels of the other four species of porpoises.

BLACK PORPOISE

Like some other cetaceans, Burmeister's porpoise turns entirely black almost as soon as it dies. Early descriptions of this animal were based on dead specimens, so scientists mistakenly named the animal the "black porpoise." Although Burmeister's porpoise is mostly dark gray with a paler underside, the name stuck, and it is still often called the black porpoise today.

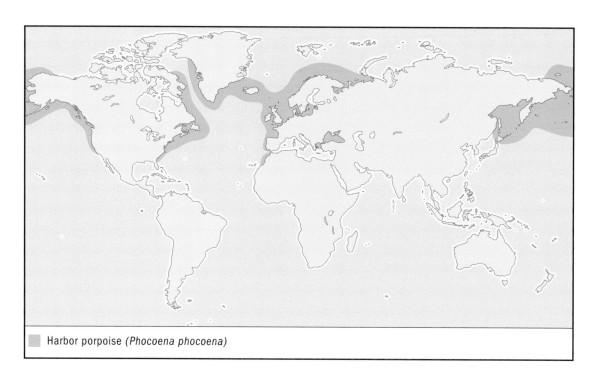

Harbor porpoise (*Phocoena phocoena*)

SPECIES ACCOUNTS

HARBOR PORPOISE
Phocoena phocoena

Physical characteristics: Harbor porpoises have short, thick bodies with brown or dark gray backs and whitish bellies. Their lips and chin are black. They have a rounded forehead and no beak. Females are larger than males with an average weight of 130 pounds (60 kilograms) and an average length of 5.5 feet (1.6 meters). Males weigh about 110 pounds (50 kilograms) and measure about 4.8 feet (1.4 meters).

Geographic range: Harbor porpoises are found along the U.S. and Canadian coasts in the North Atlantic, around Greenland and northern Europe, in the Mediterranean Sea, and the northern Pacific along the North American coast and in Asia as far south as northern Japan.

Habitat: These animals live in cold costal waters, bays, tidal channels, and estuaries. They appear to prefer water between 65 and 200 feet (20 and 60 meters) deep.

Diet: Harbor porpoises eat cold water fish such as herring and mackerel. They also eat squid and octopus.

Behavior and reproduction: Harbor porpoises are shy and avoid people. They rarely leap out of the water when they go to the surface to breathe. They are heard more often than they are seen, because they make a loud puffing sound when they surface to breathe.

Harbor porpoises and people: From 1830 to about 1950, these animals were hunted for food and oil, but today little hunting takes place.

Conservation status: Harbor porpoises are considered Vulnerable, because they are often drowned accidentally by commercial fishing gear. ■

Harbor porpoises live in cold coastal waters, and feed on fish, squid, and octopus that live there. (© Armin Maywald/ Seapics.com. Reproduced by permission.)

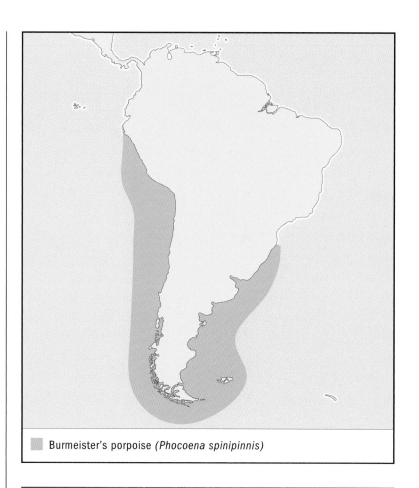

Burmeister's porpoise (Phocoena spinipinnis)

BURMEISTER'S PORPOISE
Phocoena spinipinnis

Physical characteristics: Burmeister's porpoise, sometimes called the black porpoise, measures between 4.6 and 6 feet (1.4 and 1.8 meters) and weighs 88 to 154 pounds (40 to 70 kilograms). This porpoise has a dark gray to black back and a dark gray belly. Its small dorsal (back) fin is located farther back on its body than the fin of any other porpoise.

Geographic range: Burmeister's porpoise is found in South America from Brazil south to Tierra del Fuego in the Atlantic Ocean, and then north in the Pacific Ocean as far as the coast of Peru. It is more common on the Atlantic side of South America than on the Pacific side.

Habitat: This porpoise prefers cold, coastal water no more than 500 feet (152 meters) deep.

Diet: Burmeister's porpoise eats about nine species of fish, mainly hake and anchovies. It also eats squid, small shrimp, and mollusks.

Behavior and reproduction: Burmeister's porpoises make quick, jerky movements when they swim. They do not leap out of the water and are barely visible when they come up to breathe. They seem to live in groups of fewer than eight individuals. They are very shy and difficult to study, so little is known about their behavior or reproductive cycle. They appear to mate between June and September and give birth about ten months later.

Burmeister's porpoise and people: Burmeister's porpoises have been hunted for meat in Chile and Peru.

Conservation status: Information about the population of Burmeister's porpoise is not known, so they have been given a Data Deficient conservation rating. The greatest threat to this species is drowning by becoming caught in fishing gear. This species became protected by law in 1994, and since then the number of individuals killed has decreased. ■

Burmeister's porpoises make quick, jerky movements when they swim, and are barely visible when they come up to breathe. (Illustration by Michelle Meneghini. Reproduced by permission.)

FOR MORE INFORMATION

Books:

Carwadine, Mark, and Martin Camm. *Smithsonian Handbooks: Whales, Dolphins and Porpoises.* New York: DK Publishing, 2002.

Ellis, Richard. *Dolphins and Porpoises.* New York: Knopf, 1989.

Nowak, Ronald. M. *Walker's Mammals of the World Online 5.1.* Baltimore: Johns Hopkins University Press, 1997. http://www.press.jhu.edu/books/walkers_mammals_of_the_world (accessed on July 7, 2004).

Web sites:

American Cetacean Society. http://www.acsonline.org (accessed on July 7, 2004).

Culik, Boris and Convention on Migratory Species. *Phocoena phocoena.* http://www.cms.int/reports/small_cetaceans/data/P_phocoena/p_phocoena.htm (accessed July 7, 2004).

Whale and Dolphin Conservation Society. http://www.wdcs.org (accessed on July 7, 2004).

DOLPHINS
Delphinidae

Class: Mammalia
Order: Cetacea
Family: Delphinidae
Number of species: 34 species

family

C H A P T E R

PHYSICAL CHARACTERISTICS

Dolphins are found in all oceans and many rivers of the world. They are often confused with other aquatic animals. Dolphins arose from the same ancestor as porpoises, but have been a separate family for at least eleven million years. In addition, the common names of some dolphins lead to confusion. For example, the killer whale is actually a dolphin. With genetic testing now available, some re-classification of individual dolphin species is occurring.

Dolphins have long, streamlined, torpedo-shaped bodies adapted to life in the ocean. Generally they are fast, acrobatic, agile swimmers. The bones in what would be the hand and arm of a land animal are compressed into a web of bones to make flippers. Their back legs are so reduced that all that remains are a few internal pelvic bones. They have strong, muscular tails. Dolphins breathe through a single blowhole on top of their head. All dolphins have a melon, a fatty organ on their forehead that they use for echolocation. Echolocation (eck-oh-loh-KAY-shun) involves making sounds that bounce off objects. Sense organs pick up the echo or reflected sound and use information about the echo's timing, direction, and strength to determine the location of objects. They have a single type of cone-shaped tooth, but the number of teeth ranges from four to about 260, and the size varies with the size of the species. Dolphins are able to taste, but not smell.

Within this family there are many physical differences in size and color. The smallest dolphin is the endangered Hector's

phylum

class

subclass

order

monotypic order

suborder

▲ **family**

dolphin. They are about 4.5 feet (1.4 meters) long and weigh about 117 pounds (53 kilograms). The largest is the killer whale, which can measure 30 feet (9 meters) and weigh 12,000 pounds (5,600 kilograms). Dolphins come in many colors, including black, white, gray, tan, brown, orange, and pink. Some have distinctive color patterns, while others are a single color.

GEOGRAPHIC RANGE

Dolphins are found in every ocean and sea and in many major river systems. They are the largest family of cetaceans.

HABITAT

Dolphins live in salt water, fresh water, and brackish water, a mixture of salt and fresh water. They live in both the open ocean and in coastal waters, although more live shallow water. Their distribution is determined mainly by the availability of prey.

DIET

Dolphins are carnivores, meat eaters. They eat fish and squid and capture their food one fish at a time. The type of fish they prefer depends on the zone of the ocean that they inhabit. Killer whales eat fish, but they also hunt seals, sea lions, other dolphins, whales, porpoises, and sea birds.

Dolphins use echolocation to navigate and find prey. Echolocation allows dolphins to use high-pitch sounds that bounce off objects in order to determine their location. In some species, echolocation is so sensitive that it can locate an object less than 0.5 inch across (1.25 centimeters) at a distance of 50 feet (15 meters).

BEHAVIOR AND REPRODUCTION

Dolphins are highly intelligent social animals. Many species appear to live in cooperative groups, groups that work together. They may live in groups called pods of fewer than five or as many as several thousand. To some extent, group size depends on the availability of food. Within a large group, animals often separate by age and sex.

Dolphins have excellent hearing and communicate with each other by producing a variety of different sounds, often identified as "clicks," "pulses," and "whistles." Some of these sounds may be identifiers for individual animals, but this communication is not well understood. Dolphins living in clear water may also communicate by flipping and flashing patches of color on their bodies.

There are many examples of dolphins working cooperatively. They may work together to locate and round up a school of fish or chase them into shallow water or to attack a predator, an animal that hunts them for food. They have been seen helping newborn or injured animals to the surface to breathe. They are best known for their acrobatics. They often leap and spin out of the water, sometimes in large, coordinated groups. They are curious and playful. Some dolphins will catch a ride on the waves a boat makes as it passes through the water. Dolphins can be taught behaviors or tricks when in captivity.

Dolphins mate and give birth in the water. From an early age, both sexes do a lot of touching and stroking, rubbing and sex play behavior with their own and the opposite sex. Sexual maturity, the ability to reproduce, occurs when individuals are between five and sixteen years old. Larger species tend to mature later than smaller ones. A single calf is born after a pregnancy lasting ten to fifteen months.

The bond between mother and calf is extremely important and may last many years. Calves begin to catch fish when they are a few months old, but may continue to nurse for three-and-a-half years or more. Even after they are weaned, no longer nursing, they remain with their mother for a year or longer.

DOLPHINS AND PEOPLE

Dolphins are familiar to most people from exhibitions at marine parks and movies and television programs such as "Flipper." Dolphin-watching tours attract thousands of ecotourists, who travel to observe these animals without interfering with them. More controversial are resorts where tourists can swim with captive dolphins. Dolphins are hunted for food in some places in the world. They are also trained by the United States military to retrieve small underwater objects.

DOLPHIN COMMUNICATION

Scientists who have recorded dolphin whistles have found that individual animals react much more strongly to the whistle of an individual that is related to them than to a whistle of a stranger. It appears that each dolphin has a signature whistle all its own that is recognized by its family.

CONSERVATION STATUS

The conservation status of dolphins depends upon the species. Hector's dolphin is considered Endangered, facing a very high risk of extinction in the wild, because it is often killed accidentally by fishing gear. Population estimates are not available for most species.

Dolphins are threatened by hunting, accidental capture in fishing nets, pollution, and capture for display in captivity. In the 1990s public pressure resulted in the development of dolphin-free fishing nets and the sale of dolphin-free tuna. These changes have resulted in a substantial decrease in the number of dolphins accidentally harvested during fishing. Dolphins are protected in the United States under the 1972 Marine Mammal Protection Act and are the focus of many conservation and research organizations.

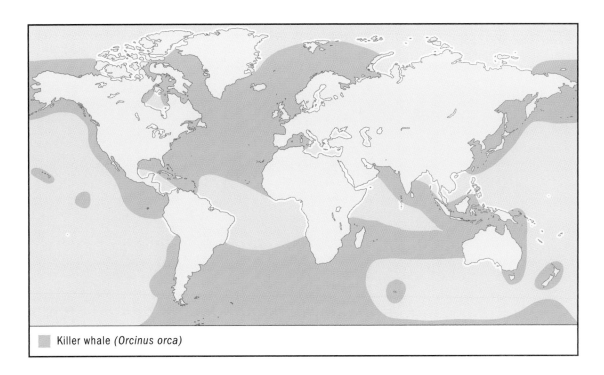

Killer whale (*Orcinus orca*)

KILLER WHALE
Orcinus orca

Physical characteristics: Killer whales, or orcas, are the largest dolphins, measuring 30 feet (9 meters) and weighing up to 12,000 pounds (5,600 kilograms). They have a striking black and white pattern of mainly black above and white below, and they have the tallest dorsal fin of any cetacean. The dorsal fin can reach 6 feet (2 meters) in height. They are the top predators in the ocean.

Geographic range: Killer whales live in all the oceans of the world, but are most abundant in cold water areas such as the Arctic and Antarctic.

Habitat: Killer whales prefer cold water, but can live in warmer temperatures. They tend to live in water that is less than 650 feet (200 meters) deep. Rarely they have been known to swim up rivers such as the Columbia in the United States and the Thames in England.

Diet: Killer whales have the most varied diet of any dolphin. They hunt fish, seals, sea lions, other dolphins, porpoises, and whales. Their

diet depends primarily on what is available in their region of the ocean. They are swift swimmers and hunt in packs. They can successfully attack a blue whale, the largest animal on the planet, or a great white shark. In some places they chase sea lions up onto the beach and attack them. They are able to swallow a small seal whole. Adults eat 3 to 4 percent of their body weight daily.

Behavior and reproduction: Killer whales live in stable pods. Males often stay with their mothers for years after they are weaned. Like other dolphins, they use echolocation and make sounds to communicate with members of their pod.

Killer whales have pregnancies that last from fifteen to eighteen months and produce a single calf. Calves stay dependent on their mothers for several years. New calves are born only every three to eight years.

Killer whales and people: Most people know of killer whales from exhibits at marine parks and movies. Since they can regularly be seen near shore, they are often the object of dolphin-watching tours. In 1985, the first killer whale was successfully born in captivity. That whale lived to adulthood and produce calves of her own. It is not clear how long killer whales live in the wild. Estimates range from thirty to fifty years.

Conservation status: Killer whales are not threatened. Their main threat appears to be pollution of their habitat. ■

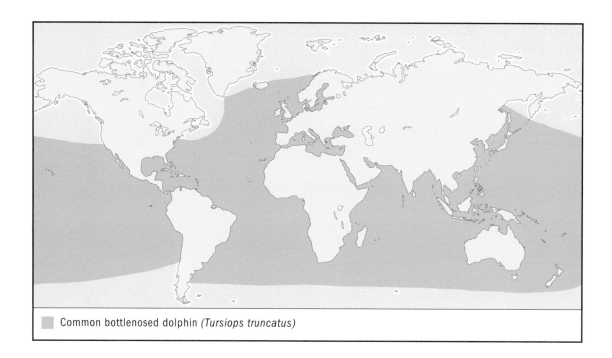

Common bottlenosed dolphin *(Tursiops truncatus)*

COMMON BOTTLENOSED DOLPHIN
Tursiops truncatus

Physical characteristics: Common bottlenosed dolphins, also called Atlantic bottlenosed dolphins, range in size from 8 to 12.5 feet (2.5 to 3.8 meters) and in weight from 500 to 1,100 pounds (227 to 500 kilograms). These dolphins can be colored brown to gray on their backs and light gray to white on their bellies. There are several distinct subpopulations in different regions of the world.

Geographic range: These dolphins are found worldwide in warm and temperate, moderate temperature, waters. In the United States they are the most abundant dolphin along the Atlantic coast from Massachusetts to Florida.

Habitat: Common bottlenosed dolphins prefer warm shallow water and are often found along the coast in harbors and bays, although they also inhabit open ocean.

Diet: These animals eat fish, squid, and shrimp. They often feed cooperatively, herding fish together to make them easier to catch. In shallow water they may chase fish into a sandbar where they are trapped.

Behavior and reproduction: Common bottlenosed dolphins form pods of varying size. Pods in the open ocean seem to be larger than those close to shore. The pods are moderately stable and tend to migrate in order to follow the fish. Those pods living in cooler waters usually migrate to warmer water in the winter.

Common bottlenosed dolphins are curious and playful. They often ride the waves produced by the passage of a boat through the water. They can jump as high as 16 feet (4.9 meters) out of the water.

Female bottlenosed dolphins have their first calf between the ages of five and twelve years. Pregnancy lasts about twelve months and produces a single calf. Calves stay with their mothers for about three years, after which another calf is born. Bottlenosed dolphins have been successfully born and raised in captivity.

Common bottlenosed dolphins and people: Common bottlenosed dolphins are the dolphins most frequently exhibited in marine park shows. They are very acrobatic and can be taught many behaviors in captivity.

Conservation status: Not enough information is available to give the common bottlenosed dolphin a conservation rating, however, they do not appear to be threatened. The main threat to their habitat is pollution. ■

Bottlenosed dolphins often ride the waves produced by passing boats. (Tom Brakefield/Bruce Coleman Inc. Reproduced by permission.)

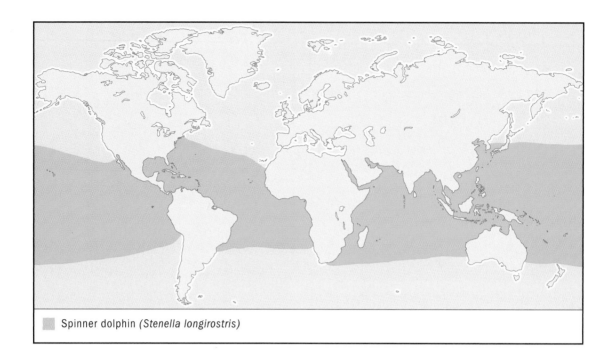

Spinner dolphin (*Stenella longirostris*)

SPINNER DOLPHIN
Stenella longirostris

Physical characteristics: Spinner dolphins, also called long-snouted dolphins, are known for their acrobatic displays. Spinner dolphins are about 7.7 feet (2.3 meters) long and weigh about 170 pounds (78 kilograms). Males are usually larger than females. They vary in color from individuals that are all gray to ones having black backs, gray sides, and white bellies.

Geographic range: Spinner dolphins are found worldwide in tropical and subtropical waters.

Habitat: Spinner dolphins mainly live in the open ocean, although they may come into shallow waters to feed.

Diet: Spinners are carnivores. They tend to feed at night and eat mainly fish, squid, octopus, and shrimp.

Behavior and reproduction: Spinner dolphins form schools or pods that may contain more than 1,000 individuals. They are very social and communicate with each other by sound and touch. They are best known for their ability to leap out of the water and turn on their longitudinal, long, vertical, axis. Some can spin as many as seven times on one jump. This behavior gave them their common name.

Less is known about the reproductive behavior of spinner dolphins than some other species because they live farther out in the ocean and they do not survive well in captivity. Females produce one calf after about a ten-and-a-half-month pregnancy. New calves are born about every three years.

Spinner dolphins and people: Spinners were the first dolphins captured for display in marine parks because of their ability to leap and spin, but they do not survive well in captivity. Their amazing leaps and spins attract ecotourists who want watch these animals in their natural habitat. Because they often associate with tuna, they are sometimes accidentally killed by fishing gear.

Conservation status: Spinner dolphins are not threatened. ■

Spinner dolphins form pods that may contain more than 1,000 individuals. They are very social and communicate with each other by sound and touch. (© Tony Wu/ www.silentsymphony.com. Reproduced by permission.)

FOR MORE INFORMATION

Books:

American Cetacean Society, Chuck Flaherty and David G. Gordon. *Field Guide to the Orcas.* Seattle: Sasquatch Books, 1990.

Carwadine, Mark, and Martin Camm. *Smithsonian Handbooks: Whales Dolphins and Porpoises.* New York: DK Publishing, 2002.

Ellis, Richard. *Dolphins and Porpoises.* New York: Knopf, 1989.

Gowell, Elizabeth T. *Whales and Dolphins: What They Have in Common.* New York: Franklin Watts, 2000.

Mead, James G., and Joy P. Gold. *Whales and Dolphins in Question: The Smithsonian Answer Book.* Washington, DC: Smithsonian Institution Press, 2002.

Nowak, Ronald. M. "Dolphins." In *Walker's Mammals of the World Online 5.1.* Baltimore: Johns Hopkins University Press, 1997. http://www.press.jhu.edu/books/walkers_mammals_of_the_world/cetacea/cetacea.delphinidae.html (accessed on July 8, 2004)

Web sites:

American Cetacean Society. http://www.acsonline.org (accessed on July 8, 2004).

"Animal Information." Sea World. http://www.seaworld.org/animal-info (accessed on July 8, 2004).

Dolphin Research Center. http://www.dolphins.org (accessed on July 8, 2004).

Whale and Dolphin Conservation Society. http://www.wdcs.org (accessed on July 8, 2004).

BEAKED WHALES

Ziphiidae

Class: Mammalia

Order: Cetacea

Family: Ziphiidae

Number of species: 21 species

PHYSICAL CHARACTERISTICS

Beaked whales are the second largest family of living whales. They get their name from their long, narrow snout, or beak. In some species, the snout slopes gradually into the forehead. In others, the forehead bulges out over the beak. Beaked whales breathe through a blowhole on top of their head. They have a melon, a fatty organ in their forehead that they use for echolocation (eck-oh-loh-KAY-shun).

Beaked whales are toothed whales. However, all species except Shepherd's beaked whale have very few teeth. Males usually have only one or two teeth in the lower jaw and just stubs or no visible teeth at all in the upper jaw. The lower jaw teeth grow into tusks in some species. In females of some species, the teeth never erupt, or break through the skin, although in x rays they can be seen in the jaw.

Beaked whales are medium-sized whales ranging from about 13 to 42 feet (4 to 13 meters) in length and weighing up to 25,000 pounds (11,500 kilograms). They have cigar-shaped bodies that are thicker in the middle than at either end. Their dorsal (back) fin is small and set farther back toward the tail than in other whales. The bones in what would be the hand and arm of a land animal are compressed into a web of bone to make small flippers that fit against their body in depressions called flipper pockets. The back legs are so reduced that all that remains are a few internal pelvic bones. Beaked whales have strong, muscular tails that, unlike most other whales, are not notched. They range in color from light brown to gray to black. Males and females may have different color patterns.

phylum

class

subclass

order

monotypic order

suborder

▲ **family**

GEOGRAPHIC RANGE

Beaked whales live in every ocean of the world. The only place they are not found is under the permanent ice pack at either pole.

HABITAT

Beaked whales are mainly deep water whales. They can be found beyond the continental shelf in water as shallow as 660 feet (200 meters) and as deep as 9,900 feet (3,000 meters). Most live at depths of 3,300 to 9,900 feet (1,000-3,000 meters). These whales are often found around underwater formations such as canyons, shelf edges, and seamounts. A seamount is an underwater mountain that does not break the surface.

DIET

Beaked whales are good divers. Scientists believe that they feed on squid, fish, shrimp, and crabs that live on or near the ocean floor, because they have discovered these animals plus stones in the stomachs of dead beaked whales.

Beaked whales have well-developed melons and use echolocation to find and catch their prey. Echolocation involves making sounds or clicks that are then focused through the melon and skull. These to sounds bounce off objects. Sense organs pick up the echo or reflected sound and use information about its the timing, direction, and strength to determine the location of objects. This is particularly useful, since little sunlight penetrates to the depths where these animals feed.

Since beaked whales have few teeth, they feed by sucking in their food. They have up to six groves in their throat that can expand and along with their strong tongue suck prey into their mouth. These whales also have between four and fourteen chambers, or sections, to their stomach.

BEHAVIOR AND REPRODUCTION

Not too much is known about beaked whale behavior or reproduction, because these animals live mainly in the open ocean and are hard to observe. They usually are seen in pods (groups) of ten or fewer animals, and within a pod they seem to swim or dive all at the same. This suggests that like other cetaceans, they have a good communication system. Some species regularly migrate, while others seem to stay within a home range.

From the scars that appear on the skin of some males, it appears that they fight each other with their tusks for the right to mate with females. One calf is born at a time. It stays with the mother and nurses for at least one year.

BEAKED WHALES AND PEOPLE

Three species of beaked whale were hunted mainly from the 1880s to the 1920s for their oil and spermaceti: the northern bottlenosed whale, Cuvier's whale, and Baird's whale. Otherwise beaked whales have few interactions with humans because they live so far off shore.

CONSERVATION STATUS

Not enough is known about most species of beaked whale to give them a conservation rating. However, four species, the northern bottlenose whale, the flathead bottlenose, Baird's beaked whale, and Arnoux's beaked whale, although not vulnerable to extinction, are listed as in need of conservation efforts.

STRANDED ON LAND

Scientists cannot explain why whales strand themselves on shore. Individual whales that strand are usually old or sick. However, sometimes whole pods, meaning dozens of animals, will strand at once. Usually these are deep-water toothed whales. Some scientists believe that their echolocation system does not function well when they accidentally stray into shallow water. Others think the whales are escaping a predator or are frightened by human-made underwater noises. Another theory is that disease or pollution makes them disoriented. Whatever the reason, people have recorded strandings for hundreds of years all over the world. Stranded animals that cannot be re-floated often die because they are so heavy out of water they cannot expand their lungs to breathe.

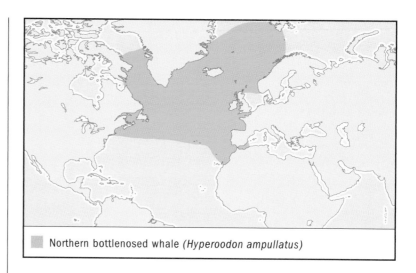

Northern bottlenosed whale (*Hyperoodon ampullatus*)

NORTHERN BOTTLENOSED WHALE
Hyperoodon ampullatus

Physical characteristics: The northern bottlenosed whale is also called the Atlantic bottlenosed whale, the flathead, or bottlehead. Males reach a maximum length of about 30 feet (9 meters), while females grow only to about 25 feet (7.5 meters). In addition, males develop a large, bulging forehead. The forehead of the female is much smoother. Both sexes have a short beak or snout and range in color from dark brown on the back to pale yellow on the belly. Mature males often have a white or light patch on the forehead. Males have one pair of small teeth in the lower jaw. In females, the teeth never break through the skin.

Geographic range: These whales are found in pockets in the North Atlantic off Norway, Finland, Greenland, Iceland, and as far south as Spain and North Africa on the European side. On North American side, they are found off the Labrador and Nova Scotia in Canada and as far south as Rhode Island in the United States. One particularly well-studied group lives in an area called the Gully, a deep canyon off Sable Island, Nova Scotia.

Habitat: Northern bottlenosed whales prefer deep, cold to moderate (32 to 63°F; 0 to 17°C) water, and sometimes travel into broken ice fields. They are usually seen in areas where the water is more than

Northern bottlenosed whales can stay underwater for seventy minutes before they need to surface for air. (Flip Nicklin/ Minden Pictures. Reproduced by permission.)

3,300 feet (1,000 meters) deep and are more common in the northern part of their range than in the southern part.

Diet: Northern bottlenosed whales feed near or at the ocean floor. They eat mainly squid, but will also eat fish, sea cucumbers, starfish, and shrimp. Like all toothed whales, they use echolocation to hunt their prey.

Behavior and reproduction: Northern bottlenosed whales live in groups of four to ten individuals. They are excellent deep divers and have been known to regularly dive to depths of between 2,600 and 4,600 feet (800-1400 meters) and stay under water for seventy minutes. These whales seem to migrate north in the summer and south in the winter in a regular pattern.

Not much is known about bottlenosed whale reproduction, although it is believed that males buck each other in the head in competitions to breed with females. Females are thought to be sexually mature (able to reproduce) at about seven to ten years old. A single calf is born in the spring or early summer after a twelve-month pregnancy. It stays with its mother and nurses for at least one year. Northern bottlenosed whales are thought to live for thirty to forty years.

Northern bottlenosed whales and people: These whales have few interactions with people.

Conservation status: These whales were hunted from the 1880s until the 1970s, mostly in Norway. One estimate is that Norwegian fisherman killed 60,000 northern bottlenosed whales between 1880 and 1930 and 5800 from 1930 to 1973. Hunting stopped in 1973, and in 1977 the whale became legally protected from hunting. Another threat to this species is human development. In Nova Scotia, a large undersea oil and gas field is being developed only about 3 miles (5 kilometers) from the Gully where these whales live. ■

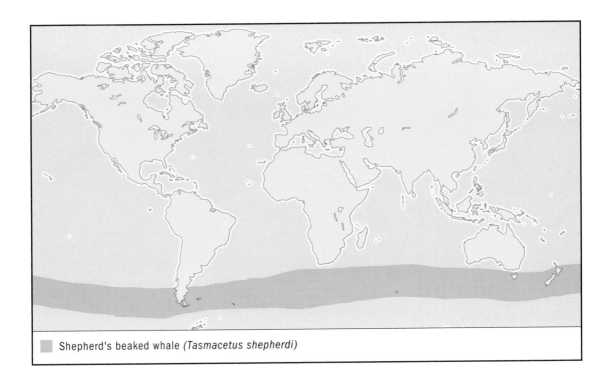

Shepherd's beaked whale (*Tasmacetus shepherdi*)

SHEPHERD'S BEAKED WHALE
Tasmacetus shepherdi

Physical characteristics: Shepherd's beaked whale, also called the Tasman beaked whale, has not been well studied. What is known about it comes mainly from about twenty stranded whales that have been found in various places in the Southern Hemisphere.

Shepherd's beaked whale is the only whale in this family to have more than half a dozen teeth, It has about 90 to 100 small peg-like teeth in both the upper and lower jaw. Two teeth in the lower jaw of males develop into tusks. Shepherd's beaked whale is about 23 feet (7 meters) long. It has a dark brown or gray back, two light stripes along its side and a light cream-colored belly.

Geographic range: These whales are found in temperate (moderate) water from Chile to South Africa to New Zealand.

Habitat: Shepherd's beaked whale lives in deep water in open ocean.

Shepherd's beaked whale lives in deep water in the open ocean, and was not discovered until 1937. Scientists do not know much about its behavior. (Illustration by Bruce Worden. Reproduced by permission.)

Diet: Unlike other members of this family that eat squid, the Shepherd's beaked whale appears to eat mainly fish.

Behavior and reproduction: This whale was not discovered until 1937. It is very rare. Almost nothing is known about its behavior or reproduction.

Shepherd's beaked whale and people: There have been only about half a dozen sightings of this whale outside of strandings.

Conservation status: Not enough information is available to give this whale a conservation ranking, although the absence of sightings suggests that it is rare. ■

FOR MORE INFORMATION

Books:

American Cetacean Society, Chuck Flaherty, and David G. Gordon. *Field Guide to the Orcas.* Seattle: Sasquatch Books, 1990.

Carwadine, Mark, and Martin Camm. *Smithsonian Handbooks: Whales Dolphins and Porpoises.* New York: DK Publishing, 2002.

Mead, James G., and Joy P. Gold. *Whales and Dolphins in Question: The Smithsonian Answer Book.* Washington, DC: Smithsonian Institution Press, 2002.

Nowak, Ronald. M. *Walker's Mammals of the World Online 5.1.* Baltimore: Johns Hopkins University Press, 1997. http://www.press.jhu.edu/books/walkers_mammals_of_the_world (accessed on July 8, 2004)

Web sites:

American Cetacean Society. http://www.acsonline.org (accessed July 8, 2004).

Culik, Boris. *"Hyperoodon ampullatus."* Convention on Migratory Species. http://www.cms.int/reports/small_cetaceans/data/H_ampullatus/h_ampullatus.htm (accessed July 8, 2004).

Whale and Dolphin Conservation Society. http://www.wdcs.org (accessed July 8, 2004).

PHYSICAL CHARACTERISTICS

The family of sperm whales contains the largest toothed whale—the giant sperm whale—and two smaller toothed whales. All are dark gray above, lighter gray on the belly, and have erupted (visible) teeth only in the lower jaw. Although these animals range in size and weight from 9 feet (2.7 meters) and 600 pounds (270 kilograms), to 60 feet (18.3 meters) and 125,000 pounds (57,000 kilograms), they have other physical features in common.

All members of this family have a spermaceti (spur-mah-CEE-tee) organ in their forehead. This produces a waxy substance called spermaceti. At the animal's body temperature, it is a clear yellowish liquid. After processing, it becomes a white waxy solid. It was prized in the 1800s and 1900s for making smoke-free candles and soap and as a way to waterproof cloth (called oil-skins). Later it was used in cosmetics, ointments, as a lubricant for watches and machinery, and in automatic transmission fluid. Today it has been replaced by human-made oils and waxes.

The purpose of the spermaceti organ is not clear. Some scientists think that it helps the whale regulate its buoyancy, or ability to sink or float, during dives. Others believe that it is used to focus the sounds made for echolocation (eck-oh-loh-KAY-shun) and communication. Echolocation involves making sounds that bounce off objects. Sense organs pick up the echo or reflected sound and use information about the timing, direction, and strength to determine the location of objects. Echolocation allows whales to find food in water so deep that there is no natural sunlight.

Members of the sperm whale family share other physical characteristics. Their heads are asymmetrical, meaning that if they were divided in half along the long axis of the body, the features in the right half would look different from the features in the left half. This is not common in mammals. As a result, a single S-shaped blowhole that allows the whale to breathe is located on the left side of the body. The left nasal passage is used for breathing, but the right one is narrower and is thought to be used to produce sounds.

GEOGRAPHIC RANGE

Members of this family are found in oceans worldwide.

HABITAT

These are deep-water whales, living in water over 3,300 feet (1,000 meters) deep. Smaller species may live in slightly shallower water.

DIET

Sperm whales eat mainly squid, although they will also eat fish, crabs, and octopus that live on or near the ocean bottom.

BEHAVIOR AND REPRODUCTION

Sperm whales appear to be very social, communicating through a series of clicks, whistles, and similar sounds. It appears as if each whale has a personal identification sound called a coda, that it makes when it meets other whales. These animals live in small groups. The composition of the group with regard to age, gender, and size changes as these animals age.

Almost nothing is known about reproduction in the smaller species of this family. Female giant sperm whales give birth about every five years after a pregnancy that lasts between fourteen and sixteen months. Mothers and calves have strong social bonds, and calves nurse for many years after birth.

WHAT IS SPERMACETI?

Spermaceti or sperm oil is a waxy substance, not a true oil, found in the head of marine mammals, especially the giant sperm whale. At the animal's body temperature, it is a clear yellowish liquid. After processing, it becomes a waxy solid. It was prized in the 1800s for making candles and soap and as a way to waterproof clothing (called oilskins). It was later used in cosmetics, ointments, and as a lubricant for watches. Today man-made oils and waxes are used in its place. An average sperm whale has 1,900 liters (500 gallons) of spermaceti.

WHAT IS AMBERGRIS?

Ambergris is a substance made in the digestive system of sperm whales. Sperm whales eat squid, which have sharp beaks that they use for biting food. The whales cannot digest the beaks of the squid, and eventually they begin to irritate the whale's digestive system. In response, sperm whales produce a material to cover the beaks. This is known as ambergris. It is rare and valuable. Since ancient times, ambergris has been used in perfumes to make the scent remain longer. Today human-made additives are available that do the same thing.

SPERM WHALES AND PEOPLE

Sperm whales were hunted for their spermaceti, blubber, and meat for many years. Minimal hunting still occurs. In parts of New Zealand, sperm whales form the basis of whale watching ecotoursism, where tourists observe whales without disturbing them.

CONSERVATION STATUS

Not enough is known about the smaller sperm whales to give them a conservation rating. Although there is some debate about population size, giant sperm whales are considered Vulnerable, facing a high risk of extinction, because of slow recovery from population declines that resulted from hunting.

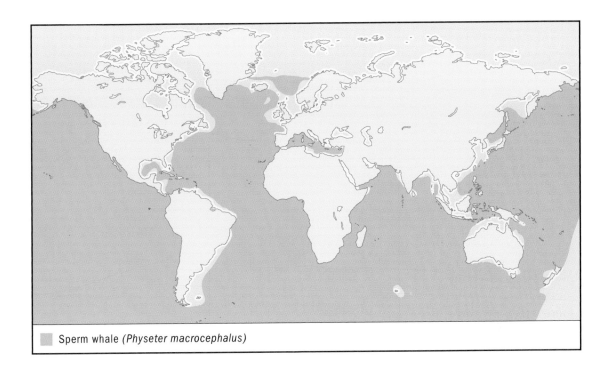

Sperm whale *(Physeter macrocephalus)*

SPERM WHALE
Physeter macrocephalus

Physical characteristics: Sperm whales, sometimes called giant sperm whales to distinguish them from the smaller members of this family, are the largest toothed whales. They can reach 60 feet (18.3 meters) in length and weigh 125,000 pounds (57,000 kilograms). Males are much larger than females, who reach only about 36 feet (11 meters) and 33,000 pounds (15,000 kilograms). Although these whales are usually dark gray, they can also be black or white (albino). An albino sperm whale is famous as the monster great white whale in Herman Melville's story *Moby Dick.*

Sperm whales, especially males, have huge square asymmetrical heads that take up about one-third the length of their body. They have the largest brain of any mammal, larger even than the brain of the giant blue whale, the largest mammal on earth. Their brain weighs an average of 20 pounds (9.2 kg). For comparison, the average adult human brain weighs less than 3 pounds (1.3 kilograms). The spermaceti organ can contain more than 500 gallons (1,900 liters) of spermaceti

Sperm whales can dive to depths of more than a mile (2.2 kilometers), and stay underwater an hour before coming to the surface to breathe. (© François Gohier/Photo Researchers, Inc. Reproduced by permission.)

oil. Their blubber can be almost 14 inches (35 centimeters) thick. Sperm whales have about thirty-five to fifty large cone-shaped teeth in their lower jaw only. When the whale closes its mouth, these teeth fit into pockets in the roof of the mouth. These teeth were prized by sailors who carved pictures on them in an art form known as scrimshaw.

Geographic range: Giant sperm whales are found in every ocean of the world.

Habitat: These whales live in deep water and are often found near underwater features such as seamounts (underwater mountains that do not rise above the surface of the ocean) and sharp drop-offs.

Diet: Sperm whales hunt their prey by echolocation deep in the ocean where there is no sunlight. They mainly eat squid, including the giant squid that can be over 50 feet (15 meters) long. Many whales have scars on the head made by the suckers of these squid as they battle the whale. They also eat smaller squid, fish, and sharks.

Behavior and reproduction: Giant sperm whales are champion divers and are able to dive deeper than any other whale. They can dive to depths of more than a mile (2.2 kilometers), and stay under water for an hour. Some scientists believe that they may be able to dive to depths of 10,000 feet (3,000 meters). More typically, these whales dive to depths of 1,000 to 2,600 feet (300-800 meters) and remain under water for thirty to forty-five minutes. They then rest at the surface for about ten minutes before diving again. Females do not dive as deep as males and may spend more time at the surface with their calves. These whales swim at about 6 miles per hour (10 kilometers per hour) but can reach speeds of 19 miles per hour (30 kilometers per hour) when hunting or avoiding danger.

Females become sexually mature and able to reproduce when they are about eight years old. Males may be capable of reproducing earlier, but usually do not do so until they are nineteen or twenty years old. Females give birth every five to seven years. The mother-calf bond is strong and socially important. Mothers may continue to nurse their young for up to thirteen years. Mothers and calves form groups of about twenty to forty individuals (although one group of 3,000 to 4,000 animals was seen off the coast of South America) that appear to stay together and assist each other. For example, since calves cannot make deep dives, some females will take turns staying at the surface guarding the young from killer whales while their others dive for food.

As the young mature, the males leave the group and swim with other young males in groups of about twelve to fifteen individuals. As they grow older, they split off into smaller and smaller groups. It is common for an old male to swim alone. Males tend to move toward the poles and come back to warmer water where the female groups stay when it is time to breed. The males fight for the right to breed, which is why young males rarely start reproducing until age twenty. Once mating has occurred, the males leave the group of females and calves and go off on their own again. Sperm whales are thought to live about seventy years.

Sperm whales make a wide variety of sounds with the help of specially modified nasal passages and air sacs. The sounds they make are loud and carry well over long distances. It appears that each whale has a signature "song" to identify it to other whales. They also make clicks for echolocation and ringing sounds that may be involved in attracting a mate.

Sperm whales and people: Sperm whales have been hunted since the early 1700s, with peak whaling activity between 1880 and 1930 and 1950 to 1975. They are valued for their spermaceti, oil, and ambergris (AM-bur-gris), a waste product used in manufacturing perfumes. Whale meat is also eaten in some countries such as Japan.

Conservation status: Sperm whale hunting stopped in 1985. However, in 2000, Japan resumed hunting for what they called "scientific research" and has continued to kill between five and ten sperm whales each year. Sperm whales are considered Vulnerable. Because it takes them so long to mature and they have calves only every five to seven years, it will take a long time for their populations to recover from hunting. They are also at risk from collisions with ships and accidental entanglement in fishing nets and transatlantic communication cables. ■

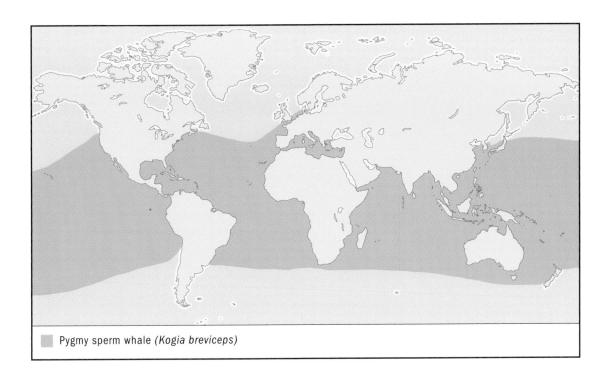

Pygmy sperm whale *(Kogia breviceps)*

PYGMY SPERM WHALE
Kogia breviceps

Physical characteristics: The pygmy sperm whale is one of two small species in this family. These whales are about 11 feet long (3.4 meters) and weigh about 600 pounds (400 kilograms). They have blue-gray backs and a shape that makes them look something like a shark. Unlike the giant sperm whale, their head is only about 15 percent of their body length. They also have a much smaller spermaceti organ, and their blowhole is located on the left side of the forehead. Pygmy sperm whales have about thirty sharp, curved teeth only in the lower jaw.

Geographic range: These whales are found worldwide in temperate and tropical water.

Habitat: Pygmy sperm whales live in deep ocean and less deep water over continental shelves. They prefer moderate or warm waters and avoid the very cold waters of the Arctic.

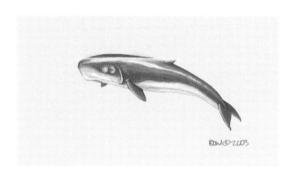

Pygmy sperm whales are rarely seen, and little is known about their behavior. (Illustration by Bruce Worden. Reproduced by permission.)

Diet: Pygmy sperm whales feed on squid, octopus, fish, and crabs. They eat deep-dwelling species as well as species that live in the less deep waters over continental shelves.

Behavior and reproduction: Little is known about these animals. They have been seen floating without moving on the surface or swimming slowly. They are not often observed, but when they are seen, they are often in mother-calf pairs or in groups of fewer than five animals. These animals appear to give birth to a single calf every year after a pregnancy lasting eleven months. Beyond that, little is known about their mating behavior.

Pygmy sperm whales and people: These animals are rarely seen. Occasionally they are accidentally caught in fishing gear.

Conservation status: Too little is known about the population of pygmy sperm whales to give them a conservation rating. ∎

FOR MORE INFORMATION

Books:

American Cetacean Society, Chuck Flaherty, and David G. Gordon. *Field Guide to the Orcas.* Seattle: Sasquatch Books, 1990.

Carwadine, Mark, and Martin Camm. *Smithsonian Handbooks: Whales Dolphins and Porpoises.* New York: DK Publishing, 2002.

Mead, James G., and Joy P. Gold. *Whales and Dolphins in Question: The Smithsonian Answer Book.* Washington, DC: Smithsonian Institution Press, 2002.

Nowak, Ronald. M.*Walker's Mammals of the World Online 5.1.* Baltimore: Johns Hopkins University Press, 1997. http://www.press.jhu.edu/books/walkers_mammals_of_the_world (accessed on July 8, 2004).

Web sites:

American Cetacean Society. http://www.acsonline.org (accessed on July 8, 2004).

Bird, Jonathan. "Sperm Whales: The Deep Divers of the Ocean." Oceanic Research Group. http://www.oceanicresearch.org/spermwhales.htm (accessed on July 8, 2004).

Culik, Boris. *"Kogia breviceps."* Convention on Migratory Species. http://www.cms.int/reports/small_cetaceans/data/K_breviceps/K_breviceps.htm (accessed on July 8, 2004).

Whale and Dolphin Conservation Society. http://www.wdcs.org (accessed on July 8, 2004).

BELUGA AND NARWHAL

Monodontidae

Class: Mammalia

Order: Cetacea

Family: Monodontidae

Number of species: 2 species

phylum

class

subclass

order

monotypic order

suborder

▲ **family**

PHYSICAL CHARACTERISTICS

Beluga whales and narwhals are the only two living species in this family. Although they look quite different, these species share certain physical characteristics, including a very small beak and small head. Their neck bones (cervical vertebrae) are not fused or joined together, giving them the ability to turn their head without turning their entire body. Neither species has a dorsal (back) fin, only a ridge where the fin normally is found. The lack of a fin is unusual in whales. Members of this family range in size from 13 to 16 feet (4 to 5 meters) and in weight from 1,500 to 3,500 pounds (680 to 1,600 kg).

Both species change color as they age. Belugas are born gray, but gradually become white by the time they reach maturity at seven to nine years. Narwhals are born gray. As young animals, they become almost completely blue-black. In adulthood they become mottled (spotted) dark gray, with more dense splotches on the back and less dense ones on the belly. In old age, they become white.

The main difference in these species is in their teeth. Belugas have simple teeth in both the upper and lower jaw. Narwhals have only two teeth in the upper jaw. In females, these teeth do not erupt or become visible. In males, one tooth becomes a spiraled tusk that may be 10 feet (3 meters) long.

GEOGRAPHIC RANGE

Both these species live in the Arctic oceans, although their distribution is not continuous.

HABITAT

Narwhals live in deep water farther north than any other whale, following the ice pack as it grows and recedes. Beluga whales live in shallower water and are sometimes found farther south. In the summer, they move into estuaries (places where rivers empty into the ocean). They can survive in fresh water and have occasionally been found swimming hundreds of miles (kilometers) up river from the ocean.

DIET

Both these species are bottom feeders, diving deep to eat squid, fish, and shrimp. Narwhals have a more limited diet than belugas.

BEHAVIOR AND REPRODUCTION

Both narwhals and beluga whales live in small groups or pods, although these pods may gather in groups of hundreds or thousands of animals during migrations. These species are social and communicate with a wide range of sounds. Both species migrate. The narwhal follows the ice pack, moving north as it melts in summer and south as it grows in winter. The migration of belugas appears to be triggered by day length. Not all groups of belugas migrate. One well-studied group that live at the mouth of the St. Lawrence River in Canada appears to stay there year round.

These whales give birth to a single calf at a time after a pregnancy lasting thirteen to sixteen months. The calf nurses, feeds on breast milk, and remains dependent on its mother for up to two years. Mating usually occurs in late winter or early spring and births occur in the summer of the following year.

BELUGAS, NARWHALS, AND PEOPLE

The native people of the Arctic, the Inuit, have hunted narwhals and beluga whales for hundreds of years. These animals are an important part of their diet and culture. Both species have also been hunted commercially.

CONSERVATION STATUS

Beluga whales are considered Vulnerable, facing a high risk of extinction, dying out. Not enough is known about the size of the narwhal population to give them a conservation rating. All narwhals that have been taken into captivity have lived only a few months. However, beluga whales do well in captivity and are often exhibited at marine parks.

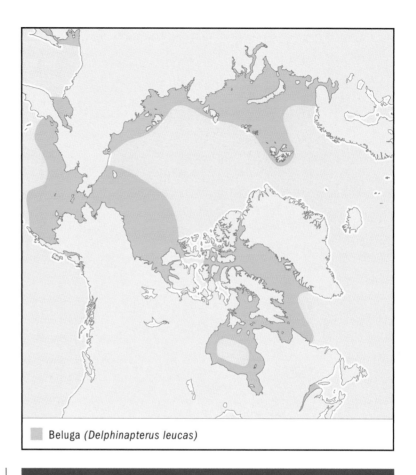

Beluga *(Delphinapterus leucas)*

BELUGA
Delphinapterus leucas

Physical characteristics: Beluga whales, sometimes called white whales, begin life colored light gray, then turn darker gray and become white as they mature. They are the only species of whale that is completely white. Beluga whales range in length from 13 to 16 feet (4 to 5 meters) and in weight from 1,500 to 3,500 pounds (700 to 1,600 kilograms). Males are about 25 percent larger than females.

Geographic range: These whales are found worldwide in the Arctic. Isolated populations also exist in the Gulf of St. Lawrence, Canada, and in Cook Inlet, Alaska.

Habitat: Belugas live in cold water of almost any depth. During the summer they gather in shallow water at the mouths of rivers. At other

times, they migrate through deep, open ocean. They can survive in fresh water, and have been occasionally found in rivers far from the ocean.

Diet: Belugas eat a wide variety of squid, fish, crabs, shrimp, clams, worms, and octopus that they find by echolocation (eck-oh-loh-KAY-shun). They can easily dive to depths of 3,300 feet (1,000 meters). Their teeth are not made for capturing prey. Instead, they suction food into their mouths and swallow it whole.

Behavior and reproduction: Belugas are some of the most playful whales. They have been seen swimming and playing either alone or with other whales with all kinds of floating objects. They live in pods of less than ten animals, but these pods often gather into large herds of hundreds of animals.

Belugas are the most vocal species of whale. Their voices are loud and varied. They make clicks, chirps, whistles, squawks, and other high-pitched sounds.

Mating occurs in early spring and a single calf is born about fourteen months later. During the summer, females gather in shallow waters at the mouths of rivers to give birth, probably because the water there is warmer than in the open ocean. Calves nurse for about two years. A new calf is normally born every three years. Belugas are thought to live between thirty-five and forty years in the wild.

Natural predators, animals that hunt them for food, of the beluga whale include killer whales and polar bears. Polar bears lie in wait at breathing holes in the ice and attack when the whale surfaces to take a breath.

Beluga whales and people: Belugas have been hunted commercially for food mainly by the Russians. They adapt well to captivity and are also captured for display in marine entertainment parks. Ecotourists visit the population in the St. Lawrence River to observe them in their natural environment.

Conservation status: Beluga whales are considered Vulnerable. Some populations, like the one at the mouth of the St. Lawrence River are coming under increasing pressure from chemical pollution, shipping, and the development of undersea oil and gas fields. ■

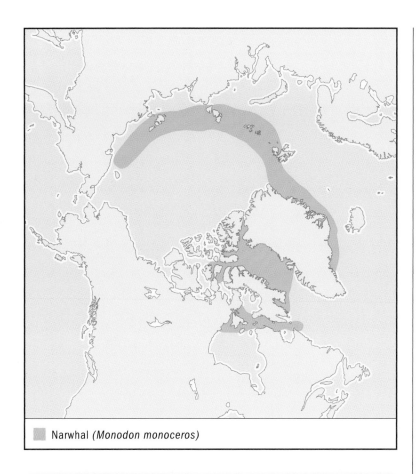

Narwhal (*Monodon monoceros*)

NARWHAL
Monodon monoceros

Physical characteristics: Narwhals grow to be about 14 to 15.5 feet (4.2 to 4.7 meters) long and weigh 2,200 to 3,500 pounds (1,000 to 1,600 kilograms). Males are much larger than females.

The most outstanding physical feature of the narwhal is its ivory tusk. The tusk is a tooth that in males grows out of the left side of the upper jaw in a counter-clockwise spiral. Tusks can grow to be one-third the length of the body, or 30 feet (10 meters) long, and weigh 20 pounds (10.5 kilograms). Narwhals have two teeth in the upper jaw, and occasionally the right tooth will also grow into a tusk. Once in a great while, a female will develop a tusk. Tusks are often broken, but will heal and continue to grow.

The male narwhal's tusk is a tooth that grows out of the left side of the upper jaw in a counter-clockwise spiral. (© Goran Ehlme/Seapics.com. Reproduced by permission.)

Geographic range: Narwhals are limited to the coldest Arctic waters. They are not evenly distributed and are rare along Alaska, Siberia, and parts of Arctic western Canada.

Habitat: Narwhals live in colder water than any other whale. They follow the ice pack, moving north in the summer as it retreats and south in the winter as it grows. They often swim long distances under thick ice, coming up to breathe in small cracks called leads.

Diet: Narwhals feed along the sea bottom, eating squid and deep water fishes. They can dive to depths of about 3,300 feet (1,000 meters) and stay under water for up to twenty-five minutes. They locate their food by echolocation. Echolocation involves making sounds that bounce off objects. Sense organs pick up the echo or reflected sound and use information about its the timing, direction, and strength to determine the location of objects.

Behavior and reproduction: Narwhals are social animals. They live in groups or pods of three to eight individuals, usually of the same sex and age. When they migrate, these pods may gather to form groups of hundreds or even thousands of animals. Narwhals have been known to work cooperatively to open breathing holes in the ice. Several animals will simultaneously butt their foreheads against the ice sheet in order to break it. This suggests that they have some form of group communication.

Narwhals mate in the early spring and have a single calf in July or August of the following year. Scientists are not sure, but they think that males fight each other with their tusks for the right to mate. Females normally produce a calf every three years. Pregnancy lasts about fifteen months. Newborns are 5 feet (1.6 meters) long and weight about 175 pounds (80 kilograms). They are born with a 1-inch (2.5-centimeter) thick layer of blubber to protect them from the cold water. Calves nurse for about twenty months and may remain with their mother longer. They become physically mature between four and seven years of age and can live fifty years in the wild. Natural predators of the narwhal are the killer whale and the Greenland shark.

Narwhals and people: The ivory in the tusks of narwhals has commercial value. It is often carved into jewelry or decorations. The tusks are also sold as curiosities to collectors. In earlier times, narwhal tusks brought back by sailors may have given rise to the story of the unicorn, a one-horned horse.

Conservation status: Not enough is known about the population of narwhals to give them a conservation ranking. Threats include being hunted for food and for their tusks. Global warming is of particular concern to the survival of this species, because they live in and around the ice pack. ■

FOR MORE INFORMATION

Books:

American Cetacean Society, Chuck Flaherty, and David G. Gordon. *Field Guide to the Orcas.* Seattle: Sasquatch Books, 1990.

Carwadine, Mark, and Martin Camm. *Smithsonian Handbooks: Whales Dolphins and Porpoises.* New York: DK Publishing, 2002.

Mead, James G., and Joy P. Gold. *Whales and Dolphins in Question: The Smithsonian Answer Book.* Washington, DC: Smithsonian Institution Press, 2002.

Nowak, Ronald. M. *Walker's Mammals of the World Online 5.1.* Baltimore: Johns Hopkins University Press, 1997. http://www.press.jhu.edu/books/walkers_mammals_of_the_world (accessed on July 8, 2004).

Web sites:

American Cetacean Society. http://www.acsonline.org (accessed on July 8, 2004).

Drury, C. *"Monodon monoceros* (Narwhal).*"* Animal Diversity Web http://animaldiversity.ummz.umich.edu/site/accounts/information/Monodon_monoceros.html (accessed on July 8, 2004).

Whale and Dolphin Conservation Society. http://www.wdcs.org (accessed on July 8, 2004).

Williams, S. *"Delphinapterus leucas* (Beluga).*"* Animal Diversity Web http://animaldiversity.ummz.umich.edu/site/accounts/information/Delphinapterus_leucas.html (accessed on July 8, 2004).

PHYSICAL CHARACTERISTICS

Gray whales are very large animals that weigh 30 to 40 tons (27,200 to 36,300 kilograms) and are 45 to 50 feet (13.8 to 15 meters) in length. Females are larger than males. These whales have a streamlined body with a narrow head. The upper jaw overlaps with the lower jaw, and they have two to four throat grooves. Each groove is about 5 feet (1.4 meters) long and allows the throat to expand when the whale takes in water for filter feeding.

Gray whales are baleen (buh-LEEN or BAY-leen) whales. They do not have teeth. They filter feed using 130 to 180 overlapping plates called baleen plates that hang from the upper jaw. These plates are made of a material called keratin (KARE-ah-tin). This fingernail-like material frays out into thin hairs at the end of each strand to make a strainer. Each baleen plate is white and about 2 to 10 inches (5 to 25 centimeters) in length.

Gray whales have a 10-inch (25-centimeter) layer of blubber, or fat, to keep them warm in freezing cold water. Their skin is dark with gray patches and white splotches. Their skin also shows many scars and patches from white barnacles and orange whale lice. Often many more of these patches are found on the left side of the whale than on the right because of the way the whale scrapes along the ocean floor while feeding.

Although the gray whale does not have a dorsal (back) fin, it does have a large dorsal hump about two-thirds of the way back on its body. Behind the hump is a row of six to twelve knuckles that extend to its fluke, otherwise known as its tail.

phylum

class

subclass

order

monotypic order

suborder

▲ **family**

DEVIL FISH

Gray whales got the nickname "devil fish" from early whalers who hunted off the coast of the Baja Peninsula. They got this name because the gray whale mother is so protective of its calf. The mother will make any sacrifice, including death, to protect her young. Soon whalers found that it was too dangerous to hunt these whales from boats in the water, so they started a new technique where they would herd the whales toward the beach and harpoon them from land.

The fluke is 10 to 12 feet (3.7 meters) across with a deeply notched center and pointed tips. The flippers are shaped like paddles and are also pointed at the tips.

GEOGRAPHIC RANGE

Gray whales migrate between northwest Alaska in the Chukchi Sea, where they live during the summer, and the Baja Peninsula of Mexico, where they live during the winter. A few individual gray whales live year-round in the Straits of Juan de Fuca, located between the state of Washington and Vancouver Island, Canada, and off the coast of California. Most whales, however, make the 10,000-mile (16,000-kilometer) trip from Mexico to the Arctic yearly.

HABITAT

Gray whales prefer shallow coastal water but dive to the ocean floor to feed. Every year gray whales spend two to three months migrating 10,000 miles (16,000 kilometers) from their summer home in Alaska to the warmer coastal waters off of the Baja Peninsula, Mexico, where they stay all winter.

DIET

Gray whales eat a variety of small shrimp, krill, squid, and octopus, along with plankton and mollusks. They are seasonal feeders, doing most of their feeding between May and November in the Arctic, but they are unique among baleen whales because they are bottom feeders. To eat, they dive to the bottom and roll on to their right side. They suck the stirred-up bottom mud and water into their mouth. This is filtered through the whale's baleen plates, trapping the food near the tongue where it can be eaten.

BEHAVIOR AND REPRODUCTION

Gray whales live in small groups (called pods) of about three whales, although some pods may have as many as sixteen whales. In feeding waters, pods come together, and hundreds of whales will temporarily feed in the same area.

Although gray whales are large, they are quite agile. Normally gray whales swim only 2 to 6 miles per hour (3 to 10 kilometers per hour), but when in danger, they can reach speeds of 10 to 11 miles per hour (16 to 17.5 kilometers per hour). While feeding, gray whales usually swim at speeds of 1 to 2.5 miles per hour (1.6 to 4 kilometers per hour).

Gray whales can do many different maneuvers (mah-NOO-verz) including breaching, where they jump partially out of the water and fall back in at an angle. This makes a loud noise and is thought to either help clean off some of the barnacles and lice on their skin or to communicate with other gray whales. Spy hopping is another favorite maneuver. This is when the whale pokes its head up to 10 feet (3 meters) out of the water and looks around while turning slowly.

Gray whales can stay underwater for thirty minutes and dive to depths of 500 feet (155 meters) while searching for food. When they come back to the surface, they take in air through two blowholes located near the top of their head. Before they go under water for a long time, they spend two to five minutes taking deep, slow breaths. When at rest, gray whales breathe about two to three times per minute. While sleeping, they keep their blowhole just above the surface. Each spout, or breath, is very noisy and can be heard up to a half mile away. The stream of water that comes from the blowhole rises 10 to 13 feet 3 to 4 meters) above the water and is a very impressive sight.

Gray whales reach sexual maturity when they are about 36 to 39 feet (11 to 12 meters) long. This usually occurs between five and eleven years of age. Courtship and mating involves three or more whales of both sexes and is very complex. Both mating and calving usually occur off the coast of Baja California, Mexico. After breeding, which usually takes place in late winter or early spring, females are pregnant for twelve to thirteen months. When the calf is born, it is about 15 feet (4.5 meters) long and weighs somewhere between 1,100 and 1,500 pounds (500 to 600 kilograms). The calf spends seven to eight months nursing on its mother's milk, which is 53 percent fat. Females have a single calf only every two to four years.

When the calf is born, it immediately swims to the surface. Its mother helps it, because the newborn cannot swim for the first half hour of its life. Gray whales stop growing at the age of forty and usually live to be between fifty and sixty years old.

A LONG TRIP

Gray whales migrate 10,000 miles every year between Alaska and Mexico. This is the longest migration of any mammal. During this time, they do not eat, but live off their stored blubber.

Adult gray whales can stay underwater for thirty minutes. But when calves are first born, their mothers must help them to swim to the surface for air, because the newborn cannot swim for the first half hour of its life. (© François Gohier/Photo Researchers, Inc. Reproduced by permission.)

Gray whales do not have many predators, animals that hunt them for food. The largest and most significant are humans, who spent thousands of years hunting these whales almost to extinction. Killer whales, also known as orcas, will attack gray whales and often kill them. Killer whales make most of the scars on the backs of gray whales. Most of these attacks happen off the coast of northwest Oregon. Large sharks have also been known to attack gray whales, but that is much less common.

GRAY WHALES AND PEOPLE

For thousands of years, people have hunted the gray whale for oil, meat, hide, and baleen. This has caused a major decline, and two of the three populations located throughout the world were killed off. As the gray whale became protected by the International Whaling Commission, whale watching has replaced hunting. Now millions of people watch gray whales along the peninsula of Baja California and as they migrate along the West Coast of North America. Some gray whales are known as "friendlies" and will come up to small boats and allow themselves to be touched.

CONSERVATION STATUS

At one time there were three separate gray whale populations in the world. A population in the North Atlantic became

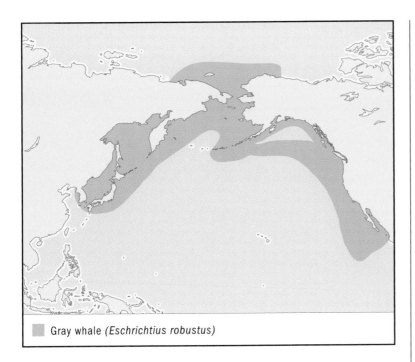

Gray whale *(Eschrichtius robustus)*

extinct during the mid-1700s because of overhunting. The western Pacific population was also overhunted to extinction in the 1930s. Now, only the eastern Pacific stock remains. These whales were hunted almost to extinction in the 1850s. In 1937, the International Whaling Commission gave the gray whale partial protection, and in 1947 this was changed to full protection. The Eastern Pacific gray whale population has made an extraordinary recovery. Their numbers now range between 19,000 and 23,000 individuals. This number is close to their original population.

FOR MORE INFORMATION

Books:

Carwadine, Mark, and Martin Camm. *Smithsonian Handbooks: Whales Dolphins and Porpoises.* New York: DK Publishing, 2002.

Gowell, Elizabeth T. *Whales and Dolphins: What They Have in Common.* New York: Franklin Watts, 2000.

Mead, James G., and Joy P. Gold. *Whales and Dolphins in Question: The Smithsonian Answer Book.* Washington, DC: Smithsonian Institution Press, 2002.

Nowak, Ronald M. *Walker's Mammals of the World.* Baltimore: Johns Hopkins University Press, 1995.

Web sites:

American Cetacean Society. http://www.acsonline.org (accessed on July 8, 2004).

"Baleen Whales." SeaWorld/Busch Gardens Animal Information Database. http://www.seaworld.org/infobooks/Baleen/home.html (accessed on July 8, 2004).

International Whaling Commission. http://www.iwcoffice.org/ (accessed on July 8, 2004).

Whale and Dolphin Conservation Society. http://www.wdcs.org (accessed on July 8, 2004).

PYGMY RIGHT WHALE
Neobalaenidae

Class: Mammalia
Order: Cetacea
Family: Neobalaenidae
One species: Pygmy right whale
(*Caperea marginata*)

CHAPTER

PHYSICAL CHARACTERISTICS

The pygmy right whale is the smallest of the baleen (buh-LEEN or BAY-leen) whales. It ranges from 5.2 to 7.2 feet (1.6-2.2 meters) in length and weighs around 4.5 tons (4,000 kilograms). Females are larger than males. The largest female ever recorded was 21.3 feet (6.45 meters), while the largest male was 20 feet (6.05 meters). The pygmy right whale is the only species in this family and should not be confused with right whales in the family Balaenidae.

Like all baleen whales, the pygmy right whale is a filter feeder. Pygmy right whales do not have teeth. Instead, it has many overlapping plates, called baleen plates, which hang like a curtain from the upper jaw. These plates are made of a material called keratin (KARE-ah-tin). This horny, fingernail-like material frays out into thin hairs at the end of each strand to make a strainer. The whale opens its mouth to feed and sucks in a lot of water. It then pushes the water out through the baleen plates and uses its tongue to lick up food that remains.

The pygmy right whale's head is one-fourth the size of its body. Its most noticeable characteristics are a highly arched jaw and large lips. Inside the pygmy's mouth are 460 ivory-colored baleen; these are lined up, with 230 on each side of the upper jaw. This baleen is thought to be more flexible and tougher than the baleen of any other species. Each piece varies from 1 to 28 inches (2.5 to 70 centimeters) wide and can be as long as 4 inches (10 centimeters). The size of each baleen depends on where it is in the mouth.

phylum

class

subclass

order

monotypic order

suborder

▲ **family**

THE RAREST WHALE

The pygmy right whale is the rarest and least understood of all the baleen (filter feeding) whales. Only about two dozen specimens have been studied. Some things about this whale resemble whales in the rorqual family. Other characteristics are similar to whales in the right whale family. In the past, pygmy right whales have been classified as part of the right whale family, but today, scientists believe that it is different enough to be put in a family of its own.

The head of the pygmy right whale has more hair than most other whales, with 100 hairs on the upper jaw and over 300 on the tip of the lower jaw. This whale has very small eyes, but good sight is not very important to it in finding food.

The pygmy right whale has a dark gray head that, with age, gets lighter along the lower jaw until it turns white on its underside. The back of the whale is also dark gray and has two blowholes located near the front of the head. Two-thirds of the way back is a very small dorsal (back) fin. The fin grows to be only about 6 inches (15 centimeters) high. The flippers are darker than the rest of the body. They are very narrow and are rounded at the ends.

GEOGRAPHIC RANGE

The pygmy right whale lives deep in Southern Hemisphere in the Atlantic, Pacific, and Indian Oceans. Most often this species is seen around Australia, Tasmania, New Zealand, South Africa, and the southern tip of South America.

HABITAT

Pygmy right whales live where the surface water is between 41 and 68°F (5 and 20°C). Not much else is known about the habitat preferences of this whale.

DIET

The pygmy right whale eats small squid, octopus, krill, and shrimp-like marine animals. Their method of feeding has never been observed, but it is thought that this whale uses a surface-skimming technique instead of diving deep to feed.

BEHAVIOR AND REPRODUCTION

There have been very few sightings of pygmy rights, so little is known about their behavior. They are often seen in pairs or pods of up to ten individuals, but there have been occasional sightings of groups as large as eighty. To communicate, pygmy right whales use intense thumps or tones, each quickly rising and slowly falling, as the frequency drops.

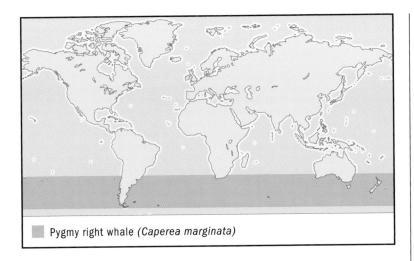

Pygmy right whale (*Caperea marginata*)

The pygmy right whale is a very slow swimmer. It often spends only a few seconds on the surface when it comes up for air, usually just sticking its snout out of the water. The longest recorded dive of a pygmy lasted only four minutes. This whale is not known to do any acrobatic leaps out of the water. It is rarely seen at sea.

Since so little is known about the pygmy whale, there is little information about the mating season, mating practices, or length of pregnancy. Calves are around 6.5 feet (2 meters) at birth. Many researchers believe that calving may take place year-round. Calves stop nursing when they are between 9 and 11.2 feet (3 and 3.5 meters) long. Sexual maturity (the ability to reproduce) is reached when the animals are about 16 to 20 feet (5 to 6 meters) in length. Their average lifespan has not been determined.

PYGMY RIGHT WHALE AND PEOPLE

The pygmy whale has little to no contact with humans. Because it is so rare, the pygmy has never been hunted. The only human-caused deaths come from occasional entanglement in fishing nets.

CONSERVATION STATUS

Only a few dozen pygmy right whales have ever been examined, and only a few hundred have been identified. They are not on the endangered species list because of a lack of information, but are still thought to be threatened with extinction.

Only about two dozen pygmy right whales have been studied, and they are rarely seen at sea. There is still a lot to learn about how they live. (Illustration by Brian Cressman. Reproduced by permission.)

They are the only baleen whales not to have been threatened by large-scale commercial hunting. There is concern that this whale might be confused with the Antarctic minke whale, which it resembles. The Antarctic minke whale is still hunted by Japanese whalers. The pygmy is thought to be threatened by global climate change, but not by toxic pollution. Overall, it seems to be so rare not because of the lack of animals, but because of a lack of data and research.

FOR MORE INFORMATION

Books:

Nowak, Ronald. M. *Walker's Mammals of the World.* Baltimore: Johns Hopkins University Press, 1995.

Web sites:

American Cetacean Society. http://www.acsonline.org (accessed on July 8, 2004).

"*Caperea marginata:* Pygmy Right Whale." Cetacea. http://www.cetacea. org/pright.htm (accessed on July 8, 2004).

Cover, Sarah. "*Caperea marginata* (Pygmy Right Whale)." Animal Diversity Web. http://animaldiversity.ummz.umich.edu/site/accounts/ information/Caperea_marginata.html (accessed on July 8, 2004).

"Fishin' for Facts: Pygmy Right Whale." Whale Times. http://www. whaletimes.org/pygrtwha.htm (accessed on July 8, 2004).

Whale and Dolphin Conservation Society. http://www.wdcs.org (accessed on July 8, 2004).

RIGHT WHALES AND BOWHEAD WHALES
Balaenidae

Class: Mammalia
Order: Cetacea
Family: Balaenidae
Number of species: 4 species

family
CHAPTER

PHYSICAL CHARACTERISTICS

Right whales and bowhead whales are baleen (buh-LEEN or BAY-leen) whales. Like all baleen whales, these whales are filter feeders. Right whales and bowhead whales do not have teeth. Instead, they have many overlapping plates, called baleen plates that hang like a curtain from the upper jaw. These plates are made of a material called keratin (KARE-ah-tin). This horny fingernail-like material frays out into thin hairs at the end of each strand to make a strainer. The whale opens its mouth to feed and sucks in a lot of water. It then pushes the water out through the baleen plates and uses its tongue to lick up food that remains, caught by the plates.

Right whales and bowhead whales are generally between 43 and 65 feet (13 to 20 meters) long. They weigh between 168,000 and 224,000 pounds (76,200 to 101,600 kilograms). They have large heads and a curved mouth that allows them more baleen surface than baleen whales with a straight mouth. Because they are mammals, whales must come to the surface of the water to breathe. They breathe through a blowhole located on top of their head. The blowhole is connected to the lungs.

Bowhead and right whales are almost entirely black, but they do have a patch of white around their chin, as well as a band of lighter color on their tail. The easiest way to tell the difference between a bowhead whale and a right whale is that right whales have bumps around their head, near their mouth, and around their eyes. These bumps are actually places where small animals known as whale lice live. These parasites are not

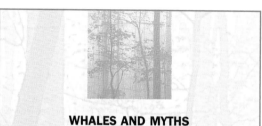

WHALES AND MYTHS

Whales have played an important role in popular culture. In the story of Pinocchio, a father and his wooden boy are swallowed by a whale. In *Moby Dick,* Captain Ahab pursues a white whale that attacks his ship. While these tales tell us of the fear that people have had of whales for centuries, it is important to remember that whales do not feed on people. Most large whales are not even capable of swallowing a person.

thought to be harmful to the whales. Bowhead whales do not have these bumps.

GEOGRAPHIC RANGE

Right and bowhead whales can be found throughout most of the world's oceans and seas. They go farther into the Arctic than many other whales and are capable of breaking through newly formed ice up to 9 inches (23 centimeters) thick. These whales do not generally enter the warmest waters close to the equator.

HABITAT

Right whales and bowhead whales travel long distances and can live in a variety of habitats. They generally find warmer temperatures for birthing along coastal regions and bays. They are capable of traveling far into the polar regions and navigating through icy waters to find krill for feeding.

DIET

Right whales and bowhead whales feed on small marine animals called krill by using their baleen. They do this by taking in water and krill as they open their large mouth. Next, they close their mouth most of the way, until only the baleen is exposed between their lips at the sides of the mouth, like a sieve (SIV). Then they push the water through the baleen and out between their lips, but the krill are trapped in the baleen and are left in the whale's mouth. By scraping the baleen with their huge tongue, the whales are able to swallow the food that is left after the water rushes out.

BEHAVIOR AND REPRODUCTION

Like all baleen whales, bowhead whales and right whales migrate. They spend the colder times of the year in warmer water closer to the equator and then move towards the polar regions of the Arctic and Antarctica where they spend the rest of the year. They do most of their feeding in the colder regions, and give birth in the warmer areas. Female right whales and bowhead whales give birth to one young at a time after a year of pregnancy. The young are nursed for about six months. They reach maturity after eight or nine years. Right whales can live as long as seventy years, but bowheads can live even longer, some past one hundred years.

Right and bowhead whales are known for their songs and the other types of sounds they make. Some people have described these sounds as grunts, roars, growls, belches, complex screams, or pulses. In the spring-time, bowhead whales send out complicated songs with themes, sets of notes that are repeated. It is thought that these serve as communication between males and females.

ANCIENT TREASURES

In 1995, a bowhead whale was killed in Alaska. When it was processed, it was found to have two stone harpoon blades in its flesh. This type of harpoon has not been used to hunt whales since the late 1800s. This means that the whale had to be over one hundred years old when it was killed.

RIGHT WHALES AND BOWHEAD WHALES AND PEOPLE

Throughout the nineteenth century and until recent times, right and bowhead whales were among those whales most sought by hunters. Whalers would bring in thousands of whales every year. Not only were whales a plentiful source of meat, but their blubber could be used to make oil for lamps. The baleen whales were particularly prized, because baleen could be used to make hoop skirts, shirt collars, and other clothing items because it was stiff, yet flexible. The invention of electric lighting, as well as new kinds of metal and plastic, has eliminated the need for almost all whale products in the modern world. In the 1930s, the International Whaling Commission banned the hunting of right and bowhead whales, although some hunting still occurs illegally. Native people of the Arctic are still allowed to hunt whales, and they use them for food, oil, and in the construction materials of sleds, baskets, traps and other items.

CONSERVATION STATUS

Bowhead whales and southern right whales are considered at low risk for extinction, dying out. However northern Pacific right whales and northern Atlantic right whales are considered Endangered, facing a very high risk of extinction in the wild, and it is thought that fewer than 250 mature individuals remain. Since commercial whaling began, the population of these two endangered species has been reduced by 95 percent. It is questionable whether they will ever recover.

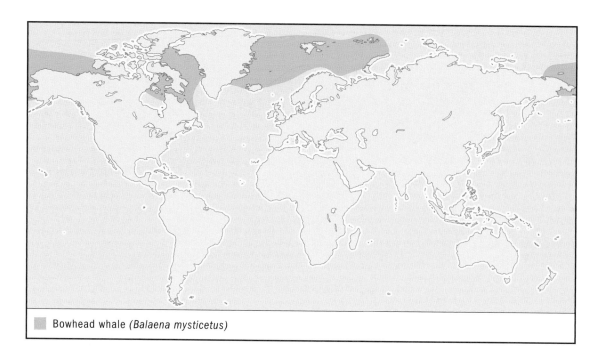

Bowhead whale (*Balaena mysticetus*)

SPECIES ACCOUNTS

BOWHEAD WHALES
Balaena mysticetus

Physical characteristics: Bowhead whales grow to a length of 46 to 65 feet (14 to 20 meters) and can weigh as much as 112 tons (102 metric tons). They have the longest of all whale jaws and can have as many as 350 baleen plates in their mouth. They have no dorsal, or back, fin, but they do have a muscular bulge around the blowhole. They are almost entirely black except for a white patch at the front of their jaw. The bowhead has longer baleen than any other whale—its baleen can measure 25 feet (4.5 meters) long.

Geographic range: Bowhead whales are found mostly in the northern polar regions.

Habitat: Bowhead whales are accustomed to the icy waters found in the northern polar region and can navigate waters where there is a lot of ice.

Diet: Bowheads feed both near the surface and on the ocean floor. This gives them a highly varied diet of small marine animals. They eat as many as sixty different species.

Behavior and reproduction: Bowhead whales swim slowly and migrate with the forming and melting of ice in the northern pole region. In females pregnancy lasts fourteen months, and young are fed for a year after birth.

Bowhead whales and people: Inuit in Alaska have hunted and eaten bowhead whales for centuries. During the nineteenth century, bowhead whales were hunted commercially by a number of countries. This commercial whaling was one of the reasons that people first began to explore the Arctic region.

Conservation status: It is estimated that 10,000 bowheads still exist, and they are considered at low risk for extinction. However, certain populations have been greatly diminished and it is questionable whether the few animals left in these areas will be able to recover their once great numbers. ■

Bowheads eat as many as sixty different species of small marine mammals. They feed both near the surface and on the ocean floor. (Illustration by Michelle Meneghini. Reproduced by permission.)

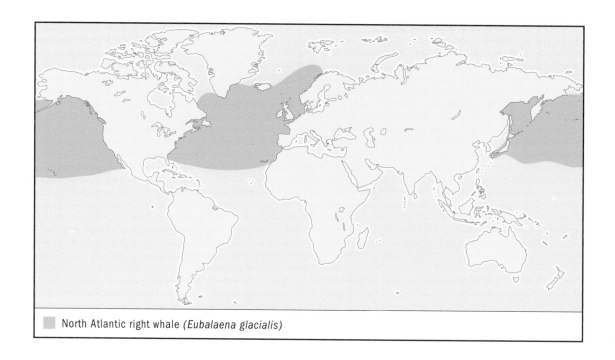

North Atlantic right whale (*Eubalaena glacialis*)

NORTH ATLANTIC RIGHT WHALE
Eubalaena glacialis

Physical characteristics: North Atlantic right whales are usually 43 to 53 feet (13 to 16 meters) in length and can weigh up to 100 tons (91 metric tons). They are black, but can have white areas on their belly and chin. Like other right whales, they have rough areas of skin that appear bumpy around their head. Barnacles and whale lice live in these bumps.

Geographic range: North Atlantic right whales are found throughout the seas and oceans of the Northern Hemisphere.

Habitat: These whales spend most of their time in shallow coastal waters. They migrate between cold polar waters for feeding and warmer southern waters for birthing and feeding their young.

Diet: North Atlantic right whales feed on almost any small marine animal that it can filter through its baleen. They are known to feed at the surface and to also dive in order to feed off the ocean floor where the water is not too deep.

Behavior and reproduction: These whales usually dive for ten to twenty minutes. They are slow swimmers. Males compete over a female by pushing and shoving each other. The young are born in the warmer waters during winter and they are fed by their mother for a year after birth.

North Atlantic right whales and people: North Atlantic right whales have been hunted for almost a thousand years because of the meat, oil, and baleen that they can provide. Today large amounts of money are spent on preserving and restoring the small remaining population. They are also an important part of the whale watching industry.

Conservation status: North Atlantic right whales are Endangered. It is estimated that fewer than 250 exist in the world today. Because of accidents with fishing vessels and accidental entanglement in fishing nets, these whales have had a difficult time recovering their numbers. ■

North Atlantic right whales migrate between cold polar waters for feeding and warmer southern waters for birthing and feeding their young. (Illustration by Michelle Meneghini. Reproduced by permission.)

FOR MORE INFORMATION

Books:

Hess, Bill. *Gift of the Whale: The Inupiat Bowhead Hunt, a Sacred Tradition.* Seattle: Sasquatch Books, 1999.

Kraus, Scott, and Ken Malory. *The Search for the Right Whale.* New York: Crown Publishers, 1993.

Paulson, Dennis, and Les Beletsky. *Alaska: The Ecotravellers' Wildlife Guide.* San Diego, CA: Academic Press, 2001.

Web sites:

"Family Balaenidae (Bowhead Whales and Right Whales)." Animal Diversity Web. http://animaldiversity.ummz.umich.edu/site/accounts/information/Balaenidae.html (accessed on July 8, 2004).

International Whaling Commission. http://www.iwcoffice.org (accessed on July 8, 2004).

PHYSICAL CHARACTERISTICS

Rorquals (ROAR-kwulz) are large baleen (buh-LEEN or BAY-leen) whales. Like all baleen whales, they are filter feeders. These whales do not have teeth. Instead, they have many overlapping plates called baleen plates that hang like a curtain from the upper jaw. These plates are made of a material called keratin (KARE-ah-tin). This horny, fingernail-like material frays out into thin hairs at the end of each strand to make a strainer. Rorquals also have a set of ridges and groves along the bottom of their mouth and throat. When they open their mouth to feed, the grooves expand and make the inside of their mouth very large so that they can suck up a lot of water. They then push the water out through the baleen plates and use their tongue to lick up food that remains.

Rorqual whales can be anywhere between 32 to 102 feet (10 to 31 meters) long and weigh as much as 200 tons (181 metric tons). Some rorquals have a dorsal fin on their backs, and others have particular bumps or ridges on their head and back that help to distinguish them from other rorquals. Females are usually larger than males.

GEOGRAPHIC RANGE

Rorquals are found in all of the oceans of the world and the seas that connect to these oceans. They do not live in the parts of the Arctic and Antarctic Ocean that are covered by ice, since they must come to the surface to breathe. Rorquals are more often found in shallower parts of the ocean that are closer to land. These areas are called continental shelves.

HABITAT

Rorquals can be seen most often in open waters over continental shelves. They can sometimes be found in bays and inlets near land.

DIET

Rorqual whales eat small fish, squid, and other small marine animals. Much of their diet is made up by krill, which are tiny shrimp-like animals. They obtain their food by filtering large quantities of water through their baleen. Normally they feed at depths no greater than 300 feet (91 meters) and stay under water no longer than ten minutes.

To capture the large amount of food that they need, rorquals expand their mouth and open it wide. Then they close their mouth most of the way, leaving only the baleen exposed, like a sieve (siv) between their lips, and squeeze the water out by ramming their tongue against the baleen. This pushes out the water and leaves the food behind. The blue whale, the largest rorqual, can eat 8 tons (7.3 metric tons) of krill per day.

BEHAVIOR AND REPRODUCTION

Rorquals normally swim at around 10 to 20 miles per hour (16 to 32 kilometers per hour). Some species, such as the fin whale can swim at speeds of 23 miles per hour (37 kilometers per hour) for short periods. Groups, or pods, are usually made up of two to five individuals, but sometimes large groups of rorquals come together where food is abundant. Generally rorquals do not dive deeper than 300 feet (91 meters) below the surface.

Even though different rorqual species live in different parts of the world, they all follow a migration pattern. This means that they spend part of the year in a warmer area and then move, often over great distances, to a cooler area for the other part of the year. Rorquals time their reproduction with this yearly cycle by giving birth in the warmer area and feeding in the cooler area. A female rorqual is pregnant for about a year, depending on the species, before she gives birth to a single calf. When the calf is born, it measures between 9 and 23 feet (2.7 and 7 meters) long. The young nurse, feed on their mother's milk, for about a year and grow rapidly. They become mature between five and fifteen years and live, on average, fifty to eighty years.

RORQUALS AND PEOPLE

All species of rorquals have been hunted by people for their oil and meat. Their oil was used in making margarine, soap, and lubricants, or industrial oils, until the 1980s. During the early 1900s humpback whales were hunted heavily, because they live close to land and their population was severely reduced. Hunters then began hunting of a number of other rorqual species. The blue whale became a preferred target of whalers, whale hunters, because of its size and the quantity of oil, meat, and blubber that it could provide. Larger blue whales could contain as much as 9,000 gallons (34,000 liters) of oil. Through efforts of the International Whaling Commission, environmental groups and other agencies, large scale commercial whaling ended by 1990. Today, whale watching is more popular and profitable than hunting. According to the World Wildlife Fund, this ecotourism, travel for the purpose of observing wildlife and learning about the environment, generated approximately one billion dollars in 2000.

A WHALE'S FINGERPRINT

Scientists have discovered that each humpback whale's dorsal, back, fin and tail markings are unique. This is the whale's fingerprint. Knowing this, scientists can follow individual whales by photographing them when they leap out of the water and matching their fin and tail pattern to known individual whales. Being able to track a single whale has helped scientists learn where they migrate, when they mate, how long they live, and other important information.

CONSERVATION STATUS

The International Whaling Commission, set up in 1946 by twenty countries, has attempted to monitor and establish limits on the number of whales and the kinds of whales that are killed each year. In 1972, the United States Congress passed the Marine Mammal Protection Act banning hunting of marine mammals and the purchasing of their products from other countries. While these efforts have brought an end to most whale hunting worldwide, they may have been too late for many rorqual species. Today, the blue whale, the sei whale, and the fin whale are considered Endangered, facing a very high risk of extinction in the wild. Humpback whales are considered Vulnerable, facing a high risk of extinction in the wild. Studies done by the International Whaling Commission have estimated that there are fewer than five hundred blue whales remaining in the world.

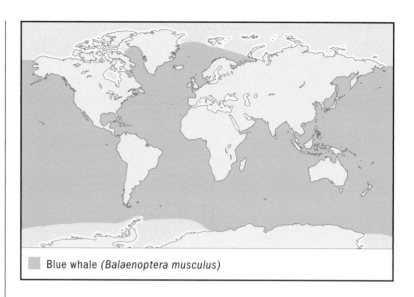

Blue whale (*Balaenoptera musculus*)

BLUE WHALE
Balaenoptera musculu

Physical characteristics: The blue whale is the largest animal on the planet. Their skin is gray or blue-gray with lighter colored splotches. Blue whales grow to between 74 and 79 feet (23 and 24 meters) and weigh up to 200 tons (181 metric tons). Females are slightly larger than males.

Geographic range: Blue whales are found in all oceans worldwide.

Habitat: Blue whales spend the spring months in the colder waters close to the poles, but migrate toward the warmer regions closer to the equator for the other eight months.

Diet: Blue whales eat only during the spring for about four months when they feed in colder waters. The rest of the year, they live off stores of blubber, fat, that they build up during the feeding season. Blue whales eat krill and generally avoid other marine life. When they are feeding, they can eat 8 tons (7.3 metric tons) of krill per day.

Behavior and reproduction: Although they usually swim at about 14 miles per hour (22 kilometers per hour), blue whales have been

known to swim as fast as 30 miles per hour (48 kilometers per hour). They dive for ten to twenty minutes to feed and generally do not dive more than 300 feet (91 meters) below the surface. Female blue whales give birth in late spring and summer after twelve months of pregnancy to young that are about 23 feet (7 meters) long. Blue whales can live past one hundred years of age.

Blue whales are the largest mammals on Earth, and can live over one hundred years. (Phillip Colla/Bruce Coleman Inc. Reproduced by permission.)

Blue whales and people: When whalers began using ships that allowed them to haul up whales no matter how large they were, the blue whale populations dropped dramatically. Because of their size, blue whales were highly prized, as whalers could bring in large amounts of oil, blubber, and meat with a single kill. During the years of 1930 and 1931, almost 30,000 blue whales were killed. During the 1960s, the blue whale gained protection from the International Whaling Commission. The blue whale may not survive much longer. Some scientists predict that the remaining population of about five hundred whales is not large enough to support a recovery. In recent decades the blue whale has taken a place in popular culture, and its image has helped to promote conservation efforts and ecotourism activities such as whale watching.

Conservation status: Blue whales are Endangered.   ■

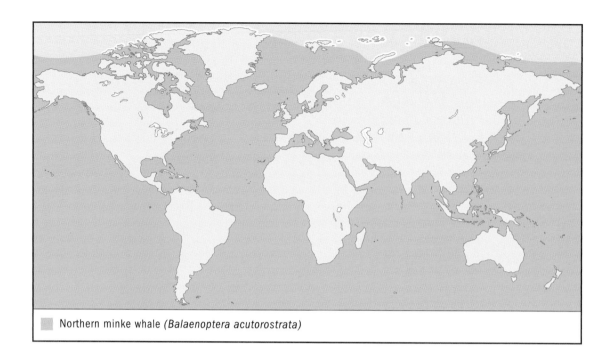

Northern minke whale (*Balaenoptera acutorostrata*)

NORTHERN MINKE WHALE
Balaenoptera acutorostrata

Physical characteristics: The northern minke whale is the smallest rorqual whale, but is still between 26 and 33 feet (8 and 10 meters) long. They are sleek whales with black, brown or gray backs and lighter bellies. They have light stripes across their flippers.

Geographic range: Northern minke whales migrate from tropical waters to the polar oceans in the Northern Hemisphere. There are two separate populations, one in the North Atlantic and one in the North Pacific.

Habitat: Northern minke whales live at the edge of the polar ice fields, and sometimes even enter the fields of ice. They prefer water close to shore, and will enter bays and inlets.

Diet: Although a large part of their diet is krill and small schooling fish, the northern minke whale feeds on many foods that other rorquals generally avoid, including larger fish such as salmon, cod, and mackerel.

Behavior and reproduction: Northern minke whales are most often seen alone, in pairs, or groups of three. However, there are times when they gather in large groups of up to fifty in rich feeding areas. Female northern minke whales are pregnant for ten months, after which the calves nurse for about six months. Calving usually occurs in the winter. Calves stay with their mothers for about two years, even when they have stopped nursing. These rorquals often live to be sixty years old.

Northern minke whales and people: Meat from this rorqual, as well as many other rorquals, is sought after in Japan and Korea as a special delicacy. Their meat is extremely expensive. Despite the International Whaling Commission's 1986 ban on hunting, these whales are still taken illegally because of the high price their meat brings.

Conservation status: Northern minke whales, unlike many of their fellow rorquals, are abundant and considered at low risk for extinction. ■

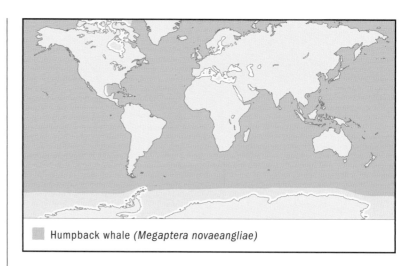

Humpback whale (*Megaptera novaeangliae*)

HUMPBACK WHALE
Megaptera novaeangliae

Physical characteristics: Humpback whales grow to between 38 and 49 feet (12 to 15 meters) in length and weigh between 27 and 33 tons (25 to 30 metric tons). The tail can be 18 feet (5.5 meters) wide. They are black except for their underside, flippers, and throat, which are white. Their head, jaw, and flippers are covered with bumps. Each bump has at least one hair growing out of it. Scientists do not know what these bumps or hairs are for. The humpback whale has the longest flippers of any whale.

Geographic range: Humpback whales live in the Pacific and Atlantic Oceans.

Habitat: Humpback whales spend the cooler months closer to the equator and then migrate towards the north or south pole for the warmer months.

Diet: Like most rorquals, humpback whales eat krill or small marine animals that they catch by filtering large quantities of water through their baleen. While the largest part of their diet is krill, the humpback whale also eats a variety of small fish. Each whale eats about 1.5 tons (1.4 metric tons) of food a day.

Behavior and reproduction: Humpback whales tend to gather in groups of two to five. Not only are they known for their acrobatic ability to leap out of the water and slap the water with their tail and flippers, but humpback whales do some of the most complex and intricate singing of any mammal. These songs last about twenty to thirty minutes and are repeated for hours. The North Atlantic whales all sing the same song, and it is different from the song the North Pacific humpback whales sing. Females are pregnant for twelve months and nurse their young for another year after birth. They usually have a new calf every other year. Humpback whales can live up to seventy-five years.

Humpback whales and people: Because humpback whales tend to stay closer to the land than other rorquals, they were hunted heavily. Although their numbers have decreased substantially, the humpback whale is less likely to go extinct than several other whales.

Conservation status: Humpback whales are considered Vulnerable. ■

FOR MORE INFORMATION

Books:

Clapham, Phil. *Humpback Whales (World Life Library)*. Stillwater, MN: Voyageur Press, 1996.

Cooper, Jason. *Baleen Whales*. Vero Beach, FL: The Rourke Book Company, 1996.

Miller-Schroeder, Patricia. *Blue Whales*. Austin, TX: Raintree Steck-Vaughn, 1998.

Web sites:

American Cetacean Society. http://www.acsonline.org (accessed on July 8, 2004).

International Whaling Commission. http://www.iwcoffice.org/ (accessed on July 8, 2004).

Myers, Phil. "Family Balaenopteridae (Rorquals)." Animal Diversity Web. http://animaldiversity.ummz.umich.edu/site/accounts/information/Balaenopteridae.html (accessed on July 9, 2004).

Whale and Dolphin Conservation Society. http://www.wdcs.org (accessed on July 8, 2004).

Female humpback whales nurse their young for about one year, and have a new calf about every other year. (V. & W. Villoch/ Bruce Coleman Inc. Reproduced by permission.)

Class: Mammalia

Order: Tubulidentata

One family: Orycteropodidae

One species: Aardvark (*Orycteropus afer*)

monotypic order
CHAPTER

PHYSICAL CHARACTERISTICS

Aardvarks have elongated, or stretched-out, heads with a pig-like snout and tubular ears. Their muscular, arched bodies are protected by a thick, grayish brown skin that is covered with bristles. The front feet have four toes as well as sharp claws, while the back feet have five toes. The cone-shaped tail is short and tapered, smaller at the end. The long tongue is sticky to help catch insects. Adult aardvarks are 67 to 79 inches (170 to 200 centimeters) long and weigh anywhere from 88 to 143 pounds (40 to 65 kilograms).

The word aardvark means "earth pig" in Dutch. In addition to having a pig-like snout, this mammal resembles a pig in the way it uses its front feet to dig. Like the tail, the snout tapers at the end, and it has two nostrils that can be closed. Although the legs are short, they are powerful—strong enough to break through rock-solid termite mounds. The back legs are slightly longer than the front legs. Despite having soles on the hind feet, aardvarks move on their toes and use the front feet, with their long claws, for digging.

Adults have about twenty teeth, and they are located in the back of the mouth. These column-shaped teeth grow throughout the aardvark's lifetime and, unlike human teeth, do not have protective enamel coating. Instead, each tooth is made of dentin, a material that is harder than bone.

GEOGRAPHIC RANGE

Though not common anywhere, aardvarks live primarily in the grassland and woodlands of the part of Africa south of the Sahara desert. They have also been seen in rainforests.

HABITAT

The deciding factor for where aardvarks live is availability of food. They also require sandy soil, as opposed to rocks, so that they can dig for termites. Aardvarks live in underground burrows that are 6.5 to 9.8 feet (2 to 3 meters) long, at 45 degree angles. At the end of the tunnel is a rounded "room" where the aardvark curls up to sleep. Female aardvarks give birth in this chamber. Although burrows usually have just one entrance, some have numerous entryways as well as several tunnels extending from the main passage.

DIET

Aardvarks began eating termites thirty-five million years ago, and that's still their preferred meal. A hill of termites is not enough to satisfy an aardvark, however, so it searches for entire termite colonies. These colonies march in columns 33 to 130 feet (10 to 40 meters) long, which makes it easy for the aardvark to suck the termites through its nostrils. When attacking a termite mound, the aardvark starts digging at the base with his front claws. Once the termites begin escaping, it extends its tongue and traps them with its sticky saliva. Aardvarks also eat ants and locusts, a type of grasshopper.

In addition to these insects, aardvarks eat an underground fruit of the cucumber species, probably as a source of water. *Cucumis humifructus* is known in South Africa as the "aardvark pumpkin" or "aardvark cucumber." One tribe of native people, the !Kung San, call this plant "aardvark dung" because the aardvark buries its feces outside abandoned aardvark burrows and the plant grows from seeds left in the aardvark's feces.

Termites are the aardvark's preferred food. Aardvarks will dig at a termite mound and eat the escaping termites, or look for a whole colony on the move and eat them as they march along. (© Nigel J. Dennis/Photo Researchers, Inc. Reproduced by permission.)

BEHAVIOR AND REPRODUCTION

Aardvarks are solitary creatures, they prefer to live alone and have never been found in large numbers. Because they are nocturnal, nighttime, animals, they are not seen very often. In the warmer seasons, they come out of their burrows just after the sun sets. They are able to hunt and forage, gather food, even if it is a moonless night because they rely on their sense of smell to locate termites. Aardvarks cover 1.2 to 3 miles (2 to 5 kilometers) each night at a rate of 1,640 feet (500 meters) per hour.

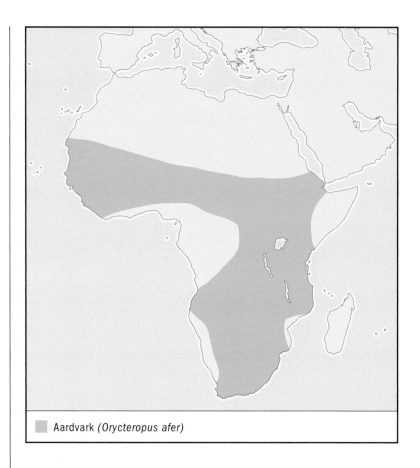

Aardvark *(Orycteropus afer)*

When searching for food, aardvarks move about in a zigzag formation with their noses to the ground. It is thought that the fleshy tentacles, hair-like growths, around the nostrils might actually be chemical receptors that help find food.

Aardvarks are known for their digging abilities. In fact, aardvarks can dig a burrow 3.3 feet (1 meter) deep faster than a group of six adults with shovels!

The mating season of the aardvark varies. In some areas, mating occurs between April and May, with offspring born in October or November. In other regions, offspring are born in May or June. Females carry their offspring for seven months before giving birth, and they bear only one offspring with each pregnancy. The baby weighs approximately 4 pounds (2 kilograms). Newborn aardvarks are hairless with pink, tender skin. They remain in the burrow with their mothers for two weeks. After two weeks they follow their mothers in the nightly search for food. The infant aardvark does not eat solid food until around three months, preferring its mother's milk until that time.

Aardvarks move away from the mother's den after six months and build burrows a few feet (meters) away, but they continue to forage together. Male aardvarks leave their mothers completely during the next mating season, but females stay with mothers until the birth of the next baby. Male aardvarks roam while females remain in a consistent home range. Because of this, experts believe aardvarks to be polygamous (puh-LIH-guh-mus), having more than one mating partner.

Humans are not the only hunters of aardvarks. Lions, leopards, and hyenas are the main predators, animals that hunt them for food, of aardvarks. Pythons feed on young aardvarks as well. When they sense danger, aardvarks retreat to the nearest hole. If a hole is not nearby, they use their powerful claws to dig one. The claws push the dirt backwards while the tail sweeps it away. In the event they cannot get to safety, aardvarks will lie on their back and fight with all four feet.

AARDVARKS AND PEOPLE

European colonialists hunted aardvarks for their meat and hide. Africans continue to hunt aardvarks and consider it a sport as well as a means of survival.

CONSERVATION STATUS

Aardvarks are classified as Vulnerable, facing a high risk of extinction in the wild, by the World Conservation Union (IUCN).

FOR MORE INFORMATION

Books:

Joyce, Peter. *From Aardvark to Zebra: Secrets of African Wildlife.* Cape Town, South Africa: Struik, 2000.

McColaugh, Doreen Wolfson. *Wild Lives Guidebook.* African Wildlife Federation, 1997. Online at http://www.awf.org/wildlives/60 (accessed on July 9, 2004).

Web sites:

African Wildlife Federation. http://www.awf.org (accessed on July 9, 2004).

"Science & Nature: Animals." *BBC.* http://www.bbc.co.uk/nature/reallywild/amazing/aardvark.shtml (accessed on July 9, 2004).

Class: Mammalia

Order: Proboscidea

One family: Elephantidae

Number of species: 3 species

monotypic order
C H A P T E R

phylum

class

subclass

order

● **monotypic order**

suborder

family

PHYSICAL CHARACTERISTICS

Elephants weigh 200 to 265 pounds (90 to 120 kilograms) when they are born. Even after they reach adulthood, elephants continue to grow. Females stop growing between twenty-five and thirty years and males between thirty-five and forty-five years. Adult females weigh anywhere from 3.3 to 7.7 tons (3 to 7 metric tons), depending on the species of elephant.

When compared to the size of its body, an elephant's head is large. It weighs up to half a ton (half a metric ton) and is supported by a short neck. Elephants have four, very strong legs with feet containing five splayed, spread out, toes. The toes are buried inside the flesh of the foot so that they are invisible to the naked eye. When elephants stand, they are actually on their tip-toes, and though the first visible joint looks like a knee, it is more like a wrist or ankle. Elephant feet also have pads of tissue to help support their massive weight. The long tail ends in a cluster of coarse, rough, hair.

Elephants have no sweat glands, but their large ears contain a great number of blood vessels to assist with heat loss to help keep them cool. Their gray hide is sparingly covered with tiny, short hairs.

The tusks of an elephant are actually teeth and are covered in dentin, a material that is harder than bone. A third of each tusk is hidden inside the skull, and additional dentin forms there, pushing each tusk out at a rate of up to 6 inches (15 centimeters) yearly. The tusks of a male elephant can weight 110 pounds (50 kilograms) each and measure 79 inches (200 centimeters). If an elephant were human, its trunk would be comparable to the nose and upper lip. The trunk is extremely sensitive and flexible and contains no bone or cartilage. Instead, it is made up of about 150,000 moveable muscles, which makes it incredibly powerful. An elephant's nostrils run the whole length of the trunk.

GEOGRAPHIC RANGE

African elephants live in central Africa, from Democratic Republic of the Congo to Mauritania. Asian elephants inhabit India, Sri Lanka, Myanmar, Indonesia, Thailand, Cambodia, Vietnam, Laos, Malaysia, Nepal, Bangladesh, and southern China.

HABITAT

Elephants live only in tropical and subtropical regions, but they occupy a wide range of habitats, including savannas (a mixture of grassland and woodland), rainforests, mountains, semi-deserts, and deciduous (trees that lose their leaves every year) forests. Elephants eat a wide variety of plants, so it is important that they live in an area that provides this essential diversity. Water is another requirement. They must live within a day's walking distance of water in order to survive. Also of great importance is that the elephant has room to move about freely without coming into contact with humans.

Elephants have been known to change wooded area into open grassland by destroying trees.

DIET

Elephants are herbivores, plant eaters, who eat a wide range of various plant types, including grasses, trees, vines, and shrubs. They consume between one hundred and five hundred species of plants, and eat everything edible on each plant, including twigs, bark, flowers, roots, bulbs, leaves, and shoots. Tree bark is favored because it provides essential minerals and other nutrients.

What elephants eat depends on the season. During the rainy season, 50 to 60 percent of an elephant's diet is made up of new grasses. As those grasses dry out in the African and Asian sun, the elephants eat more fruit and shrubs, which account for about 70 percent of their diet. Bamboo is a staple, basic food, for elephants residing in the forests of Asia. Elephants in the rainforests of Africa and Malaysia eat more leaves and fruits.

Elephants eat 220 to 660 pounds (100 to 300 kilograms) of food daily. Anywhere from twelve to eighteen hours of each day is spent eating. Where elephants live determines their behavior in terms of food gathering. Elephants in forest areas travel slowly, eating plants as they cover about 3 miles (5 kilometers) each day. Elephants who live in woodlands and grasslands spend the hottest parts of the day in the wooded areas and graze in the grassland as the temperatures cool down. Elephants drink up to 53 gallons (200 liters) of water each day in hot weather. When water is hard to find, they dig holes in dried-up streams or lake beds until water seeps in, then they suck it up through their trunks.

An elephant's trunk is a major eating utensil. Smaller items are plucked or picked up with the trunk while larger items like branches are torn away from the tree by putting the trunk around them and twisting. To reach the top of trees, elephants stand on their hind legs, which give them a total reach, combined with the stretch of the trunk, of 26 feet (8 meters). Elephants have also been observed pushing over and uprooting trees. The trunk is also important for drinking and is used like a straw. The elephant sucks water up its trunk only until it can be squirted into its mouth. Water never reaches the elephant's nose. An elephant's trunk can hold 2.2 gallons (8.5 liters) of water. The only time elephants eat without the use of their trunks is when they are nursing from their mothers.

Tusks are also useful for eating. They can strip bark from trees, dig for roots and water, and scrape salt and other nutrients from soil or rock. Food is chewed by grinding the lower jaw against the upper jaw, using a forward and backward motion. The molars, back teeth, of an elephant are flat-topped, each one independent from its own root. The molars are held together by a cement-like material and form blocks of enamel and dentin about 11.8 inches (30 centimeters) long. As each set wears down, another larger set moves forward to replace it. Elephants have a total of six pairs of teeth blocks, each weighing up to 8.8 pounds (4 kilograms). The final pair emerges into place around forty years of age and takes about twenty years to wear out. At that time, the elephant dies of a combination of starvation, malnutrition, and old age.

Because elephants do not digest food effectively, only about 40 percent of food by weight is used. The intestine is 115 feet (35 meters) long in comparison the human adult intestine is about 12 to 13 feet (3.7 to 4.0 meters) long. When the elephant is full the intestine weighs up to a ton (0.9 metric tons). An elephant expels an average of 220 pounds (100 kilograms) of feces daily.

BEHAVIOR AND REPRODUCTION

The female elephant, or cow, is sexually mature between the ages of twelve and fourteen and begins to reproduce shortly after that. Cows typically give birth to one calf at a time every four or five years. One of every one hundred births results in a twin delivery. The gestation period, length of pregnancy, for an elephant cow is twenty-two months. This ensures that the calf will be born during the rainy season, when grass will be plentiful for both mother and baby. Mating takes place at sixteen-week intervals year round.

Elephant cows give birth standing up, with the help of other females. Within hours, the calf will stand and take its first steps. Calves nurse, feed on their mother's milk, until they are two or three years old, sometimes longer, depending on the timing of the mother's next birth. Male calves nurse more frequently than do females, which becomes evident by the difference in size after the first few years.

Elephants have socially complex lives. The social structure is matriarchal (may-tree-ARK-ul), female-led, and the family is at the core. Each family unit has three to twenty-five members of adult females and their offspring. The females remain close throughout their lifetimes. Male elephants are typically solitary, preferring their own company to that of herds. They leave their birth families between the ages of twelve and fifteen and have no long-term bonds with them or any other elephants.

Groups are led by the older females, who make all decisions. Calves remain very close to their mothers, but all the females of the group will assist in raising the calves. Elephants are highly intelligent, and social interaction is complex. For example, within families, individuals greet one another by making sounds and touching each other with their trunks.

ELEPHANTS AND PEOPLE

Elephants and humans have interacted for tens of thousands of years. As long ago as thirty thousand years, people in Europe carved tools and ornaments from ivory tusks. Ivory has

ELEPHANT EMOTIONS

Studies have shown that elephants lead highly complex social lives marked by emotions such as joy, grief, and compassion. In a 2001 *Los Angeles Times Syndicate* article, Steve Newman reported on a train wreck in India that killed a group of elephants. The rest of the herd began trumpeting and giving off shrill cries as they encircled their dead. The police official described the grieving elephants "with tears rolling down their faces." In *The Astonishing Elephant,* Shana Alexander recalled an incident when a young circus elephant began to sob when scolded during a circus training session.

been used for carving because it's hard yet has elasticity, flexibility. Elephants play an important role in Asian culture especially. Evidence points to their domestication, taming for human use, as early as the third millennium B.C.E. in India. Soon after, they were used in the military to knock down enemy buildings. Royalty used to hunt while riding on elephants' backs. In the United States, elephants are raised in captivity in zoos and circuses.

CONSERVATION STATUS

All elephants are listed as Endangered, facing a very high risk of extinction in the wild, by the World Conservation Union (IUCN). They are threatened by habitat loss and poaching, illegal hunting, for ivory, meat, and hides.

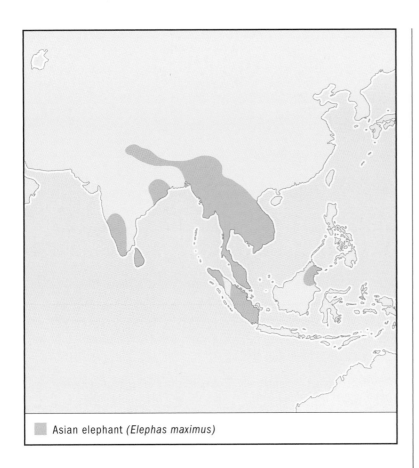

Asian elephant (*Elephas maximus*)

ASIAN ELEPHANT
Elephas maximus

Physical characteristics: Asian elephants weigh 3.3 to 5.5 tons (3 to 5 metric tons) with shoulder heights of 6.6 to 9.8 feet (2 to 3 meters). They have heads that are large compared to their bodies with large ears—but smaller ears than the African elephant—that fold forward at top. Their trunks have one finger at tip. Asian elephants have gray skin that fades to pink spotting on ears, face, and trunk with age. Only males have tusks. Some males lack tusks but make up for this by have an especially strong upper trunk region.

Geographic range: Asian elephants live in Myanmar, Cambodia, India, Indonesia, Laos, Malaysia, Sri Lanka, Thailand, and Vietnam.

Smaller populations can be found in Bangladesh, Bhutan, southwest China, Indonesia, and Nepal.

Habitat: Asian elephants live primarily in forests that are wet or partially moist, those containing bamboo, and grassland. They must live with a day's walking distance of water.

Diet: Asian elephants spend eighteen to twenty hours a day eating and searching for food. Adults eat 220 to 440 pounds (100 to 200 kilograms) of food daily. They consume a variety of plants, which they chew with their molars, and drink up to 53 gallons (200 liters) of water each day.

Behavior and reproduction: Asian elephants have matriarchal social structures that are complex. They live in family units within larger groups. Asian elephants mate throughout the year, and the gestation period lasts twenty-two months. Females assist each other in raising the calves within family units. They communicate by touching one another and making sounds. Given their size, elephants do not have many predators. Calves and weakened adults may be attacked by hyenas, lions, and tigers.

Asian elephants and people: Asian elephants are important in Asian cultures. They are revered in religion. Asian elephants are also used for domestic work and in the military.

Conservation Status: Listed as Endangered by the IUCN due primarily to habitat loss, but also because of poaching for ivory, meat, and hides, especially in southern India. ■

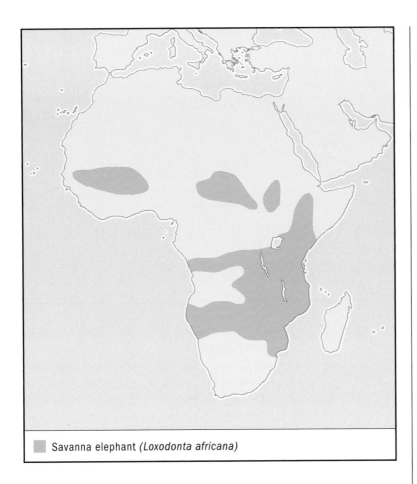

Savanna elephant (*Loxodonta africana*)

SAVANNA ELEPHANT
Loxodonta africana

Physical characteristics: The savanna elephant, the better-known of the two African elephants, weighs anywhere from 4.4 to 7.7 tons (4 to 7 metric tons), with a shoulder height of 8.2 to 13 feet (2.5 to 4 meters). The savanna elephant's head is not as high as the Asian species and has just a single dome; their ears are larger and fold back at the top. The trunk has two fingers on its end. Both sexes have tusks, but the females have smaller tusks.

Geographic range: Savanna elephants live in Mali, Namibia, Botswana, Zimbabwe, and South Africa.

Habitat: There are 250,000 to 350,000 savanna elephants living in Africa. Savanna elephants also live in dry woodlands as well as on savannas, which are a combination of woodland and grassland.

Diet: Adults consume 220 to 660 pounds (100 to 300 kilograms) of plant food daily, which they chew with their molars. These elephants tend to spend the hottest parts of the day in the wooded areas and graze in the grassland as the temperatures cool down. Savanna elephants drink up to 53 gallons (200 liters) of water each day.

Behavior and reproduction: A female cow will signal her readiness to mate by making loud sounds through her trunk. She also has a special courtship walk, in which she holds her head high while looking back over her shoulder. Gestation period lasts twenty-two months. Newborns weigh 265 pounds (120 kilograms). Males are competitive and solitary. Savanna elephants live in a matriarchal society of family units within the larger social structure, with up to seventy elephants in a multi-family group. Females remain bonded for life.

Savanna elephants and people: The savanna elephant is at higher risk of habitat loss than the forest elephant because it prefers environments similar to those that humans prefer.

Conservation status: Because the savanna elephant was not recognized as a species separate from the African forest elephant until 2001, both species are still considered together in legal terms. Excessive hunting and habitat loss has caused the African elephant to be listed as Endangered by the IUCN. ■

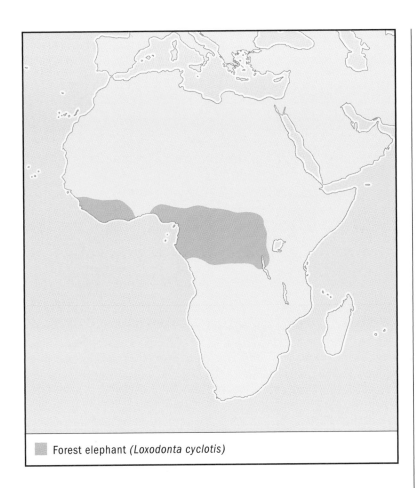

Forest elephant *(Loxodonta cyclotis)*

FOREST ELEPHANT
Loxodonta cyclotis

Physical characteristics: Forest elephants weigh 2.2 to 4.4 tons (2 to 4 metric tons), with a shoulder height of 6 to 9.8 feet (1.8 to 3 meters). Compared to the savanna elephant, it is smaller physically. Their heads are not as high as the Asian species, nor as large as the savanna elephant, and it has just a single dome. Forest elephant ears are rounded and fold back at the top. The trunk has two fingers on its end. Both sexes have tusks, but the female's tusks are smaller. The ivory is long and thin, straight with a pinkish hue to it. It is a harder material than the ivory of the savanna elephant.

After a pregnancy of twenty-two months, female African forest elephants give birth to a newborn that weighs 265 pounds (120 kilograms). (© Christophe Ratier/Photo Researchers, Inc. Reproduced by permission.)

Geographic range: The forest elephant is thinly scattered throughout West Africa but has substantial populations in Central African rainforests.

Habitat: Forest elephants must live near water, and in areas with varied vegetation.

Diet: Adults consume 220 to 660 pounds (100 to 300 kilograms) of plant food daily, which they chew with their molars. Forest elephants drink up to 53 gallons (200 liters) of water each day.

Behavior and reproduction: Similar to the savanna elephants, a female cow signals her readiness to mate by making loud sounds through her trunk, and has a special courtship walk, in which she holds her head high while looking back over her shoulder. Gestation period lasts twenty-two months. Newborns weigh 265 pounds (120 kilograms). Males are competitive and solitary. Forest elephants live in a matriarchal society of family units within the larger social structure, though group size is much smaller for forest elephants than for the savanna elephants. Females remain bonded for life.

Forest elephants and people: African elephants are rarely domesticated. Their numbers have been reduced by hunting for ivory and meat as well as by loss of habitat due to logging.

Conservation status: Because the forest elephant was not recognized as a species separate from the African savanna elephant until

2001, both species are still considered together in legal terms. Excessive hunting and habitat loss has caused the African elephant to be listed as Endangered, by the IUCN. ■

FOR MORE INFORMATION

Books:

Alexander, Shana. *The Astonishing Elephant.* New York: Random House, 2000.

de Waal, Frans. *Good Natured: The Origins of Right and Wrong in Humans and Other Animals.* Cambridge, MA: Harvard University Press, 1997.

Masson, Jeffrey Moussaieff, and Susan McCarthy. *When Elephants Weep: The Emotional Lives of Animals.* Surrey, U.K.: Delta, 1996.

Moss, Cynthia. *Echo of the Elephants: The Story of an Elephant Family.* New York: William Morrow, 1992.

Moss, Cynthia. *Elephant Memories.* New York: William Morrow, 1988.

Payne, Katy. *Silent Thunder: In the Presence of Elephants.* New York: Penguin USA, 1999.

Periodicals:

Newman, Steve. "Elephants in Mourning." *Los Angeles Times Syndicate* (November 2001).

Web sites:

African Wildlife Foundation: Amboseli Elephant Research Project. http://www.awf.org/wildlives/elephant.php (accessed July 9, 2004).

"The Elephants of Africa." Public Broadcasting Service (PBS). www.pbs.org/wnet/nature/elephants (accessed on July 9, 2004).

"Elephant Information." Friends of Elephants. http://www.friendsofelephants.org/links/elephantInfo.html (accessed July 9, 2004).

The Elephant Information Repository. http://elephant.elehost.com/ (accessed July 9, 2004).

"Understanding Elephants." The Africa Guide. http://www.africaguide.com/features/trvafmag/005.htm (accessed July 9, 2004).

World Wildlife Fund: Endangered Flagship Species. http://www.panda.org/about_wwf/what_we_do/species/what_we_do/flagship_species/index.cfm (accessed July 9, 2004).

monotypic order
CHAPTER

PHYSICAL CHARACTERISTICS

Hyraxes are herbivores, plant eaters, that resemble guinea pigs. They have short legs, a stubby tail, and round ears. There is no average size, as the species vary greatly across Africa, but the growth of the hyrax seems to be directly linked to precipitation, or rainfall—the largest hyraxes are in the areas with the most rainfall.

The feet have pads on them that contain sweat glands. The hyrax sweats as it runs, which help its feet pads grip, making it easier to climb. The feet are flexible and can turn upwards. The front foot has four toes and the hind foot has three toes. All toes have flat nails except for the second toe of the hind foot. This toe sports a long, curved claw used for grooming.

All hyraxes have fur, but the length of it depends on the climate in which they live. The colder the temperature, the longer the fur. Coat color ranges from light to dark, and may be brown, white, or gray. The bulging eyes are framed by bushy white eyebrows. The head is flat on top, and the muzzle, nose and mouth area, is shaped like a skunk's muzzle.

GEOGRAPHIC RANGE

Hyraxes live mainly in Africa. The rock hyrax has been seen from Lebanon to Saudi Arabia.

HABITAT

Hyraxes easily adapt to their surroundings and can work with any kind of shelter so long as it provides the necessary protection from weather and predators, animals that hunt them for food.

Each species is distinct in terms of where it lives. The bush and rock hyraxes need mountain cliffs and an abundance of rocks for refuge. Tree hyraxes prefer moist forests and savannas, a tropical environment that contains trees and shrubs and has a dry season. At higher elevations they can survive among rocks.

DIET

The hyrax eats mostly twigs, fruit, and bark as well as leaves, but it also feeds on lizard and bird eggs. Because their food is plant based, hyraxes can go for long periods of time without water, getting the moisture they need from the plants they eat.

BEHAVIOR AND REPRODUCTION

Rock and bush hyraxes are active during daylight hours and tend to live in groups whereas tree hyraxes are nocturnal, active at night, and prefer to live on their own. The social unit of the rock and bush hyraxes includes one adult male and about seventeen adult females, with their young. Though solitary, tree hyraxes have been found in groups of two or three. In this group, too, there is a hierarchy, rank structure, and the male is at the top.

Hyraxes mate once a year. Gestation, pregnancy, lasts twenty-six to thirty weeks, and the number of babies per female ranges from one to four. Mothers suckle only their own babies, and the young stop nursing anywhere from one to five months. Both sexes are ready to mate between sixteen and seventeen months of age. At this time, females join the adult female group while males take off on their own. Adult females live longer than adult males and may reach eleven years or more.

Young hyraxes are playful, with normal behavior including biting, climbing, chasing, and fighting.

HYRAXES AND PEOPLE

Some African people hunt hyraxes for food and skin. The tree hyrax is harvested to be used in medicine. Deep coughs

A PATCHWORK MAMMAL

Although the hyrax resembles a rabbit or guinea pig, it is actually closely related to elephants and other hoofed animals. Its anatomy is like an elephant and a horse. Its brain is like an elephant's while the stomach is like a horse's. It has a skeleton similar to that of a rhinoceros, and its upper incisors, chisel-shaped teeth at the front of the mouth, look like those found on rodents. The upper cheek teeth are like those of a rhinoceros and the lower cheek teeth are similar to those of a hippopotamus.

are relieved by drinking the ash of burnt hairs mixed with honey or water. Also, some tribes wrap newborn babies in hyrax skin to ensure health and vitality.

CONSERVATION STATUS

Three hyrax species are listed as Vulnerable, facing a high risk of extinction in the wild. Because these three species are found primarily in the African forests, their status is probably the result of habitat destruction, as well as being hunted for food and their fur. No other species has been given special status.

Southern tree hyrax (*Dendrohyrax arboreus*)

SOUTHERN TREE HYRAX
Dendrohyrax arboreus

SPECIES ACCOUNTS

Physical characteristics: From head to hind end, the southern tree hyrax is anywhere from 12.5 to 24 inches (32 to 60 centimeters) long and weighs 3.7 to 9.9 pounds (1.7 to 4.5 kilograms). The soft coat is made of long, dark brown hair.

Geographic range: Southern tree hyraxes are distributed throughout South Africa.

Habitat: They live in evergreen forests up to 13,500 feet (4,500 meters), and among boulders in the Ruwenzori Mountains.

Diet: Tree hyraxes eat leaves, twigs, and fruit year-round.

Behavior and reproduction: Southern tree hyraxes spend daylight hours nestled in the hollows of trees and venture out only in the safety of the night. More often heard than seen, the male tree hyrax emits shrill shrieks in order to claim his territory, and as an effort to keep in contact with his family throughout the night.

Southern tree hyraxes are very good climbers but are awkward on the ground.

Not much is known about the reproductive behavior and cycle of the tree hyrax. Gestation lasts from 220 to 240 days, and each pregnancy yields one to two babies. Babies are competent tree climbers by the end of their first day. Southern tree hyraxes live at least ten years.

Southern tree hyraxes and people: Some African people eat the southern tree hyrax and use the skin to make rugs and clothing. They are also used as medicine. Southern tree hyraxes play important roles in African spiritual traditions as well.

Conservation status: Southern tree hyraxes are not threatened. ∎

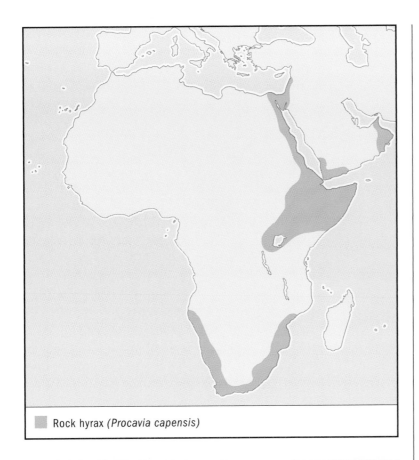

Rock hyrax *(Procavia capensis)*

ROCK HYRAX
Procavia capensis

Physical characteristics: Rock hyraxes are 17 to 21 inches (44 to 54 centimeters) long and weigh 4 to 12 pounds (1.8 to 5.4 kilograms). Their fur is light to dark brown.

Geographic range: Rock hyraxes are found from southwest to northeast Africa, Sinai to Lebanon, and the southeast Arabian Peninsula.

Habitat: Rock hyraxes prefer mountain cliffs and rocky outcrops or boulders. They live in the crevices of rocks.

Diet: Rock hyraxes eat quickly, with some members of the colony keeping watch for predators while the rest feed on leaves, fruit, lizard

Birds are important predators of rock hyraxes. Rock hyraxes have a protective film over their pupils that allows them to look directly into the sun without damaging their eyes, so they can keep a look out for birds in the sky. (Ann & Steve Toon Wildlife Photography. Reproduced by permission.)

and bird eggs, and long grasses. When they eat, rock hyraxes take a mouthful of food, then quickly check out their surroundings. Because their greatest predators are birds of prey, the rock hyrax must be able to look into the sky to avoid being swooped down upon and eaten. For this reason, they have a protective film over their pupils that allows them to look directly into the sun without damaging their eyes.

Behavior and reproduction: Rock hyraxes are social creatures and live in colonies up to fifty members. As many as twenty-five hyraxes can share one den. Unlike tree hyraxes, rock hyraxes are busy during daylight hours, but since they are unable to regulate their body temperature, they will not be found foraging during very hot or very cold temperatures.

The social unit is comprised of one adult male, up to seventeen females, and their young. Although several groups may live in one area, the head male will defend his territory from other males. Predators of the rock hyrax include leopards, snakes, and birds of prey.

Rock hyraxes have more than one mate, but they give birth just once a year. Pregnancy results in one to four babies per female after a gestation period of 212 to 240 days. Once a baby reaches one to five months of age, it is weaned, taken off its mother's milk. By sixteen or seventeen months, the rock hyrax is ready to breed.

Rock hyraxes live anywhere between nine and twelve years, with females living longer than males.

Rock hyraxes and people: Some African tribes hunt the rock hyrax for food, and it is mentioned numerous times in the Bible as "conie," which means "rabbit."

Conservation status: Rock hyraxes are not threatened. ■

FOR MORE INFORMATION

Books:

Mostue, Trude. *Wild About Animals.* London: Madcap, 1999.

Ricciuti, Edward R., Jenny Tesar, and Bruce Glassman, eds. *What on Earth is a Hyrax?* Detroit: Gale Group, 1996.

Periodicals:

Slattery, Derek M. "Kenya—the Rock and Tree Hyrax or Dassie." *PSA Journal* (September 2003): 29–31.

Web sites:

"Hyrax." Out to Africa. http://www.outtoafrica.nl/animals/enghyrax.html?zenden=2&subsoort_id=4&bestemming_id=1 (accessed on July 9, 2004).

"Hyrax." Science Daily. http://www.sciencedaily.com/encyclopedia/hyrax (accessed on July 9, 2004).

"The Hyrax: More Elephant than Rodent." BBC Science & Nature: Animals. http://www.bbc.co.uk/nature/animals/features/155index.shtml (accessed on July 9, 2004).

"Rock Hyrax." Nature Niche. http://natureniche.tripod.com/hyrax.html (accessed on July 9, 2004).

"Rock Hyrax." Wildlife Safari Info. http://www.wildlifesafari.info/hyrax_rock.html (accessed on July 9, 2004).

World Wildlife Fund. http://www.panda.org/ (accessed on July 9, 2004).

DUGONGS, SEA COWS, AND MANATEES
Sirenia

Class: Mammalia

Order: Sirenia

Number of families: 2 families

PHYSICAL CHARACTERISTICS

Dugongs, sea cows, and manatees are mammals that vary in length from 9.8 feet (3 meters) to 32.8 feet (10 meters) and weigh anywhere from 992 pounds (450 kilograms) to more than 9,920 pounds (4,500 kilograms). Sirenians (sye-REEN-ee-unz), members of the order Sirenia, are nearly hairless and skin texture varies from smooth to rough. They have no back limbs, only short, flexible forelimbs that they use to help them swim. The tail of the manatee is paddle-shaped while that of the dugong and sea cow is fluked with long, horizontal fins, like a whale. Eyes are small, and their ears are not visible. Sirenians vary in color from gray to brown. The manatee has both upper and lower molars, flat teeth suitable for chewing, which are replaced on a regular basis throughout its lifetime. Male dugongs have tusks, and all dugongs have molars that are not replaced. Sea cows were toothless. All appear to have whiskers.

GEOGRAPHIC RANGE

Sirenians live in tropical, subtropical, and temperate, or mild, regions throughout the world. The exception to this is Steller's sea cow, now extinct, which lived only in the frigid waters of the northwestern Pacific Ocean.

HABITAT

Manatees and dugongs live in shallow, warm coastal waters that contain plentiful vegetation. Some manatees exist in estuaries (EST-yoo-air-eez), mouth of a river where fresh water mixes with salt water, others occupy both sides of the Atlantic Ocean.

The Amazonian manatee lives only in fresh-water. The dugong lives in the Indian Ocean, Red Sea, Persian Gulf, and the west coast of India, in strictly saltwater habitats. The sea cow preferred an exceedingly cold environment, and history indicates it liked a mix of salt water and freshwater.

DIET

All sirenians are vegetarians, feeding on vegetation such as sea grasses and other marine plants. While the dugong is strictly a bottom-feeder, eating only what lives on the ocean floor, manatees feed from above the water's surface all the way to the bottom. Sirenians use their flippers to uproot vegetation and use their molars to chew or crush food. Although male dugongs have tusks, it is not clear what role these teeth play in feeding, if any. It takes about one week for food to digest. Manatees consume about 10 percent of their body weight every day. Because they need so much food, sirenians spend a great portion of their time feeding.

TWIN SEA COWS CAUSE FOR CELEBRATION

In December 2003, Beauval Zoo, located in France, celebrated the birth of twin sea cows—the first twin sea cow birth in captivity.

Quito, a male, and Luna, a female, weighed around 44 pounds (20 kilograms) each and measured 3.3 feet (1 meter). Although Daphne, the mother, was watched around the clock during the final days of her pregnancy, no one anticipated that she would give birth to twins.

As of mid-2004, mother and calves were doing well.

The toothless sea cow ate algae (AL-jee) and plankton, plants that are easy to digest without chewing.

BEHAVIOR AND REPRODUCTION

Sirenians are semi-social mammals with the primary unit a female and her calf. Dugongs feed in herds of tens or hundreds of individuals. They have been recorded as traveling hundreds of miles (kilometers) in a matter of days, an impressive feat given that they must surface for air every few minutes. Dugongs have poor eyesight but an acute sense of hearing.

Manatees also travel long distances in short amounts of time and have a north-south migratory pattern, the direction or path taken during seasonal movement from one region to another, that keeps them swimming in warmer waters. Although most marine mammals use echolocation (eck-oh-loh-KAY-shun), a sensory system in which high-pitched sounds are used to determine location and distance, sirenians are not known to. Little is known about the behavior of Steller's sea cow.

Manatees reach sexual maturity between the ages of two and eleven years. Gestation, pregnancy, is believed to be twelve or thirteen months. Usually a single calf is born every two-and-a-half to three years. Manatees do not bond, which means they have numerous mates throughout their lifetimes. In fact, when a female is ready to breed, she may mate with as many as twenty males, often at the same time. Calves can swim to the surface at birth, and they are nursed, fed with mother's milk, until around the age of one. Though they have no vocal cords, calves also vocalize at birth, which is an important part of the mother-calf bonding process. The calf remains close to its mother for up to two years.

Pregnancy for the dugong lasts about one year and results in the birth of a single calf, which will nurse from and remain close to its mother for about eighteen to twenty-four months. Birth takes place in shallow water and the calf will rise to the surface to take its first breath. Dugong calves are about 3.3 to 3.9 feet (1 to 1.2 meters) and weigh 44.1 to 66.2 pounds (20 to 30 kilograms). Dugongs can live for seventy years.

Because Steller's sea cow died out so quickly, most of what we know is speculation, an educated guess based on facts. Gestation lasted at least one year, and calves were seen throughout the year, suggesting that there was no specific breeding season. Pregnancy resulted in single births, but physical data is not available. It is believed that the sea cow was monogamous (muh-NAH-guh-mus), having only one mate.

SIRENIA AND PEOPLE

Sirenians have been hunted by humans for food, hides, and bone, a fact that has endangered a number of their species. Steller's sea cow lived for just a few decades before hunting caused its extinction. Manatees and dugongs help balance the marine ecosystem by recycling nutrients in sea grass beds and keeping the plants in a continual state of growth. Without them, the biodiversity, variety, of marine life would be in danger.

Manatees are being closely studied by scientists in hopes that their immune systems can provide clues as to how humans can fight cancer. Because their immune systems, which protect against disease, are very powerful, doctors are looking for tips on how to boost human immune systems. Specifically, they are studying a manatee population that has become infected with papillomavirus (pap-ih-LOH-mah-vye-rus), a virus that develops into cervical cancer in humans. The manatees became infected in the wild and seem to fall victim to cancers as a result. Researchers study tumor tissue and blood samples taken from the infected population, which live in a rehabilitation tank at the Harbor Branch Oceanographic Institution.

CONSERVATION STATUS

Several species of manatees are threatened, according to the World Conservation Union (IUCN). The dugong is listed as Vulnerable, facing a high risk of extinction. It is also listed as Endangered under the U.S. Endangered Species Act. Sirenia are in danger due to habitat destruction brought on by human activities such as recreational boating and fishing. Today great conservation efforts are being made around the world in hopes of keeping the dugong and manatee from the sharing the fate of Steller's sea cow.

FOR MORE INFORMATION

Books:

Harman, Amanda. *Manatees and Dugongs.* New York: Benchmark Books, 1997.

Glaser, Karen, and John Elliott Reynolds III. *Mysterious Manatees.* Gainesville, FL: University Press of Florida in association with Santa Fe, NM and Harrisburg, VA: The Center for American Places, 2003.

Powell, James. *Manatees.* Stillwater, MN: Voyageur Press, 2003.

Ripple, Jeff, and Doug Perrine. *Manatees and Dugongs of the World.* Stillwater, MN: Voyageur Press, 2002.

Silverstein, Alvin and Virginia. *The Manatee.* Brookfield, CT: Millbrook Press, 1995.

Web sites:

"Dugong, a Sea Cow." BBC Science & Nature: Animals. http://www.bbc.co.uk/nature/wildfacts/factfiles/3073.shtml (accessed on July 9, 2004).

"Dugong (Seacow)." Unique Australian Animals. http://australiananimals.net/dugong.htm (accessed on July 9, 2004).

"Dugongs." Enchanted Learning. http://www.enchantedlearning.com/subjects/mammals/manatee/Dugongprintout.shtml (accessed on July 9, 2004).

"France Celebrates Twin Sea Cows." BBC News. http://news.bbc.co.uk/1/hi/world/europe/3290551.stm (accessed on July 9, 2004).

Lundberg, Murray. "The Steller's Sea Cow." Explore North. http://www.explorenorth.com/library/yafeatures/bl-seacow.htm (accessed on July 9, 2004).

"Manatees." Defenders of Wildlife. http://www.defenders.org/wildlife/new/marine/order.html (accessed on July 9, 2004).

"Manatees: Birth and Care of Young." Sea World. http://www.seaworld.org/animal-info/info-books/manatee/birth-&-care.htm (accessed on July 9, 2004).

Save the Manatee Club. http://www.savethemanatee.org/ (accessed on July 9, 2004).

"'Sea cow' could give cancer clues." BBC News. http://news.bbc.co.uk/1/hi/health/2212081.stm (accessed on July 9, 2004).

Sirenian International. http://www.sirenian.org (accessed on July 9, 2004).

DUGONG AND SEA COW

Dugongidae

Class: Mammalia

Order: Sirenia

Family: Dugongidae

Number of species: 2 species

phylum

class

subclass

order

monotypic order

suborder

▲ **family**

PHYSICAL CHARACTERISTICS

The near-hairless dugong and sea cow can be as long as 9.8 feet (3 meters) for the dugong and from 23 to 33 feet (7 to 10 meters) for Steller's sea cow. They have no hind limbs, and the tail is forked, similar to that of a whale. Their front limbs are flipper-like and without nails. Dugongs are found in various colorations of gray and brown, though it is unknown what color the sea cow was. Dugongs can weigh more than 881 pounds (400 kilograms), and scientists estimate that Steller's sea cow weighed more than 9,920 pounds (4,500 kilograms).

GEOGRAPHIC RANGE

Dugongs live in the tropical and subtropical Indo-Pacific. Steller's sea cow was found in the western North Pacific Ocean.

HABITAT

Dugongids live in coastal waters that contain sea grass. Steller's sea cow lived with macroalgae, large, plant-like algae (AL-jee) also called kelp.

DIET

Dugongs primarily feed on sea grasses that grow on the ocean's floor in shallow water. Steller's sea cow reportedly fed on the surface and was never recorded as diving. Because the sea cow was toothless, it had to crush its food between studded plates at the front of their upper and lower jaws.

DUGONGS AND SHARKS: AN UNLIKELY DUO

Shark Bay, Australia has a dugong population estimated at ten thousand to fifteen thousand. Dugongs seasonally migrate to the warmer waters off Australia's coast. Tiger sharks prey on dugongs and recognize their migration pattern. As the dugongs migrate, so do the tiger sharks.

Dr. Aaron Wirsing of th e Behavioral Ecology Research Group at Simon Fraser University studied the dugong-tiger shark relationship. Wirsing determined that Shark Bay has an abundance of sea grass and dugongs may spend more time there because the sea grass allows dugongs to escape sharks more easily.

BEHAVIOR AND REPRODUCTION

Dugongs are semi-social and can be found in units that include the mother and her most recent calf. These pairs have been known to live together in herds of up to hundreds when sea grass is abundant. Not much is known about Steller's sea cow behavior or reproduction.

Female dugongs give birth every three to seven years. The typical pregnancy, which lasts for about one year, usually results in the birth of one calf; twins are rare. The female provides all care for the calf, and nurses, feeds with the mother's milk, until eighteen months to two years of age. Georg Wilhelm Steller, a naturalist and physician who was responsible for the first recorded observations of the sea cow, reported seeing calves year-round, which suggests that mating occurred any time of year. According to Steller's accounts, only single calves were born after a gestation period, pregnancy, of around one year, possibly longer.

DUGONGS, SEA COWS, AND PEOPLE

Steller's sea cow was hunted to extinction within thirty years of its discovery. Dugongs have been hunted for their meat and other body parts, and increasingly are victims of boating and fishing accidents.

CONSERVATION STATUS

The sea cow is Extinct, no longer exists, and the dugong is Vulnerable, facing a high risk of extinction in the wild, primarily due to habitat destruction and human activities such as recreational boating and fishing. In 2004, the largest dugong population was located in Australia.

HERE AND GONE IN THIRTY

Georg Wilhelm Steller, a naturalist and physician, recorded the first descriptions of the sea cow while at sea. His physical measurements and descriptions of anatomy allowed scientists to reconstruct the sea cow's skeleton, though it is unlikely that the reconstruction is 100 percent accurate.

Steller went home with his reports as well as samples of the meat and almond-tasting fat. Hunters flocked to Kamchatka, Russia, the location of Steller's discovery, where they quickly destroyed the sea cow population.

Steller discovered the sea cow in 1741, and in 1768, explorer Martin Sauer recorded the death of the last known sea cow.

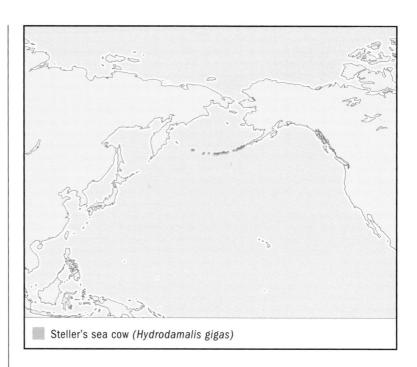

Steller's sea cow (*Hydrodamalis gigas*)

STELLER'S SEA COW
Hydrodamalis gigas

Physical characteristics: Steller's sea cow was 23 to 33 feet (7 to 10 meters) long and weighed anywhere from 9,920 to 13,000 pounds (4,500 to 5,900 kilograms). The tail resembled that of a whale. The sea cow had a small head and no teeth.

Geographic range: Unlike other sirenians (sye-REEN-ee-unz) that prefer warm water, Steller's sea cow lived in frigid waters in the northwestern Pacific Ocean.

Habitat: Steller's sea cow lived in coastal waters where kelp grew.

Diet: The sea cow ate kelp by crushing it with studded plates located at the front of its mouth, on both the upper and lower jaw.

Behavior and reproduction: Steller's sea cow lived in coastal waters but reportedly had some affinity, preference, for the mouths of freshwater creeks as well. Steller's sea cow did not migrate, but could

be found near islands year-round. Very little is known about this mammal's reproductive behavior.

Steller's sea cow and people: Steller's sea cow was a source of meat for sailors. Within the span of three decades, it was hunted to extinction.

Conservation status: Steller's sea cow is Extinct. ■

Steller's sea cow was hunted to extinction within thirty years of its discovery. (Illustration by Wendy Baker. Reproduced by permission.)

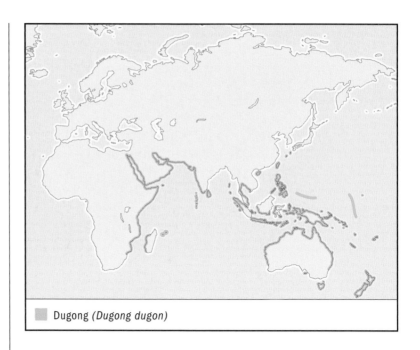

Dugong (*Dugong dugon*)

DUGONG
Dugong dugon

Physical characteristics: Dugongs are usually gray, with nearly hairless skin. They can grow to be 9.8 feet (3 meters) and weigh around 880 pounds (400 kilograms). Their whale-like tail helps them navigate the waters, as do their flipper-like front limbs. Although both sexes have tusks, they rarely can be seen in females.

Geographic range: Dugongs live in sea grass beds and shallow tropical and subtropical waters of the Indo-Pacific from eastern Africa to the Philippines and the South China and East China Seas.

Habitat: Dugongs live only in shallow coastal saltwater up to about 98 feet (30 meters) deep. The waters must contain sea grass beds.

Diet: Dugongs eat various sea grasses from the ocean floor. Sometimes, in its consumption of sea grass, it will ingest bottom-dwelling invertebrates such as crabs and shrimp. Unlike other sirenians, dugongs cannot hold their breath for long and must surface often for air, which is why the shallow waters are their preferred habitat.

Behavior and reproduction: Despite their large size, dugongs are graceful swimmers. Their tails propel them slowly through the water while the flippers help keep balance. Although their eyesight is poor, dugongs have a well-developed sense of hearing and find sea grass with the help of whiskers that line the upper lip of their large snout.

Dugongs migrate, travel from one region to another on a yearly basis, making regular, short distance (9 to 25 miles [15 to 40 kilometers]) round-trip journeys between feeding areas and warmer coastal areas. In Australia, they have been recorded as making longer trips, ranging from 62 to 373 miles (100 to 600 kilometers).

Dugongs are semi-social, often found in mother-calf pairs, sometimes in a herd with hundreds of individuals. They do not reproduce quickly, just once every three to seven years. After a year of pregnancy, the dugong gives birth to one calf, which will be nursed for anywhere from eighteen to twenty-four months. Dugongs are ready for mating around ten years of age. Males compete for mating rights, and mating often involves numerous males with one female. Male dugongs do not seem to participate at all in the care of the calf.

Dugongs can live for seventy years.

Dugongs and people: Of cultural significance to many native peoples of the Indo-Pacific region, the dugong has been hunted for meat, bones, and hide.

Conservation status: Listed as Vulnerable, the dugong is a protected species in Australia. Dugongs are often victims of boating and fishing accidents. Pollution and dredging, a form of fishing in which nets are scraped along the ocean floor to catch shellfish, are also responsible for the declining dugong population. ■

Dugongs live shallow waters of the Indian and western Pacific Oceans. (Kelvin Aitken/Bruce Coleman Inc. Reproduced by permission.)

FOR MORE INFORMATION

Books:

Bryden, M. M., H. Marsh, and P. D. Shaughnessy. *Dugongs, Whales, Dolphins and Seals: A Guide to the Sea Mammals of Australasia.* St Leonards, Australia: Allen & Unwin, 1998.

Reeves, Randall R., and Pieter A Folkens. *Sea Mammals of the World.* London: A. & C. Black, 2002.

Web sites:

"Dugong, a Sea Cow." BBC Science & Nature: Animals. http://www.bbc.co.uk/nature/wildfacts/factfiles/3073.shtml (accessed on July 9, 2004).

"Dugongs." CRC Reef Research Centre. http://www.reef.crc.org.au/aboutreef/wildlife/dugong.html (accessed on July 9, 2004).

"Dugongs." Humane Society of the United States. http://www.hsus.org/ace/18871 (accessed on July 9, 2004).

"Facts About Dugongs." Great Barrier Reef Marine Park Authority. http://www.gbrmpa.gov.au/corp_site/info_services/publications/dugong/ (accessed on July 9, 2004).

Vernon, Jennifer. "Dugongs Draw Hungry Sharks to Australia Bay." *National Geographic News* (January 23, 2004). Online at http://news.nationalgeographic.com/news/2004/01/0123_040123_dugongcam.html (accessed on July 9, 2004).

MANATEES
Trichechidae

Class: Mammalia
Order: Sirenia
Family: Trichechidae
Number of species: 3 species

family
CHAPTER

phylum

class

subclass

order

monotypic order

suborder

▲ **family**

PHYSICAL CHARACTERISTICS

The almost-hairless manatee is 9 to 13 feet (3 to 4 meters) long and weighs between 1,100 and 3,300 pounds (500 to 1,500 kilograms), depending on the species. Manatees never stop growing as long as they are alive. The tail is paddle-like, and the flipper-like forelimbs have three to four fingernails except in the Amazonian manatee, which has no fingernails. Manatees are brownish gray. Their eyes are tiny and are placed on the sides of the head. Their flexible lips help them manipulate food so that they can get it into their mouths.

Manatees have a well-developed sense of smell and hear very well. Their eyesight, however, is not very good. Manatees communicate through a series of whistles and chirps.

The manatee is a relative of the elephant. The nose or snout of a manatee acts much like the trunk of an elephant in that it is used to gather food and bring it to the mouth. Their fingernails or toenails, depending on how you look at it, are also similar to those of the elephant.

GEOGRAPHIC RANGE

Manatees live on both sides of the Atlantic Ocean. In the west, they are found from the southeastern United States throughout the Caribbean region to southeastern Brazil and in rivers of the Amazon River Basin. Manatees migrate, travel from one region to another, seasonally, to Florida coastal waters during the winter months. In the east, they live along the African coast, from Senegal to Angola.

YOU ARE NOT THE ONLY ONE WHO CATCHES A COLD

Water colder than 68°F (20°C) can lead to sicknesses, such as pneumonia, in manatees. The colder waters make it harder for the manatees to get proper nutrients, so they are more likely to get sick. That is why they migrate to warmer waters in Florida during the winter, but even those waters can get too cold.

The waters surrounding Florida's power plants are warmer and 60 percent of manatees now spend time there. Scientists are worried because some of these power plants are getting too old and must be closed, and without the warmer waters more manatees may die as a result of illness.

HABITAT

Manatees live in shallow coastal waters and estuary (EST-yoo-air-ee) waters, where saltwater and fresh water mix. They also need areas where marine vegetation is plentiful.

DIET

Manatees are primarily vegetarian, though they do sometimes ingest shrimp, snails, or crabs as they feed on ocean-floor plants. A large manatee eats up to 200 pounds (91 kilograms) of sea grass and algae (AL-jee) each day.

BEHAVIOR AND REPRODUCTION

Manatees are semi-social and usually found in mother-calf pairs. They communicate using sound, sight, taste, and touch. Communication is particularly important for developing and maintaining the cow-calf bond.

Manatees are polygamous (puh-LIH-guh-mus), having more than one mate. In fact, a female can be pursued by as many as twenty males during the breeding season, so it is virtually impossible to determine who the father of a calf is. Males do not seem to take part in caring for the young.

Female manatees give birth every two-and-a-half to three years. Usually only one calf is born after a year-long pregnancy. Depending on the species, manatees are ready to breed anywhere between the ages of two to eleven, and they do so throughout the year. Calves are born weighing 60 to 70 pounds (27 to 32 kilograms).

Manatees are unable to hold their breath for long periods of time, so they surface for air about every three minutes except during sleep, at which time they can rest for twenty minutes before surfacing. Manatees have no large predator, animal that hunts them for food, other than humans.

MANATEES AND PEOPLE

It is not uncommon for a manatee to have scars on its back due to collision with a recreational boat, and these accidents are the primary cause of death for the manatee population.

Though law prohibits the deliberate killing of manatees, they are still hunted for food in many areas.

CONSERVATION STATUS

All manatees are considered Endangered, facing a very high risk of extinction in the wild, according to the World Conservation Union (IUCN). The main cause of death is habitat destruction and human activity, specifically recreational boating accidents.

West Indian manatee *(Trichechus manatus)*

WEST INDIAN MANATEE
Trichechus manatus

Physical characteristics: Also known as the Florida manatee, the West Indian manatee grows to 13 feet (4 meters) in length, and can weigh up to 3,300 pounds (1,500 kilograms). The nearly hairless skin is gray, and the body has no hind limbs. The tail is wide and paddle-like, and the front limbs each have three to four fingernails. The eyes

are small and located on the sides of the head, and though there are only tiny ear openings, the manatee has a keen sense of hearing. The West Indian manatee uses its flexible lips in conjunction with its flippers to get food into its mouth.

Manatees communicate by whistling, chirping, and squeaking.

Geographic range: Found in the eastern coastal waters of the United States, from upper Virginia to the tip of Florida, around the west coast of Florida to Louisiana. Rare sightings have occurred in waters off New York, Texas, and the Bahamas.

Habitat: The West Indian manatee lives in coastal and estuary waters.

Diet: West Indian manatees eat more than sixty species of vegetation including sea grasses, algae, and water hyacinths. They eat between 10 and 15 percent of their body weight every day.

Behavior and reproduction: The basic social unit of the Florida is the female-calf pair, although these manatees do congregate in herds

West Indian manatees live in shallow water—they must surface for air about every three minutes while they are active. (Douglas Faulkner/Bruce Coleman Inc. Reproduced by permission.)

during mating season as well as the winter months, when they migrate to seek refuge in warmer waters.

These polygamous manatees are ready to breed between the ages of two-and-a half and six years, and females give birth every two-and-a-half to three years. Each one-year pregnancy results in the birth of one calf, though twins make up 1 to 2 percent of all births. Mothers nurse, feed with mother's milk, their young. The West Indian manatee can live for more than fifty years.

The manatee has no major predator. Death is usually caused by human activity.

West Indian manatees and people: The West Indian manatee has been hunted as a source of meat, fat, oil, bone, and hide, though it is now protected under law. Those laws, however, are difficult to enforce. The U.S. Fish and Wildlife Service estimates that 25 percent of all Florida manatee deaths are due to boating accidents.

Conservation status: The West Indian manatee is Endangered according to the IUCN, and is protected throughout its range. It is not known how many are illegally hunted for food each year. The primary reason for the decimation of the population is human activity, including pollution, habitat destruction, and recreational boating and fishing.

According to *Boat/US Magazine*, 2003 proved one of the most deadly years for the West Indian manatee. A record 380 manatees were killed that year. Ninety-eight of those deaths were the result of red tide. Red tide is a naturally occurring phenomena that happens when a type of phytoplankton, microscopic plants, produces chemical toxins, or poisons. These toxins are then released into the water, killing thousands of fish, dolphins, manatees, and other marine life.

Seventy-three Florida manatees died from boating accidents in 2003, the lowest total since 1997. The most recent surveys indicate that the Florida manatee population is over three thousand, a significant increase from six hundred recorded in 1974.   ∎

FOR MORE INFORMATION

Books:

Faulkner, Douglas. *Of Manatees and Man.* Philadelphia: Xlibris Corp., 2000.

Foott, Jeff, and Barbara Sleeper. *In the Company of Manatees: A Tribute.* New York: Three Rivers Press, 2000.

Periodicals:

Bryner, Jeanna. "Brrr…Manatees Catch Cold." *Science World* (January 12, 2004): 4–5.

Kalvin, Jim. "Weighing In On the Manatee Debate." *Boat/US Magazine* (September 2002). Online at http://articles.findarticles.com/p/articles/mi_m0BQK/is_5_7/ai_91085603 (accessed on July 9, 2004).

"Manatee Deaths Up, Boat Toll Down." *Boat/US Magazine* (March 2004). Online at http://articles.findarticles.com/p/articles/mi_m0BQK/is_2_9/ai_114604599 (accessed on July 9, 2004).

Web sites:

Bayan-Gagelonia, Ruby. "The Florida Manatee." *Ecofloridamag.com* http://www.ecofloridamag.com/archived/manatees.htm (accessed on July 9, 2004).

Manatee Junction. http://www.manateejunction.org/ (accessed on July 9, 2004).

"Manatees." Defenders of Wildlife. http://www.defenders.org/wildlife/new/manatees.html (accessed on July 9, 2004).

Wonderful World of the Manatee. http://www.manateeworld.net/index.php (accessed on July 9, 2004).

order
CHAPTER

phylum

class

subclass

● **order**

monotypic order

suborder

family

PHYSICAL CHARACTERISTICS

Ungulates (UNG-gyuh-luhts) are hoofed mammals. What makes perissodactyls (puh-RIH-suh-dack-tuhlz) different from artiodactyls (ar-tee-oh-DACK-tuhlz), is the number of toes. The presence of a single toe links the horse family (including horses, zebras, and asses), tapir, and rhinoceros together. This single toe is actually a combination of three toes that bear the weight together, with the middle toe being the largest of the three. Tapirs have four toes on the front feet and three on the back, while rhinoceroses (frequently called "rhinos") have three on all feet, and horses have just one.

The smallest perissodactyl is the mountain tapir, which weighs up to 485 pounds (220 kilograms). The white rhinoceros is the largest and can weigh more than 7,700 pounds (3,500 kilograms). Male rhinos and horses are bigger than females, but the opposite is true for tapirs.

Horses are medium sized with long heads and the ears stand up. The long neck is covered by a short-haired mane except in the domestic horse, whose mane falls to one side. All horses have long tails, and the ass and zebra have short hair at the tip.

The large, heavy body of the rhino sits on top of short, thick legs. The eyes are small and located on each side of the head. Though their vision is not well developed, their hearing is excellent and their erect ears are rather big. Some rhinos' skin is all but naked, while other rhinos are covered with fine hair. The horns of the white rhino can grow to reach 70 inches (175 centimeters).

Rhinos' horns continue to grow throughout their lifetimes, and if lost, will grow back.

Tapirs are heavy with short, fat limbs, a short tail, and medium-sized ears that grow out and up. Their eyes are small. The hind legs of the tapir are about 4 inches (10 centimeters) higher than the front legs. Due to this difference, most of the weight is supported by the longer hind legs. Tapir skin is tough and sparingly covered with hair except for the mountain tapir, whose hair is thick to protect against the cold.

Because perissodactyls eat large quantities of hard-to-chew food, their lower jaw is deep and the mouth muscles are large. The lips are thick and flexible. The stomach is simple and food passes through the digestive system quickly. This makes digestion less efficient than in other animals with more than one stomach, such as the cow. In fact, a horse digests food only 70 percent as efficiently as a cow does.

GEOGRAPHIC RANGE

Perissodactyls are found in Asia, Africa, and America in limited populations. Tapirs are found in Central and South America and in southeastern Asia. Rhinos live throughout Central and East Africa below the Sahara Desert and in the tropical region of Asia. Horses are found in eastern and southern Africa and Asia from Near East to Mongolia. Domestic horses live throughout the world, and there are several wild populations in North America and western Australia.

HABITAT

Tapirs prefer to live near permanent bodies of water and enjoy tropical forests. The exception is the mountain tapir, who lives in the Andes Mountains.

Rhinos can be found in rainforests, grasslands, and scrublands (region similar to grassland but which includes scrub vegetation). These mammals must live near water for drinking and bathing. Asian rhino fossils have been found in the Himalayas at an altitude of 16,100 feet (4,900 meters), though today they're found at altitudes of up to just 6,600 feet (2,000 meters).

Horses live in grasslands and desert scrublands. Plains zebra and the mountain zebra prefer greener grasslands and savannas where vegetation is more plentiful.

DIET

Perissodactyls are herbivorous (plant-eating). The plants they eat depend on what is available in the region in which they live. Tapirs eat leaves, twigs, fallen fruit, and aquatic vegetation. Rather than eat entire plants, they consume just a few leaves from a plant and move on.

Using their upper lip to grab plants, rhinos prefer woody or grassy vegetation. They will eat fruit occasionally, but leafy greens are their favorite food. Because of their size, rhinos eat a large amount of food and drink a large amount of water almost daily. The African species, however, can live for up to five days without water if their food is moist. While black rhinos will eat bushes and trees, the white rhino prefers short grasses.

Horses eat primarily grasses, but they will also eat bark, leaves, fruits, and roots. Wild asses have adapted to their drier environment and are able to graze the desert. Horses spend 60 to 80 percent of every twenty-four hours foraging (browsing or grazing). Although most horses can go without water for three days, zebras must drink frequently. Some are able to dig waterbeds with their hooves.

BEHAVIOR AND REPRODUCTION

Rhinos are solitary creatures seldom seen in pairs other than the mother-offspring combination. Even mated pairs don't remain together. Rhinos are territorial and have obvious displays to prove their authority, including rolling eyes, lowered head, and strutting. Males engage in brutal fights, and African rhinos inflict injury by jabbing each other with upward blows of their horns. Rhinos enjoy wallowing in mud holes because it helps keep their body temperature down and repels insects.

Female rhinos are ready to breed between the ages of three and five years. Gestation is fifteen to sixteen months in all species but the Sumatran rhino has a gestation period of seven to eight months. Mating often takes hours to complete and usually results in the birth of one calf. Rhinos weigh 55 to 145 pounds (25 to 65 kilograms) at birth and drink up to 5.5 gallons (25 liters) of their mothers' milk each day to gain 5.5 pounds (2.5 kilograms) daily. Zebras drink their mothers' milk for up to four years, though the white rhino begins eating solid food by one week of age. Males begin breeding at age ten and rhinos can live up to fifty years. What was true in the past remains true today: humans are the main predator, hunter, of rhinos.

PRISONERS AND MUSTANGS: FORGING A FRIENDSHIP

According to HorsesAmerica.com, there are more than two hundred wild horses that are unfit for adoption and must be euthanized (YOO-thuh-nihzd), put to death, each year, so that the land can be used for the grazing of cattle. Still others are slaughtered and sold to foreign countries for human consumption. Despite this, about eight thousand mustangs (another word for "wild horses") are adopted to individuals and organizations across the country. All of this occurs under the authority of the Bureau of Land Management (BLM).

Adoption fees range from $125 to $740, and half of the horses are adopted from residents on the East Coast. Before adoption, mustangs are "re-trained" to be around humans by inmates from prisons in Colorado, New Mexico, Montana, Wyoming, Oklahoma, and California. The BLM sees this as a win-win situation. In the 90 to 150 days it takes to train a horse, the inmate develops job skills as well as a sense of trust and cooperation while the horse becomes ready for re-entry into a more domestic society.

All persons wanting to adopt a mustang must first apply and be granted approval from the BLM. Anyone with a history of physical abuse toward animals is rejected. Between two and six months after adoption, a representative from the BLM makes a surprise visit to check on the horse and determine that it is being taken care of properly.

Records show that 99 percent of (Montana) inmates who work with the mustangs and re-enter free society never commit another crime. And since 1973, more than one hundred forty thousand wild horses have been adopted.

Tapirs are also solitary mammals. They spend part of the day wallowing in mud or standing water, or simply rest in the shade. Territorial by nature, tapirs mark their territory with their urine. Most activity takes place at night. Tapirs swim with ease and water is at the center of their existence. Water provides not only food, but also safety from intruders. Able to hold their breath for minutes at a time, tapirs will seek safety from predators by immersing themselves in water. They have an acute sense of smell and hearing, but like other perissodactyls, cannot hear well. Though usually silent, they do communicate through grunts and whimpers at closer range, through whistles over greater distances.

Tapirs are sexually mature at two to four years of age. They breed year round, and females are receptive every two months.

Courtship is a noisy affair. One baby is born after a gestation (pregnancy) period of 383 to 395 days. Young tapirs stay with their mothers until six to eight months of age. Tapirs have been known to live for thirty years. The primary predator of tapirs is the jaguar.

Unlike their relatives, horses are highly social. Zebras live in families of ten to fifteen individuals. These families include a territorial male, several females, and their offspring. Home ranges overlap with ranges of other families, and measure anywhere from 31 to 232 square miles (80 to 600 square kilometers). Zebras communicate via vocalization and adult males are especially noisy at night. Within groups, other males are tolerated, but only the territorial male may mate with the numerous females of the family. The black and white stripes of the zebra trigger visual neurons that attract males and females to each other. Zebras are believed to see in color, and they have binocular vision in front.

Horses are sexually mature around the age of two years, but males do not breed until around the age of five. After a gestation period of about one year, a single foal is born. The baby is able to walk on its own within an hour of birth and doesn't mind being left alone while the mother replenishes her water supply. Offspring are weaned (removed from mother's milk) at six to thirteen months. Some horses live to see forty years. Lionesses and hyenas are the main predators of horses.

PERISSODACTYLA AND PEOPLE

Humans are largely responsible for adversely (negatively) affecting the perissodactyl populations. Tapirs and rhinos have been relentlessly hunted for food and sport, as well as for their skins, which are used to produce high quality leather goods. Rhinos are illegally hunted for their horns and other body parts, which are used in Asian medicine, supposedly to relieve headaches, heart and liver trouble, and skin disease. Horns are also used to make dagger handles. Horses are the least affected by human activity, and it wasn't until about four thousand years ago that they were first domesticated for use as transportation. Since that time, cross-breeding has become common. A mule, for example, is a cross between a male donkey and a female horse.

CONSERVATION STATUS

Nine species of Perissodactyla are listed as Endangered, facing a very high risk of extinction, or Critically Endangered, facing an extremely high risk of extinction, on the 2003 IUCN Red List. All species of rhinoceroses are included on this list. Tapir populations are declining due to deforestation leading to habitat destruction. Since 1970, the rhino population has decreased by 90 percent due to hunting. Wild horses are facing extinction due to an increase in livestock farming, which forces them from their pastures and watering holes.

FOR MORE INFORMATION

Books:

Kalman, Bobbie. *Endangered Rhinoceros.* New York: Crabtree Publishing Company, 2004.

Murray, Julie. *Zebras.* Edina, MN: ABDO Publishing Co., 2002.

Penny, Malcolm. *Zebras: Habitats, Lifestyles, Food Chains, Threats.* Milwaukee: Raintree Publishers, 2003.

Web sites:

African Wildlife Foundation. http://www.awf.org (accessed on July 9, 2004).

"Management and Protection." Horses America. http://www.horsesamerica.com/pages/management.htm (accessed on July 9, 2004).

Myers, P. "Order Perissodactyla." Animal Diversity Web. http://animaldiversity.ummz.umich.edu/site/accounts/information/Perissodactyla.html (accessed July 9, 2004).

"Wild Horses: An American Romance, Teaching Resources Page Activities." Public Broadcasting Service (PBS). http://www.pbs.org/wildhorses/wh_teaching/wh_teaching.html (accessed on July 9, 2004).

family

CHAPTER

PHYSICAL CHARACTERISTICS

Equids (EH-qwidz; horses, zebras, and asses) are built for speed, with long legs that allow them to move efficiently. Their single stomachs allow them to eat foods high in fiber because digestion occurs rapidly, and their single-toed hooves make navigating over rocks and hard surfaces easy.

There are three species of zebra, and each has a different stripe pattern. All equids have short coats, though those living in higher altitudes may grow thicker coats. There is very little size difference between the sexes.

GEOGRAPHIC RANGE

Equids live in Africa below the Sahara Desert, in the Middle East, Arabia, Central Asia, and Mongolia.

HABITAT

Equids graze throughout the day, and various species live in deserts to grassland and shrubland (similar to grassland, only with small trees and shrubs as well).

DIET

Equids eat grasses high in fiber, which makes them more difficult to chew and digest. Their teeth are made for breaking down the reedy plants, however, and their single stomach allows for quick digestion.

BEHAVIOR AND REPRODUCTION

Equids are social mammals and form groups in which individual needs for feeding, reproduction, and survival are met. Females form especially strong bonds and maintain stable communities even without the presence of a territorial male. Usually, one male heads a group and mates with several of the females. He spends a good deal of his time defending the group against "bachelor" or roaming males who might try to mate with the females. Offspring also live with the group, usually until the age of two or three years.

Groups are in the best interests of equids as they provide greater defense against predators, animals that hunt them for food, like the lion. When in herds, it is more difficult for lions to determine which zebra or horse is young, weak, or lame. When threatened, equids will run away rather than fight, but if forced to fight, they'll kick with their hind feet and bite.

Equids communicate through vocalizations but also by changing the position of their tails, ears, and mouths.

The mating system varies, depending on environmental conditions. Pregnancy lasts from eleven to twelve months and usually results in the birth of one foal. And although equids are capable of producing one foal each year, it is more likely that a foal will be born every other year if nutritional food is readily available. Wild equids are ready to breed at the age of one or two years but don't normally produce a foal until the age of three to five. There is not enough data to determine how long wild equids live. Experts estimate that 90 percent of female plains zebras die by the age of sixteen years. Their main predators are the lion and hyena.

WHY ZEBRAS NEED STRIPES

Although humans think a zebra's stripes make the horse easy to find and identify, the stripes actually act as camouflage (KAM-uh-flaj). The wavy lines of a zebra blend in with the wavy-line patterns found in nature, such as blowing grasses among which the zebra lives. The fact that zebra stripes are black and white while the lines of grass are yellowish green and brown doesn't matter. The zebra's primary predator, the lion, is colorblind!

Those stripes serve another purpose, which is to help zebras identify and recognize each other. Stripes are to a zebra as fingerprints are to humans: no two are identical. Scientists believe this is how zebras identify one another in a herd. It's how mothers and babies recognize each other, and how a zebra knows which herd it belongs to.

EQUIDS AND PEOPLE

Domestic horses have played a significant role in the social and agricultural progress of humankind. Ironically, however, it has been humankind that has decimated the wild equid populations through hunting, habitat destruction, and the demand for livestock farming.

CONSERVATION STATUS

Of the seven species, one is Extinct, died out, in the Wild; one is Extinct altogether; one is Critically Endangered, facing an extremely high risk of extinction; two are Endangered, facing a very high risk of extinction; and one is Vulnerable, facing a high risk of extinction. Wild equids are threatened primarily by hunters, but also by livestock grazing in their habitat, and inter-breeding with domestic horses and donkeys.

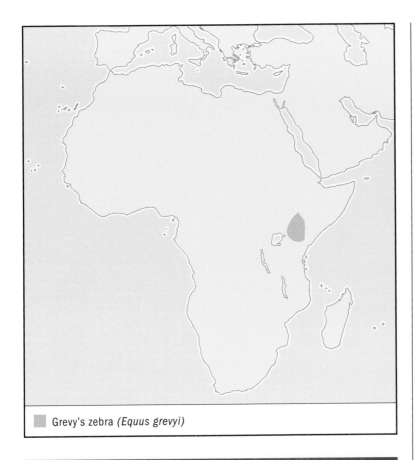

Grevy's zebra (*Equus grevyi*)

GREVY'S ZEBRA
Equus grevyi

Physical characteristics: This zebra measures about 9.8 feet (3 meters) in length, with a shoulder height of 5.3 feet (1.6 meters). It weighs around 990 pounds (450 kilograms) and is the largest wild equid. The ears are large and round, and the short coat is black and white striped. The muzzle is white, and there is a dark stripe surrounded by white running down the length of the back.

Geographic range: Grevy's zebra inhabits parts of Kenya as well as southern Ethiopia. It is believed that a small population exists in southeastern Sudan.

Habitat: Grevy's zebras live in grassland, and must live near a permanent water source.

Diet: This zebra eats grasses, but will feed on shrubs and small trees or plants if drought conditions deplete the supply of grasses.

Behavior and reproduction: As with other equids, Grevy's zebra participates in a territorial mating system in which one male resides over a large herd consisting of numerous females and their offspring. Because pregnant and nursing females need water daily or every other day, they are usually located near a permanent water source. This species differs from other zebras in that it doesn't form lasting bonds. In fact, the composition of the herd can change on an hourly basis.

Pregnancy lasts for about thirteen months, and the foal is able to recognize its mother by smell and sight within an hour of its birth. This is also the time it begins to stand up and run with the herd.

Grevy's zebra and people: Grevy's zebra is killed for its meat and hide as well as for medicinal purposes. Although these zebras eat the coarse grasses that livestock cannot feed upon, their habitat continues to be threatened and depleted by domestic livestock, which competes for grazing land.

Conservation status: Grevy's zebra is considered Endangered due to overhunting as well as competition for water and food with people and domestic livestock. ■

Kiang (*Equus kiang*)

KIANG
Equus kiang

Physical characteristics: This medium-sized wild ass stands between 3.3 and 4.7 feet (1 and 1.4 meters) and has a coat that changes with the seasons. It is dark brown in winter and chestnut red in summer. To keep warm, the length of the hair doubles in winter. The belly is white, and there are patches of white on the neck, chest, and shoulder. The muzzle, too, is white.

Geographic range: The kiang (kee-YANG) lives in China, India, Nepal, and Pakistan.

Habitat: This wild ass is found in altitudes up to 16,500 feet (5,000 meters) in grasslands and steppes (regions characterized by grasses and shrubs, with few or no trees).

Diet: The kiang eats primarily grasses and low shrubs.

Behavior and reproduction: Kiang live in close-knit herds ranging from 5 to 400 individuals, which do not scatter. The herd, composed of females and offspring, is led by an older female, and they travel in single file. The herd seems to move in unison (as one), whether they're drinking, eating, or running. Unlike other horse species, kiang do not physically touch one another. They are strong swimmers and enjoy spending hot summer days in water.

Male kiang begin following the female herds in July, and breeding takes place in August. After a year-long gestation (pregnancy) period, females form breakaway herds of two to five and retreat to nearby rocky areas to give birth to single foals. The foals thrive on mother's milk for the first year, after which time they become independent. Kiang live to be around twenty years of age; the main predator is the wolf.

Kiang and people: Kiang are hunted for their meat in some areas.

Conservation status: The kiang is listed as threatened by the IUCN. Kiang populations are most threatened by commercial hunting, habitat destruction, and competition for food and water. ■

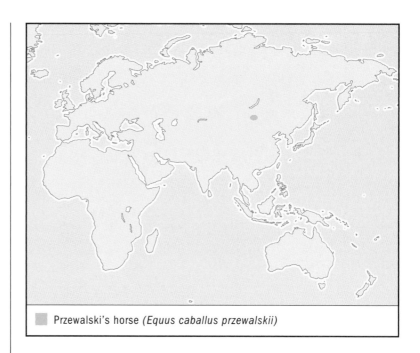

Przewalski's horse (*Equus caballus przewalskii*)

PRZEWALSKI'S HORSE
Equus caballus przewalskii

Physical characteristics: This horse stands 4 to 4.8 feet (1.2 to 1.5 meters) tall and weighs around 772 pounds (350 kilograms). Its legs are rather short while the head is large. During summertime, the coat is short and reddish brown, a color also known as "dun." The hairs grow thicker and longer during the winter to provide insulation from the cold. The mane is short and stands straight up, and the top of the tail has short hairs. The muzzle is white with gray around the nostrils.

Geographic range: Przewalski's horse is considered Extinct in the Wild, but has been reintroduced in certain areas of Mongolia.

Habitat: Like the kiang, this horse lives in grassland and steppe regions. It was last seen in the steppes of the Gobi desert.

Diet: Przewalski's horse eats whatever grasses are available.

Behavior and reproduction: These horses form a stable family composed of one male, numerous females, and their offspring. Other males form what is called "bachelor" groups.

Przewalski's wild horse spends the majority of the day foraging for food. (© Tom McHugh/Photo Researchers, Inc. Reproduced by permission.)

After 340 days of pregnancy, females deliver a single foal, usually in April, May, or June. Foals are weaned (removed from mothers' milk) around six to eight months and are ready to breed around the age of two years. Wolves are the primary predators of Przewalski's horse, and it is believed they live to an average age of twenty years.

Przewalski's horse and people: This horse is of great significance to the people of Mongolia as it is their national symbol.

Conservation status: Listed as Extinct in the Wild, though reintroduction into Mongolia has begun. They became extinct due to overhunting, capture by zoos, and loss of habitat. Today, reintroduction is difficult because there are so few left that genetic diversity (variation of genes that create distinct differences within a species) is nearly gone. ■

FOR MORE INFORMATION

Books:

Dines, Lisa. *American Mustang Guidebook: History, Behavior, and State-by-State Directions on Where to Best View America's Wild Horses.* Minocqua, WI: Willow Creek Press, Inc., 2001.

Draper, Judith. *The Book of Horses and Horse Care.* New York: Barnes & Noble, 2003.

Shah, Anup. *The Circle of Life: Wildlife on the African Savannah.* New York: Harry N. Abrams, Inc., 2003.

Periodicals:

Meadows, Robin. "An Equid Primer." *Zoogoer* (September/October 1997). Online at http://natzoo.si.edu/Publications/ZooGoer/1997/5/equidprimer.cfm (accessed July 9, 2004).

Moretti, Laura. "Mestengo. Mustang. Misfit." *Animals' Voice* Online at http://www.animalsvoice.com/PAGES/features/horses1.html (accessed July 9, 2004).

Web sites:

Ballenger, L., and P. Myers. "Family Equidae." Animal Diversity Web. http://animaldiversity.ummz.umich.edu/site/accounts/information/Equidae.html (accessed July 9, 2004).

"Grevy's Zebra." Saint Louis Zoo. http://www.stlzoo.org/animals/abouttheanimals/mammals/hoofedmammals/grevyszebra.htm (accessed on July 9, 2004).

"How Do a Zebra's Stripes Act As Camouflage?" How Stuff Works. http://science.howstuffworks.com/question454.htm (accessed July 9, 2004).

"Nature: Horses." Public Broadcasting Service (PBS). http://www.pbs.org/wnet/nature/horses/ (accessed on July 9, 2004).

"Nature: Wild Horses of Mongolia." Public Broadcasting Service (PBS). http://www.pbs.org/wnet/nature/mongolia/ (accessed July 9, 2004).

"Przewalski Horse." International Museum of the Horse. http://www.imh.org/imh/bw/prz.html (accessed on July 9, 2004).

TAPIRS

Tapiridae

Class: Mammalia

Order: Perissodactyla

Family: Tapiridae

Number of species: 4 species

family

CHAPTER

PHYSICAL CHARACTERISTICS

Tapirs (TAY-purz) have muscular bodies that are powerful enough to push through thick jungle growth. Males are slightly smaller than females. The head is small with flat sides and a slight upward arch. The front trunk acts as a nose. Eyes are small and the ears are round and able to move on their own. The rump is flat. Tapirs are skinnier than rhinos, and their short legs are powerful.

The tapir's weight rests on the third toe of each of the four feet. Hind feet are three-toed, while front feet are four-toed. In three of the four species, the coat is short; the mountain tapir has longer fur. Coat color varies and can be dun, a reddish brown color, whitish gray, coal black, and black-and-white two-tone. Newborns have horizontal stripes and dots for the first year.

GEOGRAPHIC RANGE

Tapirs live in South America, Central America, and Southeast Asia, including Myanmar, Thailand, Cambodia, Vietnam, and Sumatra.

HABITAT

With the exception of the mountain tapir, these mammals live in lowland rainforests and other moist forest regions. Mountain tapirs prefer cloud forests, tropical forests that are covered with constant clouds year-round, and paramo, treeless plateaus of tropical South America and the Andes Mountains. Lowland tapirs are found in grasslands and woodlands at lower elevations in South America. All tapirs swim and spend a good deal of time in rivers and lakes. Females often need secluded forests in which to give birth and raise their young.

DIET

Tapirs eat small branches and leaves as well as fresh sprouts. They pull the food from trees using their teeth and their mobile snout. They also eat fallen fruit and water plants. On mountains, they eat in a zigzag pattern and eat just a little bit from each plant. This method of eating keeps food plentiful. If food is out of reach, they will reach up, with hind feet planted firmly on the ground and front feet pushing against rocks or other natural objects. Lowland tapirs have been reported eating stranded fish in the Amazon. Tapirs tend to eat before the sun rises and after it sets.

BEHAVIOR AND REPRODUCTION

Despite their bulk, tapirs are swift runners and agile climbers. They are able to climb and jump vertical fences or walls measuring 9.8 feet (3 meters) high. They are shy animals and depend on concealment, being hidden, for safety. For this reason, not much is known about their sleep habits. Some tapirs have been seen sleeping in the water. In fact, tapirs will spend extra time in the water during very hot weather, a habit that not only keeps them cool, but protects them from insects. They can even walk on the bottom of rivers and lakes for short periods of time.

Although tapirs prefer the dawn and dusk hours of the day, in densely populated areas the lowland tapir becomes strictly nocturnal, active at night, for its safety. Tapirs generally establish a central location and use the same paths to travel around time after time. They mark their territory with urine and piles of dung, or feces.

Tapirs are more social during the dry season and at full moons and interact at salt licks and river banks. This is also where courtship displays take place. These rituals include grunting and squealing. After a thirteen-month pregnancy, the female secludes herself and gives birth to a single calf. The calf hides in thick shrubbery for the first two weeks, feeding off the mother's milk. After a few weeks, the calf begins foraging, or searching, for food with the mother, and begins to include the food in its diet. Calves nurse, or drink their mother's milk, for up to one year. Though it is not certain, male tapirs in the wild seem to take responsibility for some of the calf-rearing. Tapirs are monogamous (muh-NAH-guh-mus), having only one mate, during the breeding season, but change partners from year to year.

Tapirs live about thirty years in the wild. Aside from humans, it is believed that their main predators include jaguars, pumas, leopards, tigers, and anacondas.

TAPIRS AND PEOPLE

The tapir is hunted for its skin, which is used to make leather goods. It is also hunted for its meat as well as other parts of its body, which are used to make medicine.

CONSERVATION STATUS

All four species are listed as Endangered, facing a very high risk of extinction in the wild, or Vulnerable, facing a high risk of extinction in the wild, due to habitat destruction and hunting.

FOLKLORE AND FACTS ABOUT THE TAPIR

- The word "tapir" comes from a Brazilian Indian word meaning "thick," which refers to its hide.
- Some cultures claim that the powder from a tapir's ground-up hoof can cure epilepsy.
- A Malay myth claims that God made the tapir from leftover parts of other animals already created.
- The tapir is known as the "mountain cow" in Belize.

Lowland tapir *(Tapirus terrestris)*

LOWLAND TAPIR
Tapirus terrestris

Physical characteristics: Lowland tapirs are 6 to 7 feet (1.8 to 2.2 meters) in length with a tail that measures 2 to 4 inches (5 to 10 centimeters) long. They weigh 396 to 660 pounds (180 to 300 kilograms) and have a shoulder height of 2.5 to 3.5 feet (.77 to 1.10 meters). This species is tan to black or dun in color. Their black mane runs from the forehead to mid-back.

Geographic range: Lowland tapirs are found in Brazil, Bolivia, Peru, Ecuador, Colombia, Venezuela, northern Argentina, and the Guianas.

Habitat: Lowland tapirs live in lowland rainforests and mountain cloud forests up to 4,920 feet (1,500 meters) in Ecuador. They live in higher altitudes in other locations.

Diet: Lowland tapirs eat trees, bushes, and herbs. They also eat aquatic plants and walk on river bottoms as they feed. Lowland tapirs play an important role in their ecosystem by dispersing seeds. When they eat, they spit some of the seeds out, which can grow into plants. This keeps food and plant life plentiful.

Behavior and reproduction: Lowland tapirs gather together around salt licks, which they require to obtain nutrients. Otherwise, they are mostly solitary creatures. They are agile swimmers and spend time in the water. When frightened, they squeal loudly. On land they stand absolutely still to avoid detection. In the water, they immerse themselves until only the tip of their snouts is sticking out of the water.

Pregnancy lasts 385 to 412 days and results in a single birth. During the breeding season, lowland tapirs are monogamous. They will change partners from season to season. In captivity, this species lives to be about twenty-five years old. In the wild, their main predator is the jaguar.

The lowland tapir is a good swimmer, and spends time in the water to cool off during hot weather. (Tom Brakefield/Bruce Coleman Inc. Reproduced by permission.)

Lowland tapirs and people: In native religions, the tapir is endowed with magical powers. This species is hunted for its meat, leather, and body parts for use in medicine. Lowland tapirs are important to their ecosystem because of their ability to disperse seeds.

Conservation status: Lowland tapirs are listed as Vulnerable due to forest destruction, hunting, and competition from domestic livestock. A renewed interest in the wild-meat industry is also taking its toll on the population. ■

Malayan tapir *(Tapirus indicus)*

MALAYAN TAPIR
Tapirus indicus

Physical characteristics: This species is 6 to 10 feet (1.85 to 2.50 meters) long with a tail measuring 2 to 4 inches (5 to 10 centimeters). They weigh 550 to 825 pounds (250 to 375 kilograms) and have a shoulder height of 35 to 41 inches (90 to 105 centimeters). This large tapir has a black coat except for the rear half above the legs, which is white.

Geographic range: Malayan tapirs are found in Southeast Asia, including Myanmar, Laos, Cambodia, Vietnam, Malaysia, Indonesia, and Thailand.

Habitat: Malayan tapirs live in the lowland forests of swamps and mountains up to an elevation of 6,560 feet (2,000 meters). This species needs a permanent water source with plenty of water for drinking and bathing. Highest populations are found in swamps and lowland forests.

Diet: Malayan tapirs prefer tender leaves and shoots from certain trees and bushes. They eat moss and a variety of fruits. A Thailand study revealed that this species preferred thirty-nine plant species of which 86.5 percent were eaten as leaves, 8.1 percent as fruit, and 5.4 percent as twigs with leaves. Because they do not digest the seeds as well as multi-stomached animals, their feces contains seeds that eventually lead to new plant life.

Behavior and reproduction: Malayan tapirs are nocturnal and rest in seclusion during daylight hours. These excellent swimmers emit shrill whistles when alarmed or trying to settle down their offspring. They follow paths with the head down, sniffing the ground. Their sense of smell is good while their eyesight is weak.

Pregnancy lasts between 390 and 407 days and results in a single birth. The calf nurses for the first six to eight months, at which time it begins eating the vegetation of adults. This species is ready for breeding around the age of three years. Malayan tapirs live for about thirty years in the wild, and their main predators are tigers and leopards.

Malayan tapirs and people: Malayan tapirs are hunted in some areas of Asia for meat and other products and illegally traded in other areas. Humans have always been the prime enemy of the Malayan tapir.

Conservation status: This species is listed as Endangered. Their forest habitat is being destroyed at an alarming rate for agricultural purposes. Asian countries have laws protecting Malayan tapirs, but they are still killed for their meat. ■

FOR MORE INFORMATION

Books:

Emmons, Louise H. *Neotropical Rainforest Mammals: A Field Guide,* 2nd ed. Chicago: University of Chicago Press, 1997.

Kricher, John. *A Neotropical Companion,* 2nd ed. Princeton: Princeton University Press, 1999.

Web sites:

"Animal Bytes: Tapirs." Sea World. http://www.seaworld.org/AnimalBytes/tapirs.htm (accessed on July 9, 2004).

"Brazilian or Lowland Tapir." Enchanted Learning. http://www.enchantedlearning.com/subjects/mammals/tapir/Tapirprintout.shtml (accessed on July 9, 2004).

"Malayan Tapir." Animal Info. http://www.animalinfo.org/species/artiperi/tapiindi.htm (accessed on July 9, 2004).

"Malayan Tapir." Animal Planet. http://animal.discovery.com/fansites/jeffcorwin/carnival/lilmammal/malayantapir.html (accessed on July 9, 2004).

"The Tapir Gallery." Tapir Preservation Fund. http://www.tapirback.com/tapirgal/ (accessed on July 9, 2004).

Class: Mammalia

Order: Perissodactyla

Family: Rhinocerotidae

Number of species: 5 species

family

CHAPTER

phylum

class

subclass

order

monotypic order

suborder

▲ **family**

PHYSICAL CHARACTERISTICS

Rhinoceroses (commonly called "rhinos" [RYE-nose]) weigh more than 2,200 pounds (1,000 kilograms) as adults. Their barrel-shaped bodies are supported by short legs that end in three-toed feet. The mobile ears are large, tiny eyes are situated on either side of the head, and the neck and tail are short. Rhino horns are not made of bone, but of keratin (KARE-ah-tin), the same material in hooves, hair, and fingernails. They are not attached to the skull. These horns never stop growing, and they will re-grow should they be knocked out in battle or otherwise.

Skin thickness varies with the species. Rhinos have large sweat glands scattered over the skin that allows them to sweat often and a lot to help keep them cool. Their eyesight is poor, but their sense of hearing is well developed and facilitated by ears that can swivel. Their most acute sense is that of smell. Rhinos vary in coloration from gray to brown.

GEOGRAPHIC RANGE

Found in Africa and Southeast Asia.

HABITAT

Different species prefer different habitats. The white rhino likes grasslands and savannas (similar to grasslands but with small trees and bushes), while the black rhino prefers bushland and semidesert. The Indian rhino is found on meadows and swamplands, and Sumatran and Javan rhinos occupy rainforests.

DIET

Rhinos are vegetarians and feed primarily on leaves, fruit, grasses, and stems. They have one stomach, which could lead to poor digestion. Because of their large size, however, rhinos have longer periods of digestion, making it more efficient. Rhinos need water not only for drinking, but for wallowing in as well.

BEHAVIOR AND REPRODUCTION

Rhinos are solitary (lone) animals, but are primarily found in the mother-offspring pair. Their poor eyesight prohibits them from clearly seeing anything farther away than 100 feet (30 meters). Their sense of smell alerts them to danger. Rhinos are normally gentle creatures and they will only charge an intruder if they feel threatened.

Courtship behavior (mating rituals) of the rhino is so aggressive that it sometimes ends in injury to one or both parties. Rhino males are territorial and will fight with other males to defend territory or to mate with females. Rhinos do not form bonds and the sexes do not associate with each other outside of mating.

Pregnancy lasts fifteen to sixteen months and results in a single birth. Rhino calves remain with their mothers for two to four years, at which time they live independently. Baby rhinos nurse (drink mother's milk) for one year, but begin supplementing with vegetation at one to two months. Rhinos are ready to mate between the ages of four to five years, but males often wait until the age of ten due to competition from other males. Babies are born every two to five years. Rhinos can live to be forty years old and have no natural predators.

RHINOCEROSES AND PEOPLE

Humans have long been fascinated with the rhinoceros, as indicated in cave art from the Early Stone Age. Unfortunately, this fascination hasn't kept humans from reducing all rhino populations. Rhinos are especially valued for their horns, which are used to make dagger handles in Yemen (believed to give the owners invincibility) as well as medicine in China and

HUMAN GREED SPELLS DEATH FOR BLACK RHINOS

For nearly twenty years, the African Wildlife Foundation has been committed to rhinoceros conservation. Much of its funding supports black rhino protection and conservation in the Tsavo East National Park in Kenya.

In the 1970s, the black rhino population was between six and eight thousand. By 1989, however, the population had dwindled to twenty. Poaching is the sole reason for the decline of the rhino population throughout Africa. As a way to counterbalance this tragic pattern, Tsavo East created the Ngulia Rhino Sanctuary (NRS) in 1985. It began with three rhinos in a fenced-in area less than 1 square mile (less than 1 square kilometer). Today it is larger than 38 square miles (98 square kilometers) and is home to fifty-seven rhinos, half of whom were born in the sanctuary.

Although the numbers are slowly rising, it isn't happening without a cost. In May 2003 two park rangers were murdered in an effort to protect the rhinos from poachers. Poaching continues throughout rhino ranges, but sanctuaries like NRS are key to bolstering the rhino population.

India. Because the horn is made of keratin, the same as hair and fingernails, the there's no evidence to support the claim that it holds medicinal power.

CONSERVATION STATUS

The only species that isn't threatened is the white rhino, though it once was in serious jeopardy. Today, the Javan, Sumatran, and black rhinos are Critically Endangered, facing an extremely high risk of extinction, while the Indian rhino is considered Endangered, facing a very high risk of extinction. Poaching (illegal hunting) is to blame for the threat to all rhinos.

Sumatran rhinoceros (*Dicerorhinus sumatrensis*)

SUMATRAN RHINOCEROS
Dicerorhinus sumatrensis

Physical characteristics: This is the smallest and oldest living rhino species, with a weight from 2,200 to 4,400 pounds (999 to 1,998 kilograms) and a shoulder height of 48 to 58 inches (120 to 150 centimeters). From head to tail, this species measures 100 to 125 inches (250 to 315 centimeters). The body is covered sparingly with short hairs, and the hide is dark red-brown. The horn closest to the snout can measure up to 31 inches (79 centimeters), but that is unusually long, and it is normally much shorter. The other horn is no longer than 6 inches (15 centimeters). Both sexes have horns.

A newborn Sumatran rhinoceros, born at the Cincinnati Zoo in 2001, is the first Sumatran rhinoceros to be born in captivity in 112 years. (AP/Wide World Photo/Cincinnati Zoo. Reproduced by permission.)

Geographic range: Though they once roamed over Southeast Asia, they are found only on the island of Sumatra and in the Malay peninsula today.

Habitat: The Sumatran rhino lives in mountainous rainforests today, but experts believe it may have once occupied lowland forests, as well. They need to live near permanent bodies of water.

Diet: This species eats mostly twigs and leaves of small trees and shrubs. It also enjoys fruits and herbs. Although these rhinos feed on undergrowth along streams, they will reach higher shoots and twigs by walking on plants and pressing down on the trunk of saplings with their round bodies.

Behavior and reproduction: Sumatran rhinos are solitary and come together only to breed, although calves and mothers are frequently seen together. They like to wallow in mud holes, which not only keep them cool, but also protect their thin outer layer of skin from insect bites and thorns. Males roam whereas females have home ranges covering 4 to 6 square miles (10 to 15 square kilometers). Each territory has a salt lick, which the rhinos visit frequently.

Pregnancy lasts 475 days and calves weigh around 72.8 pounds (33 kilograms). While nursing, females confine their movements to small areas close to a salt lick. Calves leave their mothers between sixteen and seventeen months, at which time the mother returns to her non-breeding range. Females give birth about every four years.

Sumatran rhinoceroses and people: The number of Sumatran rhinos has decreased by 50 percent in the past twelve years due to poaching. It is believed that as of 2002, there are fewer than three hundred left in existence. Captive breeding has not been successful, as it has come to light that rhinos have strange mating habits that captivity cannot allow.

Conservation status: Listed as Critically Endangered since 1996. ■

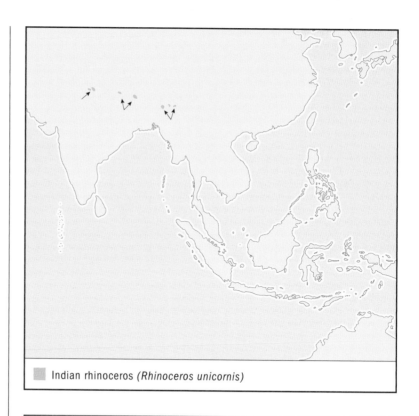

Indian rhinoceros (*Rhinoceros unicornis*)

INDIAN RHINOCEROS
Rhinoceros unicornis

Physical characteristics: This species has skin that is covered in what looks like plates of armor. Indian rhinos also have just one horn. Males can weigh up to 4,600 pounds (2,100 kilograms), while females weigh around 3,500 pounds (1,600 kilograms). Males measure to 150 inches (380 centimeters) in length, females to 135 inches (340 centimeters). Both sexes have the horn, which measures around 18 inches (45 centimeters). The hairless skin is gray and has flat bumps on it.

Geographic range: Indian rhinos are found in Pakistan, India, Nepal, and Bangladesh.

Habitat: The Indian rhino lives on floodplains and swamplands with tall grasses as well as adjoining woodlands on drier ground.

Diet: This species uses its upper lip to grasp grass stems and bushes. The lip folds back when the rhino wants to graze. The tall grasses of

the preferred region supply food year-round. During winter, woody vegetation is important. The Indian rhino also eats aquatic plants and green fallen fruits. These rhinos will step on plants and pull down stems so they can bite off the tips of vegetation. In doing so, they disperse seeds, thus guaranteeing a plentiful food supply.

Indian rhinoceros calves nurse until they are two years old, and leave their mother just before she has her next calf. (© Tom McHugh/Photo Researchers, Inc. Reproduced by permission.)

Behavior and reproduction: Solitary like other rhinos, the Indian rhino gathers around and wallows in bathing pools, as well as in feeding areas. Males are aggressive and fights break out when strange rhinos trespass on others' territory. This species is very vocal. Indian rhinos spend more than half of their time feeding.

After a courtship that includes the male chasing the female, sometimes for more than a mile (1.6 kilometers), the pair begins horn fighting. This can lead to biting, and it is common for them to inflict open wounds during mating. Pregnancy lasts sixteen months at which time the female gives birth in a secluded forest area or dense grassland region. Calves weigh 140 to 150 pounds (65 to 70 kilograms) and nurse until they are two years old. They leave their mothers a week or two before the birth of the next offspring, though females may remain on the maternal home range. Females give birth every three-and-a-half to four years. Indian rhinos can live up to thirty years in the wild with tigers as the only natural predator of the young.

Indian rhinoceroses and people: Tourists ride on elephants' backs to view Indian rhinos in some sanctuaries. Local people aren't as fond of the animals, as the rhinos tend to eat crops at night. In some instances, Indian rhinos have killed humans.

Conservation status: Indian rhinos are listed as Endangered by the IUCN due to poaching and competition from cattle and agricultural development. ■

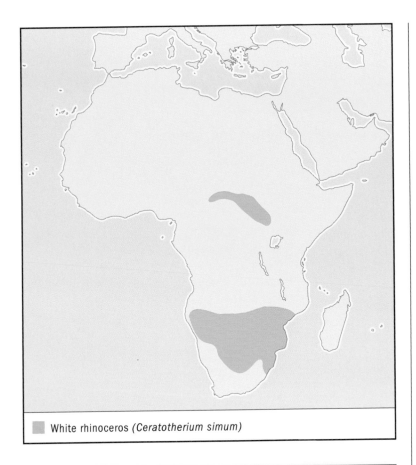

White rhinoceros *(Ceratotherium simum)*

WHITE RHINOCEROS
Ceratotherium simum

Physical characteristics: This is the largest rhino species. Males can weigh up to 5,000 pounds (2,300 kilograms), while females weigh around 3,800 pounds (1,700 kilograms). Males measure to 150 inches (380 centimeters) in length, females to 135 inches (343 centimeters). The body is covered sparingly with short hairs, and the hide is gray. The horn closest to the snout measures 20 to 62 inches (50 to 158 centimeters. The other horn is no longer than 15 inches (40 centimeters). Both sexes have horns.

Geographic range: In the nineteenth century, the white rhino was found in two separate regions of Africa: southern Chad, Central African Republic, southwest Sudan, northeast Democratic Republic of the Congo, and northwest Uganda; and southeast Angola, parts of

Mozambique, Botswana, Zimbabwe, Namibia, and northeast South Africa. Today the white rhino occupies fragments of these areas and is restricted to game preservations and national parks.

Habitat: The white rhinoceros prefers the drier savanna regions in southern Africa, yet prefers the moist savanna in the northern range.

Diet: The southern white rhino eats grasses and also ingests herbs and occasionally woody shrubs. Short grasses are the preferred food year-round, though later in the dry season, interest turns to some of the taller grasses. The northern rhino prefers short grasses but includes medium-tall grasses in its foraging.

Behavior and reproduction: White rhinos seem to be the most complex species of the family. Their range varies in size from less than 1 square mile (less than 1 square kilometer) to 5 square miles (8 square kilometers). They spend their entire lives within these ranges, and live in small groups with one dominant male, numerous females and their offspring, and even some sub-adult males. Fighting is rare. Lions have been reported to prey on young calves, but that is the extent of natural predators.

Gestation lasts sixteen months, at which time the female seeks a quiet place to birth her single calf. Calves nurse until the age of fifteen to twenty-four months, though they begin eating vegetation after a couple months of age. Females are sexually mature between the ages of six and eight years while males begin breeding around ten to twelve years. White rhinos live no longer than about forty years in the wild.

White rhinoceroses and people: White rhinos are terrified of humans. Early European hunters brought the white rhino to near extinction as they harvested populations for their meat and other body parts. The southern population has recovered well, but the future of the northern species is questionable at best.

Conservation status: The white rhino is listed as Near Threatened by the IUCN because even though population levels are higher than other rhino species, this breed is easy to track down and hunt, so reintroduced herds have been easily eliminated. The horn of the white rhino is particularly valuable, fetching a couple thousand dollars per horn on the black market. Recently, a herd of young male elephants killed a number of white rhinos. This is normally highly unlikely, but these particular elephants were orphaned at a young age and had no older bulls in the herd. Once older bulls were introduced, the aggression of the younger elephants subsided, demonstrating the importance of hierarchy in elephant populations. ■

FOR MORE INFORMATION

Books:

Cunningham, Carol, and Joel Berger. *Horn of Darkness: Rhinos on the Edge.* Oxford, U.K.: Oxford University Press, 2000.

Martin, Louise. *Rhinoceros.* Vero Beach, FL: Rourke Publishing, LLC., 2003.

Toon, Steve, Colin Baxter, and Ann Toon. *Rhinos: Natural History and Conservation (WII).* Stillwater, MN: Voyageur Press, 2002.

Periodicals:

Mill, Frances. "A Horse is a Horse, Of Course—A Rhinoceros is a Horse." *Boys' Life* (February-March, 2004).

Slattery, Derek M. "Africa Rhino Conservation." *PSA Journal* (July 1, 2003).

Web sites:

"Black Rhino Looks Tough, But is Powerless at the Hands of Man." *African Wildlife Foundation: News and Headlines* (May 12, 2004). Online at http://www.awf.org/news/17013 (accessed July 8, 2004).

Ellis, E. "*Ceratotherium simum* (White Rhinoceros)." Animal Diversity Web. http://animaldiversity.ummz.umich.edu/site/accounts/information/Ceratotherium_simum.html (accessed on July 8, 2004).

Fahey, B. "*Rhinoceros unicornis* (Indian Rhinoceros)." Animal Diversity Web. http://animaldiversity.ummz.umich.edu/site/accounts/information/Rhinoceros_unicornis.html (accessed on July 8, 2004).

"Rhino Fact Sheet." Care for the Wild. http://www.careforthewild.org/rhinos.asp (accessed on July 8, 2004).

"Rhinoceros." Defenders of Wildlife. http://www.kidsplanet.org/factsheets/rhinoceros.html (accessed on July 8, 2004).

"Sumatran Rhinoceros." Blue Planet Biomes. http://www.blueplanetbiomes.org/sumatran_rhino.htm (accessed on July 8, 2004).

"Wild Lives: Rhinoceros." African Wildlife Foundation. http://www.awf.org/wildlives/5 (accessed on July 8, 2004).

"White Rhino." Save the Rhino. http://www.savetherhino.org/rhino_facts/white_rhinoceros.phtml (accessed on July 8, 2004).

PHYSICAL CHARACTERISTICS

Because there are as many as 227 species of artiodactyls (ar-tee-oh-DACK-tuhlz), they vary greatly in physical characteristics. The smallest is the mouse deer, which weighs less than 2 pounds (1 kilogram) and stands up to 14 inches (35 centimeters) to the shoulder. The hippopotamus is the largest, weighing in at nearly 10,000 pounds (up to 4,500 kilograms). Head and ear sizes and shapes vary, as do neck lengths, but the eyes are usually big, with long lashes. Tail and leg lengths vary, and fur can be short or long.

Ungulates (UNG-gyuh-luhts) are hoofed mammals. What makes artiodactyls different from perissodactyls (puh-RIH-suh-dack-tuhlz), is the number of toes. With the exception of two species, all artiodactyls have an even number of toes (two or four) on each foot. The hooves are hard and ideal for fast running, though they vary in size depending on the size and mass of the animal. Almost all species have weapons, including horns, antlers, and tusks or canines (the four pointed teeth near the front of the mouth, two on each jaw).

Artiodactyls' coats have two layers: a short underfur and longer guard hairs on top. The top hairs repel water, and the two layers together help control body temperature. Most species have glands that are used for communication. These glands secrete strong-smelling chemicals and substances. The animals use these to mark territory. Animal behaviorists agree that the role of these glands in general is not completely clear.

GEOGRAPHIC RANGE

Artiodactyls can be found on every continent except for Antarctica and Australia. They also do not inhabit oceanic islands.

HABITAT

Habitats vary greatly. Regardless of biome, though, every artiodactyl needs abundant vegetation in order to survive. These animals are found in valleys and on mountaintops, in deserts and tundras. Depending on the species, they will choose habitats that will protect them as they go about their daily activities. For example, bighorn sheep live in open grasslands and meadows near cliffs. The meadow allows them to feed while the cliffs provide security from predators, animals that hunt them for food.

DIET

Except for two species, artiodactyls are herbivores (plant eaters). This is probably one of the reasons the order has thrived—vegetation is an abundant food source in almost any ecosystem, and so these animals are able to live almost anywhere.

All artiodactyls have at least one "false stomach" located in front of the actual stomach. Some have three. These false stomachs aid digestion. Because mammals don't have the enzymes that make digestion of plants possible, they rely on microorganisms to help break down plant tissues. These microorganisms, in combination with the action of false stomachs, make for highly effective digestion. Artiodactyls are ruminants, meaning they chew their food, swallow it, then regurgitate (re-GER-jih-tate; vomit) it back into the mouth to be chewed another time.

BEHAVIOR AND REPRODUCTION

Though often seen in pairs or trios, artiodactyls are social and live in groups. Adult sexes live separately for most of the year (though they may share a range), and offspring live with females. Males tend to live where food is more plentiful because they require more energy due to their larger size. Females, on the other hand, tend to live in areas that are more protected from predators because they have the responsibility of raising the young, which are susceptible to predation during the first few months of life.

THE BUSHMEAT CRISIS

Many of the world's tropical forests are hunting zones for bushmeat (wild meat). Not only does the meat sustain people because it is a food source, but also because bushmeat hunting is the livelihood of local people. Where once bushmeat hunting was on a smaller scale, involving only low-impact technologies, it is now a booming international business, and one that can no longer be sustained.

According to the Overseas Development Institute (ODI), there are many reasons why bushmeat hunting is no longer a sustainable activity. Some of them are:

- Remote tropical forest areas are being opened up at an alarming rate through logging. Whereas inhabitants who live there once existed without interaction in the modern world, they are now being given access to a cash economy and modern consumer markets. No longer are inhabitants native to the area, but often landless migrants searching for work.

- Many forest people have lived in a trade economy—one in which they bartered or traded goods and services. Now that they are being forced into a cash economy, there may be the tendency to over-exploit their natural resources so that they can participate in the economy. Bushmeat hunters may begin to overhunt so that they can provide large quantities of the wild meat to wholesale resources.

- New hunting technologies are killing bushmeat animals at a faster rate than they are able to reproduce, thus decimating the herd numbers. This is what leads to extinction.

The bushmeat crisis has become such a concern that in 2004, the ODI began a project titled "Wild Meat, Livelihoods Security and Conservation in the Tropics." The project's aim is to consider the bushmeat crisis in terms of livelihood for humans as well as conservation for the environment and animals.

Artiodactyls are equipped with horns or antlers used for fighting, but physical confrontation is risky because it requires energy that could be used for mating or feeding. Because of this, many artiodactyls will use displays, or behaviors, such as vocalizations or postures, to force an opponent to withdraw. During these displays, the animals do their best to appear as big as possible by raising their fur or standing sideways. They seem to use color patterns in their communications as well, though to what degree we do not know. For example, white-tailed deer raise their tails as a warning signal to other deer that danger is near. This exposes the long white hairs on the rump and underside of the tail, so as it waves the tail from side to side, the stark white contrasts with the darker fur and surroundings, such as plants, trees, etc.

Most species give birth to one or two young at a time. The pig is the exception, with four to eight young born each pregnancy. Artiodactyls breed once a year, and babies are usually born just as plants start to bloom. This allows plentiful food for mother and baby, which ensures nutrient-rich milk for the mother and a long growing period for the newborn.

Babies are able to walk and even run within hours of birth, and they either hide when mother is away or stay close to her during the first few weeks of life. Those who hide include the smaller species. The larger species live in more open habitats and have fewer places in which to hide.

Male artiodactyls mate with several females each mating season, and they usually do not form bonds. Pregnancy lasts from five to eleven months, depending on the species. Artiodactyls are ready to breed at eighteen months of age, and females give birth for the first time around the age of two. Artiodactyls can live to be ten to thirty years old, but the average age of death is much lower. Because of their keen senses and ability to run fast, artiodactyls don't often fall prey to other animals.

ARTIODACTYLS AND PEOPLE

For as long as people have inhabited the earth, artiodactyls have been hunted for their meat and skins. Still today they are valued as a source of animal protein. Domestic livestock such as cattle, pigs, goats, and sheep are artiodactyls. Historians believe sheep and goats were the first artiodactyls species to be domesticated, around nine thousand years ago. Whether domesticated or wild, humans still rely on artiodactyls for meat, bones, horns, fertilizer, milk, and other byproducts.

CONSERVATION STATUS

One hundred sixty species of Ariodactyla are on the IUCN Red List of threatened mammals. Two are Extinct in the Wild; seven are Extinct; eleven are Critically Endangered, facing an extremely high risk of extinction; twenty-six are Endangered, facing a very high risk of extinction; thirty-five are Vulnerable, facing a high risk of extinction; sixty-six are not currently threatened, but could become so; and thirteen are Data Deficient, not enough information to make a determination.

Threats include poaching (illegal hunting), habitat loss from deforestation and agricultural conversion, and competition with livestock. Regardless of the threat, all are based on human demands for natural resources that are slowly disappearing.

FOR MORE INFORMATION

Books:

Hames, Michael, Denise Koshowski, et al. *Hoofed Mammals of British Columbia.* Vancouver: University of British Columbia Press, 2000.

Nowak, Ronald M. *Walker's Mammals of the World,* 6th ed. Baltimore: Johns Hopkins University Press, 1999.

Web sites:

"Order Artiodactyla." Ultimate Ungulate. http://www.ultimateungulate. com/Artiodactyla.html (accessed on July 9, 2004).

"Artiodactyls." Enchanted Learning. http://www.enchantedlearning. com/subjects/mammals/classification/Artiodactyls.shtml (accessed on July 9, 2004).

"Artiodactyls." GeoZoo. http://www.geobop.com/mammals/art/index. php (accessed on July 9, 2004).

Myers, P. "Order Artiodactyla." Animal Diversity Web. http://animaldiversity .ummz.umich.edu/site/accounts/information/Artiodactyla.html (accessed on July 9, 2004).

The Nature Conservancy. http://nature.org (accessed on July 9, 2004).

"Wild Meat, Livelihoods Security and Conservation in the Tropics." Overseas Development Institute. http://www.odi-bushmeat.org (accessed on July 9, 2004).

Class: Mammalia

Order: Artiodactyla

Family: Suidae

Number of species: 16 species

CHAPTER

PHYSICAL CHARACTERISTICS

Pigs are medium-sized mammals whose thick bodies weigh anywhere from 77 to 770 pounds (35 to 350 kilograms). Some domesticated, tamed, breeds weigh up to 990 pounds (450 kilograms). Pigs measure 34 to 83 inches (86 to 211 centimeters) in length and stand 21 to 43 inches (53 to 109 centimeters) high. The exception is the pygmy hog, which is the smallest species and never grows longer than 28 inches (71 centimeters).

The neck is short and the head is long and pointed. The snout is able to move separately from the head. The eyes are small, the ears are long, and each foot has four toes. The two middle toes are flattened and have hooves. The upper canines, cone-shaped teeth on each side of the front of the mouth, are big and curve upward, protruding from the mouth. Skin color varies, depending on the species, from brown to near black. Some species have manes or tufts of hair. Others have warts on the face.

GEOGRAPHIC RANGE

Pigs live on every continent except Antarctica. They also occupy a number of oceanic islands. They are not indigenous (in-DIJ-un-us), native, to all ranges, but have been introduced by humans.

HABITAT

Pigs live in altitudes of up to 13,000 feet (4,000 meters) and choose their habitats depending upon the availability of food, weather conditions, and the predator, animals that hunt pigs for food, population. African pigs occupy small territories or home ranges while other pigs tend to roam in search of better feeding grounds. Regardless of species, pigs build nests out of vegetation for protection from weather as well as for resting. Warthogs do not build their own nests but use those belonging to aardvarks. Home ranges must have sources of shade as well as water and mud holes. These three characteristics are important because some pigs do not have sweat glands to cool their bodies.

DIET

Wild pigs are omnivorous, eating meat and plants, feeding on leaves, grasses, seeds, fruits, eggs, young trees, carrion, or dead animals, invertebrates, or animals without backbones, and small vertebrates, animals with backbones. They also enjoy mineral licks where they ingest nutrient-rich soil or water.

BEHAVIOR AND REPRODUCTION

The basic group is the mother-offspring pair, and group sizes vary from one to fifteen pigs. Females live alone or in a group with other females, and offspring remain with their birth group up to two years. Female offspring sometimes remain with the group permanently, but males always leave. With the exception of the African species, males and females interact only during breeding season. African males live with the group year-round and help raise the young. Male warthogs breed, leave, and then return to help care for the offspring.

Pigs vocalize when they are alarmed or in pain as well as when they are comfortable or breeding. Displays are used to ward off intruders or rivals, but if that fails, pigs will fight using tusks. Cannibalism and infanticide, killing of young, have been observed in some species, and wild piglets have been known to be playful and social.

Wild pigs are active at night. Warthogs are active during daylight hours.

Male pigs breed with several females each season, but warthogs have been known to choose one mate for life. Courtship behavior includes chasing and calling. Pregnancy lasts 100 to 175 days, and during this time the female will build a nest from vegetation. Females give birth to one to twelve piglets in this secluded spot. The litters of domesticated pigs increase in number with age and may reach eighteen piglets. Piglets nurse, drink their mother's milk, up to twenty times each day. Some piglets are

GOOD NEWS FOR THE BABIRUSA

In February 2004, the Paguyaman Forest increased in size from 120 square miles (311 square kilometers) to 200 square miles (518 square kilometers). This forest is on Sulawesi, the island home to most of the remaining babirusa population.

In addition, a poacher, illegal hunter, was prosecuted in 2002 for participating in illegal trade. Such prosecution had never taken place before that, and it has served to discourage other would-be poachers. As a result, the number of babirusas sold weekly in the local markets fell from fifteen in 1991 to two in 2004.

taken off mother's milk as early as five weeks, while others wait until thirty-two weeks of age. Sexual maturity of young is reached at eight months in some species, and at two to five years in others.

Primary predators of wild pigs are bobcats, coyotes, and black bears.

PIGS AND PEOPLE

Wild pigs and humans do not get along well. Wild pigs seriously damage crops by eating them or digging them up by the roots. Humans hunt pigs for their meat and they provide natives in Asia and parts of Africa with income through commercial hunting. Some wild pigs carry disease that threatens domestic livestock. In some cultures, pigs are used in place of money. Domestic pigs are used in scientific and medical research, and their organs have been used as replacements for human organs. Humans have been the recipients of pig hearts, kidneys, livers, lungs, and pancreas (PAN-kree-us) tissue.

CONSERVATION STATUS

The babirusa and the Philippine warty hog are Vulnerable, facing a high risk of extinction in the wild. The Javan pig is Endangered, facing a very high risk of extinction in the wild. The pygmy hog and the Visayan warty pig are Critically Endangered, facing an extremely high risk of extinction in the wild. There is no enough data about the Vietnam warty pig, but it may be extinct, died out.

The main threats to these wild pigs are hunting and loss of habitat. Although some pigs are protected by law from hunting, those laws are not well enforced.

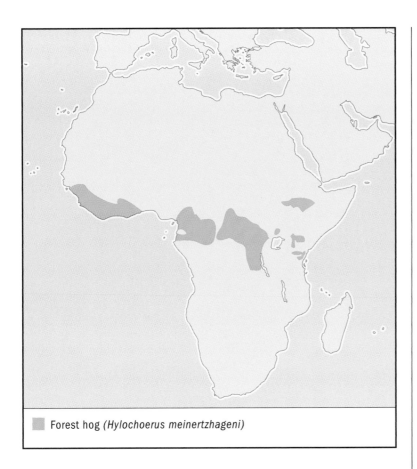

Forest hog (*Hylochoerus meinertzhageni*)

FOREST HOG
Hylochoerus meinertzhageni

Physical characteristics: Forest hogs measure 51 to 83 inches (130 to 210 centimeters) in length and stand anywhere from 30 to 43 inches (76 to 110 centimeters) high. Males weigh from 319 to 606 pounds (145 to 275 kilograms) while females weigh 286 to 449 pounds (130 to 204 kilograms). Their skin is gray to blackish gray and is sparsely covered with long, coarse hairs. Tusks are around 12 inches (30 centimeters) or shorter.

Geographic range: Western, central, and eastern tropical Africa.

Habitat: Forest hogs live in forests of all kinds up to altitudes of 12,500 feet (3,800 meters). They require a permanent water source and prefer thick vegetation that does not grow too high to easily reach.

Forest hogs are active mainly at night, though they come out during the day if humans are not around. They eat mostly grass. (David Madison/Bruce Coleman Inc. Reproduced by permission.)

Diet: Forest hogs eat mainly grass. They will eat carrion and eggs occasionally. This species also eats dung, feces.

Behavior and reproduction: Forest hogs are active mostly at night, though they will come out during daylight if humans are not around. The social group is made up of one male, several adult females, and offspring. Home ranges overlap, and each has a number of paths leading to feeding sites, mineral licks, and water holes. Hyenas are the primary predators.

Mating occurs most often towards the end of a rainy season, and pairs do not bond. After 151 days of pregnancy, sows give birth to a litter of two to four piglets, but sometimes as many as eleven. Piglets remain in thick cover for one week and then stay with the sow. Young are weaned, no longer drink mother's milk, at nine weeks.

Forest hogs and people: Forest hogs are hunted for their meat. Some tribes use the hides for war shields. Others believe that killing the forest hog brings bad luck.

Conservation status: Forest hogs are not threatened. ■

Babirusa (*Babyrousa babyrussa*)

BABIRUSA
Babyroussa babyrussa

Physical characteristics: Babirusas weigh 132 to 220 pounds (60 to 100 kilograms) and measure 34 to 39 inches (87 to 100 centimeters) in length. They stand 25 to 32 inches (65 to 80 centimeters) tall. Depending on location, some babirusas look naked while others have long, stiff coats. Skin is brownish gray, and the tusks come out the snout and curve back towards the head.

Geographic range: Babirusas are found on the island of Sulawesi, the Togian islands, the Sulu islands, and the island of Buru.

Habitat: Babirusas are found primarily in tropical rainforests and along the banks of rivers and lakes where water vegetation is plentiful.

Babirusas feed on fruit, nuts, leaves, roots, and some animal material. (© Kenneth W. Fink/ Photo Researchers, Inc. Reproduced by permission.)

Diet: Babirusas feed on fruit, nuts, leaves, roots, and some animal material. They also eat soil and rock at the mineral licks. Both sexes have been known to eat their young.

Behavior and reproduction: Babirusas are most active in the morning. Males live alone, but females form groups with one to five other adult females and their young. Tusks are used for attack as well as defense, but aggressive behavior is also met with body pushing, rubbing, and boxing. Pythons are the babirusa's main predator.

Though they give birth year-round in captivity, they may do so less frequently in the wild. Pregnancy lasts 155 to 175 days and result in a litter of one to two piglets. These small litters make for a slow-growing population. Offspring are weaned between twenty-six and thirty-two weeks, though they begin to eat solid foods at one week. Sexual maturity is reached at five to ten months of age.

Babirusa and people: Babirusas are hunted both commercially and for its meat. Babirusa skulls are sold in local markets to tourists and in department stores in Jakarta, Indonesia.

Conservation status: Babirusas are considered Vulnerable. The main threats to this species include hunting and loss of habitat. ■

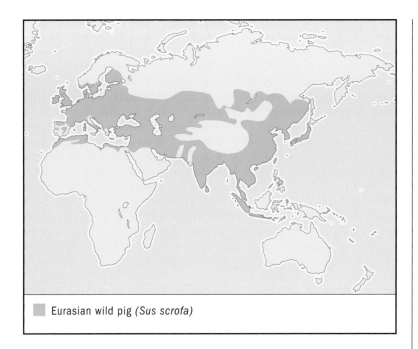

Eurasian wild pig *(Sus scrofa)*

EURASIAN WILD PIG
Sus scrofa

Physical characteristics: Eurasian wild pigs weigh from 77 to 770 pounds (35 to 350 kilograms), though domestic species can reach 990 pounds (450 kilograms). They stand anywhere from 22 to 43 inches (55 to 110 centimeters) tall. Their skin is covered with short bristles of varying color. Males have larger tusks than females.

Geographic range: Eurasian wild pigs are found on all continents except Antarctica. They also live on islands.

Habitat: Eurasian wild pigs live in a variety of habitats, including tropical rainforests, woodlands, grassland, and agricultural lands.

Diet: About 90 percent of the Eurasian wild pig's diet is vegetation. They feed on roots, grasses, fruits, seeds, nuts, agricultural crops, carrion, invertebrates and vertebrates. Eurasian wild pigs have been known to migrate, travel to another region, when food is scarce.

Behavior and reproduction: Eurasian wild pigs are mostly active in the morning and afternoon. The basic social unit is a small group of

Eurasian wild pigs have been known to travel to other areas when food is scarce. (© Uwe Walz/Jacana/Photo Researchers, Inc. Reproduced by permission.)

females and their young. Adult males are solitary, lone. These pigs are active 40 to 65 percent of the time.

Eurasian wild pigs and people: Eurasian wild pigs are eaten by humans more than any other species of pig. Because they do major damage to crops, they are considered a pest by many locals. Eurasian wild pigs are hunted commercially and for food. Their skulls are displayed as protection from evil spirits. Domesticated pigs are used as money for the payment of fines or fees for brides in some cultures.

Conservation status: Eurasian wild pigs are not threatened. ■

FOR MORE INFORMATION

Books:

Prothero, Donald R., and Robert M. Schoch. *Horns, Tusks, and Flippers: The Evolution of Hoofed Mammals.* Baltimore: Johns Hopkins University Press, 2003.

Sonder, Ben. *Pigs & Wild Boars: A Portrait of the Animal World.* New York: Todtri Productions, 1998.

Young, Allen M. *Tropical Rainforests: A Golden Guide from St. Martin's Press.* New York: St. Martin's Press, 2001.

Periodicals:

Bagla, Pallava. "World's Tiniest Wild Pig Subject of Big Rescue." *National Geographic News* (January 28, 2003). Online at http://news.nationalgeographic.com/news/2003/01/0128_030128_pygmyhogs.html (accessed on July 7, 2004).

Web sites:

Baribusa.org. http://earth-info-net-babirusa.blogspot.com/ (accessed on July 7, 2004).

"The Joy of Pigs." Public Broadcasting Service (PBS) Nature. http://www.pbs.org/wnet/nature/pigs/index.html (accessed on July 7, 2004).

"*Sus scrofa*, Eurasian Wild Pig." Ultimate Ungulate. http://www.ultimateungulate.com/Artiodactyla/Sus_scrofa.html (accessed on July 7, 2004).

Class: Mammalia

Order: Artiodactyla

Family: Tayassuidae

Number of species: 3 species

family

CHAPTER

PHYSICAL CHARACTERISTICS

Peccaries (PECK-ar-eez) weigh 30.9 to 110.3 pounds (14 to 50 kilograms), depending on the species, and are 20 to 24 inches (50.8 to 61 centimeters) tall. The body is similar to that of a pig, but the legs are longer and slimmer. Peccaries' coats are bristly and short but get longer from the midsection to the hindquarters. There is a scent gland located near the base of the tail that emits a musky smell. The snout is well developed. Peccaries have canines (the cone-shaped side teeth found in the front part of the mouth on both jaws). They have numerous stomachs, which enhance digestion, but do not have a gallbladder (a muscular organ attached to the liver used to store bile, which aids digestion).

GEOGRAPHIC RANGE

Peccaries are found in southwestern North America to Mexico and Central America, as well as South America.

HABITAT

Peccaries live in the desert areas of the southwestern United States and northern Mexico. They also occupy the tropical forests and rainforests of Central America as well as the wetlands and forests of South America. They can be found in the dry tropical thorn forests of Bolivia, Paraguay, and Argentina known as the Chaco.

DIET

Peccaries eat a wide variety of foods, allowing them to flourish in habitats other animals might find harsh. Depending on the species and where they live, they feed on fruit (especially the prickly pear), roots, bulbs, grass, acorns, pine nuts, and thistles. They find food by rooting (digging with the snout) through mud and soil. White-lipped peccaries break through seed shells using their muscular jaws and strong teeth. The food is fermented (broken down) by microorganisms in the fore stomach, which makes it easier to digest.

BEHAVIOR AND REPRODUCTION

Peccaries are social animals that live in herds ranging in number from three to more than five hundred. Home ranges vary in size, depending on the species and location. For the most part, peccaries are active during the daytime, though in Arizona and Texas, the collared peccary becomes nocturnal (active at night) in summer.

These animals are territorial and will become aggressive when threatened by trespassers. They growl, click their teeth, squeal, and make alarm-like barking sounds when threatened. When alarmed, they bristle the hairs along their neck and back. Peccaries groom one another. They are hunted by jaguars, bobcats, coyotes, and pumas.

Peccaries can give birth year-round, and litter sizes range from one to four, with the average size being one to two offspring. Pregnancy lasts 145 to 162 days, depending on the species.

PECCARIES AND PEOPLE

Peccaries are hunted throughout their range for their meat, hides, and just for sport. Books abound on the subject of trapping and hunting these animals. Selling the meat and skins is how many local populations earn their living. The peccary skin trade has slowed down considerably in recent years, and Peru is the only exporter of peccary skin today. Peccaries are considered spiritual guides of several game animals in the native communities of Amazonia.

CONSERVATION STATUS

The Chacoan peccary is listed as Endangered, facing a very high risk of extinction, by the IUCN, primarily due to habitat loss, but also because it is hunted for bushmeat (wild meat).

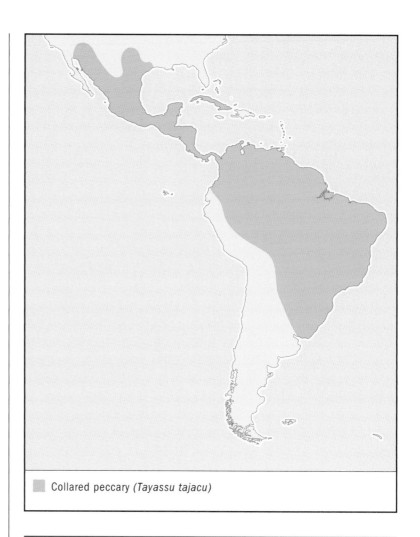

Collared peccary (*Tayassu tajacu*)

COLLARED PECCARY
Tayassu tajacu

Physical characteristics: Collared peccary adults measure 46 to 60 inches (11.8 to 152.4 centimeters) long and weigh between 40 and 60 pounds (18.2 to 27.2 kilograms). Their skin is black and gray, with a dark stripe running down their backs. They are easy to spot because of a whitish gray band of fur around their necks. Babies are yellow-brown or red.

Geographic range: Known in Spanish as the javelina (pronounced HAV-a-lee-nah), this species is found in the southwestern United

States. It also lives in Central America and on the Pacific coasts of Colombia, Ecuador, and Peru, mainly inhabiting the Chaco, or dry tropical thorn forest.

Habitat: Collared peccaries live throughout a range of habitats, from open deserts to oak forests to tropical forests. They are also found occasionally on floodplains in the Amazon.

Diet: They eat cacti (KACK-tie, or KACK-tee), roots, fruit, seeds, shrubs, small lizards and mammals, and in Arizona, the prickly pear. This is an ideal fruit for the collared peccary, as it has a high water content.

Behavior and reproduction: Herd size varies depending upon habitat, so groups can be comprised from as few as two to as many as thirty individuals. This species lives in hollowed-out logs or hollows in the ground, near water if possible. They are most active during the cooler times of day, during the morning or after sunset.

After a pregnancy of 145 days or so, the female gives birth to two offspring. The approximate age at first breeding is sixteen months. Not much else is known about the reproductive behavior of this animal, though experts believe both sexes have several mates and do not bond.

Predators of the collared peccary include bobcats, coyotes, pumas, and jaguars.

Collared peccaries and people: This species is the most widely hunted of all peccaries. Its meat is a source of food and money for many rural Peruvians.

Conservation status: Collared peccaries are not considered threatened. ■

FOR MORE INFORMATION

Books:

Yule, Lauray. *Javelinas.* Tucson, AZ: Rio Nuevo Publishers, 2004.

Periodicals:

Port-Carvalho, Marcio. "Predation of an Infant Collared Peccary by a Harpy Eagle in Eastern Amazonia." *Wilson Bulletin* (March 1, 2003).

Web sites:

"Collared Peccary." Desert USA. http://www.desertusa.com/magnov97/nov_pap/du_collpecc.html (accessed on July 9, 2004).

"Collared Peccary." Animal Planet. http://animal.discovery.com/fansites/jeffcorwin/carnival/lilmammal/javelina.html (accessed on July 9, 2004).

"Jaguar, Tapir, and Other Large Mammals." Peru Nature. http://www.perunature.com/info04.asp (accessed on July 9, 2004).

"Javelina." Big Bend National Park. http://www.nps.gov/bibe/teachers/factsheets/javelina.htm (accessed on July 9, 2004).

HIPPOPOTAMUSES

Hippopotamidae

Class: Mammalia

Order: Artiodactyla

Family: Hippopotamidae

Number of species: 2 species

phylum

class

subclass

order

monotypic order

suborder

▲ **family**

PHYSICAL CHARACTERISTICS

Hippopotamuses (often called hippos) have huge, round bodies that sit atop short legs. Males weigh 600 to 4,000 pounds (270 to 1,800 kilograms) and measure 60 to 106 inches (152 to 270 centimeters). Females weigh between 500 and 3,000 pounds (230 to 1,500 kilograms) and measure 58 to 106 inches (150 to 270 centimeters). Hippos have four toes on each foot with slight webbing between them. Though the skin looks hairless, there is a sparse covering of fine hairs over the entire body. The hippo has no sweat glands, but it does have skin glands that secrete a fluid. Experts believe this liquid acts as a sunscreen as well as an antiseptic (germ-killer). Hippos vary in color from slate brown to mud brown, and in certain lighting give off shades of purple.

The head is big with a wide mouth. The canines (pair of pointed teeth located in the front of the mouth on both jaws) and incisors (four front teeth, situated between the canines on both jaws) look like tusks and grow continuously throughout the hippo's lifetime.

The nostrils, eyes, and ears are located high on the face, which allows the animal to remain submerged for a long time with very little of its body showing. The hippo has a multichambered stomach, which allows for fermentation (breakdown) of food for more efficient digestion.

GEOGRAPHIC RANGE

Hippos live throughout Africa.

HABITAT

Common hippos like deep freshwater locations during the day, but venture out of the water at night to graze. The pygmy hippo lives in the forest and spends its day near or in water. Water is important to the hippo because if it can't submerge itself, its skin will crack from dehydration and overheating.

DIET

Hippos are vegetarians and eat mainly grasses, though the pygmy hippo also feeds on fruits and ferns. All hippos eat by nipping off the vegetation with their powerful lips. They eat about 88 pounds (40 kilograms) of grasses each night.

BEHAVIOR AND REPRODUCTION

Hippos do not feed in groups (with the exception of mother-offspring) because they are largely immune to predators and so are able to forage without fear of attack. Male hippos are in charge of home ranges, which they keep for four years in rivers and at least eight years in lakes. There have been reports of hippos retaining the same range for the entire span of their lives, twenty to thirty years. Herds average ten to fifteen in size, but vary from two to fifty. Nonbreeding males, though tolerated, are often the victims of territorial fights with breeding adult males. These "bachelor" males tend to live in herds of their own or alone.

Though large, hippos can run 18 miles per hour (30 kilometers per hour) when threatened, and they are able climbers. They are not able to jump and won't even attempt it.

Both hippo species mate and give birth in the water, but the pygmy hippo also mates and gives birth on land. Pregnancy lasts 227 to 240 days and results in the birth of a single calf. Calves nurse (drink mother's milk) underwater. Male hippos begin breeding between the ages of six and fourteen, whereas females are ready to breed between the ages of seven and fifteen. Calves are usually born in the rainy months.

Healthy adult hippos do not fall prey very often, but young hippos and old or sick hippos are in danger of being killed by lions, hyenas, and crocodiles.

HIPPOPOTAMUSES AND PEOPLE

Hippos are valued as a food source in Africa. Their teeth provide a high-quality ivory, and their hides are also of value.

HIPPO TRIVIA

- The common hippo is the second largest living land animal, surpassed only by the Indian rhinoceros.
- The word "hippopotamus" means "river horse."
- Unlike other mammals, it is the female hippo who chooses a mate. If a male hippo does not treat her with respect upon approach, she will not choose him!
- Mother hippos punish their babies by rolling them over with the mothers' heads or even slashing them with mothers' tusk-like teeth.
- When hippos fight, their goal is to break the front leg of their rival so that it can no longer walk to feed.
- Hippos use the same trails over and over to travel on their ranges. These trails can become five to six feet deep, literally turning into tunnels.
- Since hippos are often born underwater, babies can swim the instant they're born.

Hippos are considered one of the most dangerous animals in Africa because they have no fear of humans and are aggressive. They also raid and damage agricultural crops.

CONSERVATION STATUS

The pygmy hippo is listed as Vulnerable, facing a high risk of extinction, dying out, by the IUCN, and two other species are Extinct. The common hippo has a healthy population, but is vulnerable to extinction in West Africa. The primary threat to hippos is loss of habitat.

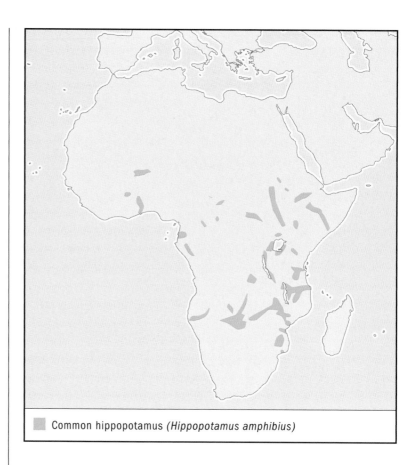

Common hippopotamus *(Hippopotamus amphibius)*

COMMON HIPPOPOTAMUS
Hippopotamus amphibius

Physical characteristics: The common hippo measures up to 106 inches (270 centimeters) in length and has a shoulder height of 54 to 60 inches (137 to 152 centimeters). It weighs up to 4,000 pounds (1,800 kilograms).

Geographic range: Although this hippo is found in thirty-five sub-Saharan countries, many of those populations are small, especially in West Africa. So, there aren't as many common hippos as it might seem there would be. Zambia, Tanzania, and the Democratic Republic of the Congo have larger populations of this species.

Habitat: The common hippo needs water deep enough to keep its body wet or the skin will crack from overheating. For the same reason, it enjoys wallowing in mud. Hippos leave the water at night to feed, sometimes traveling as far as 20 miles (32 kilometers) in one night.

Diet: The common hippo grazes on short grasses. The grasses become known as hippo lawns because they are nipped off so close to the ground. There has been one case of cannibalism (eating one's own species) documented.

Behavior and reproduction: The hippo is a difficult species to study because it is aggressive toward humans. The male common hippo is territorial in the water, where he defends mating rights with the female hippos in his range, but he is not territorial on land.

Hippos are known for their bellowing (shouting), but we don't know what role the bellowing plays in communicating between individuals. They also have at least three distinct calls underwater.

Common hippos mate and give birth in the water. Pregnancy lasts 240 days, at the end of which the female seeks solitude in the water. We do not know how long baby hippos nurse (drink mother's milk), but calves remain with their mothers until after the birth of the next calf. Common hippos are polygamous (puh-LIH-guh-mus; have more than one mate).

Common hippopotamuses and people: This species is highly dangerous to humans, particularly fishermen who invade their territories. It raids crops and is particularly fond of rice. Humans hunt the common hippo for its meat and ivory.

Conservation status: Though not listed by the IUCN, the total number of common hippos is low, especially in West Africa, where populations are as low as fifty. In order to rule out extinction, populations need to number at least five hundred in any given region or area. ■

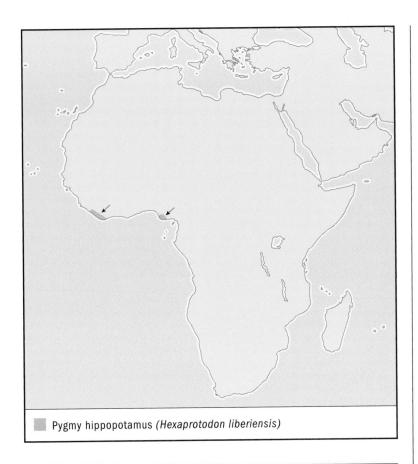

Pygmy hippopotamus (*Hexaprotodon liberiensis*)

PYGMY HIPPOPOTAMUS
Hexaprotodon liberiensis

Physical characteristics: Measures 5 to 6 feet (1.5 to 1.8 meters) in length and weighs 350 to 600 pounds (159 to 272 kilograms). Though similar to the larger common hippo in body shape, the pygmy's head is proportionately smaller. Also, its eyes, ears, and nostrils do not sit as high on the head. Its legs and neck are longer, and the skin is closer to black than brown.

Geographic range: Found in Liberia, Guinea, Ivory Coast, and Sierra Leone.

Habitat: Pygmy hippos are forest animals that spend the day in or near water and roam the land at night to forage. They also live along swamp borders.

Pygmy hippopotamus calves stay with their mothers for about three years. (Tom Brakefield/ Bruce Coleman Inc. Reproduced by permission.)

Diet: Feeds on a diet of fruits, ferns, and grasses.

Behavior and reproduction: These hippos are usually found in pairs, as they are not as social as common hippos. They also are not as aggressive.

Females give birth either on land or in water after a pregnancy lasting 190 to 210 days. Each delivery results in one calf that weighs an average of 12.6 pounds (5.7 kilograms). Unlike the common hippo calves, pygmy calves will not follow their mothers on food expeditions, but stay in hiding and wait to be nursed two or three times a day. By the age of five months, they weigh ten times more than they did at birth. These calves live with their mothers until the age of three years.

Pygmy hippopotamuses and people: Pygmy hippos are not a threat to humans but have been known to injure hunters and damage crops.

Conservation status: Listed as Vulnerable by the IUCN due to hunting and habitat loss from logging. Several national parks in the Ivory Coast and Guinea have been established to give protection to the pygmy hippo. ∎

FOR MORE INFORMATION

Books:

Eltringham, S. Keith. *The Hippos: Natural History and Conservation.* London: Academic Press, 1999.

Leach, Michael, and Frank Sloan, eds. *Hippopotamus: Habitats, Life Cycles, Food Chains, Threats.* Milwaukee: Raintree Publishers, 2000.

Perry, Phyllis J. Jean. *Freshwater Giants: Hippopotamuses, River Dolphins and Manatees.* New York: Scholastic Library Publishing, 1999.

Web sites:

"Hippopotamus." ExZooberance. http://www.exzooberance.com/virtual%20zoo/they%20walk/hippopotamus/hippopotamus.htm (accessed on May 22, 2004).

"Hippopotamus." Nature-Wildlife. http://www.nature-wildlife.com/hipptxt.htm (accessed on May 22, 2004).

"Hippopotamus." Young People's Trust for the Environment. http://www. yptenc.org.uk/docs/factsheets/animal_facts/hippopotamus.html (accessed on May 22, 2004).

"Pygmy Hippopotamus." Wonderclub. http://wonderclub.com/Wildlife/mammals/pygmyhippopotamus.htm (accessed on May 22, 2004).

Shefferly, N. *"Hippopotamus amphibius."* Animal Diversity Web. http://animaldiversity.ummz.umich.edu/site/accounts/information/Hippopotamus_amphibius.html (accessed on May 22, 2004).

"Wildlives: African Animals: Hippopotamus." African Wildlife Foundation. http://www.awf.org/wildlives/140 (accessed on May 22, 2004).

CAMELS, GUANACOS, LLAMAS, ALPACAS, AND VICUÑAS
Camelidae

Class: Mammalia
Order: Artiodactyla
Family: Camelidae
Number of species: 6 species

PHYSICAL CHARACTERISTICS

The average height of camels is 6 to 7.5 feet (1.8 to 2.3 meters), and vicuñas, guanacos, llamas, and alpacas are 3 to 4.3 feet (.90 to 1.3 meters) tall. Camels weigh between 1,000 and 1,800 pounds (454 to 816 kilograms); vicuñas, guanacos, llamas, and alpacas weigh between 88.8 and 265.5 pounds (40 to 120 kilograms).

Camelidae have long, thin necks, small heads, and slender snouts. Their tough mouths allow them to eat thick grasses and thorny plants without pain. Camels have kneepads which protect them as they fold their legs beneath their bodies to rest.

Each foot has two flat toes. Their thick coats protect them from cold temperatures, and only the camel sheds its hair as temperatures rise. Camels also have special muscles that allow them to close their nostrils and lips for long periods of time so that they do not breathe in large amounts of sand or snow.

Camels also have humps that store fat as a source of energy when food reserves are low. The better they eat, the fatter the hump or humps grow.

GEOGRAPHIC RANGE

Camelidae are found from the Arabian Peninsula to Mongolia, and in western and southern South America. Alpaca and llamas are now found throughout North America since they have become popular ranch animals.

HABITAT

Wild camelids live in the desert and semi-arid environments that have a long dry season and short rainy season. Guanacos live in warm and cold grasslands up to 13,120 feet (4,000 meters) above sea level, while vicuñas live in grasslands of the Andes Mountains above 11,482 feet (3,500 meters).

DIET

Camelids need very little water. They graze on various grasses and salty plants, which help them retain what little water they do drink. Dromedaries and guanacos drink salty water no other animals could tolerate.

Both kinds of camel eat thorny desert shrubs as well as any other vegetation found in desert or semi-arid regions. Like some other mammals, they do not chew their food completely before swallowing it. After eating, they regurgitate, bring up from the stomach, the food, re-chew it, swallow again, and digest it.

BEHAVIOR AND REPRODUCTION

Camelids are active during the day. All species will spit or kick when threatened.

Bactrian camels usually live in herds of up to thirty individuals, concentrating in the mountain areas where there are springs and snow. Dromedaries form three types of herds during the mating season. One type is that comprised of bachelor, or single, males. The next is made up of female-offspring couples, and those made up of up to thirty adult females along with their offspring, led by one adult male. Vicuñas maintain family groups of one territorial male and subadults as well as females and offspring less than a year old. The guanaco population lives in three social groups as well including families with one adult male and one or several females with their most recent offspring, male groups whose numbers may reach fifty, and solitary males. Because they are now raised domestically, llamas and alpacas have lost their social structure.

Camelids have numerous mates and do not bond with one another. After twelve to thirteen months of pregnancy, female camels give birth to one newborn, which can walk within a few hours of birth. Young remain with their mothers until the age of two years but they not considered adults until the age of five years. Female llamas and vicuñas also give birth to one offspring

ALPACAS: BIG BUSINESS

According to Lisa Olsen, an alpaca rancher in North Carolina, pregnant female alpacas can sell for $12,000 to $22,000 each. That is a nice profit considering that they are not very expensive to feed, since they live on hay, grass, and grains.

According to the Alpaca Owners and Breeders Association, the record for the highest dollar sale of a male alpaca was set in 2002, when a sire sold for $265,000. Like any other livestock ranching, alpaca breeding is a business, and it is gaining popularity.

after an eleven-month pregnancy. The babies stay with the mother until one year of age.

Pumas and foxes are the primary predators of vicuñas and llamas, while alpacas fall prey to pumas and leopards. Camels have no known predators.

CAMELIDS AND PEOPLE

Camelids have been used for transportation as well as a food and clothing source for about seven thousand years. They are especially valuable as transportation in the North African and Asian deserts because they can travel up to 100 miles (161 kilometers) without water. They are also able to carry heavy loads and still keep a steady pace.

Camels are a sign of wealth to some desert populations. These species provide humans with milk, meat, and wool used to make clothing, blankets, and tents. The fat can be removed from their humps and melted for use in cooking.

Llamas and alpacas were domesticated thousands of years ago. Alpacas were first imported to the United States in 1984, and in 2004 there were more than fifty thousand registered alpacas in the United States. Llamas are believed to be domesticated, tamed, by about 4,000 B.C.E.

Vicuñas were used in religious rituals in the Inca empire. Guanacos provided food, hides, and fibers for South American cultures, but they have never been domesticated.

CONSERVATION STATUS

Camels, alpacas, and llamas are not listed by the World Conservation Union (IUCN) because they are domestic animals. However, wild Bactrian camels are listed as Critically Endangered, facing an extremely high risk of extinction in the wild, due to heavy hunting and competition with domestic livestock for water and land. Vicuñas and guanacos are listed as Vulnerable, facing a high risk of extinction in the wild. Vicuñas had been hunted almost to the point of extinction for their fur and meat.

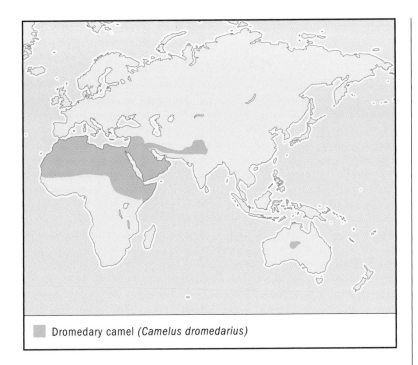

Dromedary camel (*Camelus dromedarius*)

DROMEDARY CAMEL
Camelus dromedarius

Physical characteristics: Dromedary camels are 7 feet (2.1 meters) tall at the hump and weighs 1,600 pounds (726 kilograms). Their long neck is curved, and they have one hump. Hair is caramel brown or sandy brown, though shades can range from nearly black to white. The coat is long at the throat, shoulders, and hump area, and blocks the heat of the sun. The tail is short and the eyelashes are long.

Geographic range: Dromedary camels are found in dry regions of the Middle East through northern India, and in Africa, primarily the Sahara Desert. This camel has been introduced to Australia.

Habitat: Dromedary camels like the desert where temperatures often rise above 120°F (49°C).

Diet: Dromedary camels eat thorny plants, dry grasses, and salty plants that grow in the desert. Since they eat only a few leaves from each plant, their food supply is relatively stable. Because they do not drink much water, dromedary camels need six to eight times more

A camel's hump is mostly fat, which is used by the body when food is scarce. (© Dave G. Houser/Corbis. Reproduced by permission.)

salt than other animals. Salt helps the body retain water. Dromedary camels do not sweat easily, so they lose moisture more slowly than other animals. Dromedary camels have been known to drink one-third of their weight in water within ten minutes.

Behavior and reproduction: Families include two to twenty individual camels, including one dominant male, several females, and offspring. The dominant male chases away competitor males by pushing them, snapping, and spitting.

Females are ready to mate by three years, males by six years. Pregnancy lasts up to fifteen months. Mothers nurse, feed with mother's milk, their offspring for one year. Because they have no predators, dromedary camels live anywhere from thirty to forty years.

Dromedary camels and people: Dromedary camels have been hunted for their meat and used as transportation for thousands of years. They are also valuable for their milk, wool, leather, and manure, which is used for fuel.

Conservation status: There are about fourteen million dromedary camels across the globe. They are not threatened. ■

Alpaca (*Lama pacos*)

ALPACA
Lama pacos

Physical characteristics: Alpacas reach 3 feet (.90 meters) high and weigh 154.3 pounds (70 kilograms). They have small heads, short, pointed ears, and extremely long necks. Except for the face and legs, the entire body is covered by long, thick, soft wool. Legs are short. Alpacas are generally a dark chocolate or near-black color, but the fibers used to make clothing come in twenty-two colors. Their coats are water repellant and protect them from solar radiation.

Young alpacas are called "cria." They usually nurse for five or six months. (Francisco Erize/Bruce Coleman Inc. Reproduced by permission.)

Geographic range: Alpacas live in the Andes of Peru, Bolivia, and Chile. They live in high altitudes ranging from 9,840 to 15,750 feet (3,000 to 4,800 meters).

Habitat: Alpacas prefer grasslands of the high plateaus of the Andes.

Diet: Alpacas feed on grasses, shrubs, and trees. The digestive system of an alpaca is highly efficient, which allows them to thrive on poor vegetation where other animals could not.

Behavior and reproduction: Alpacas are gentle, even-tempered animals. They are friendly and show little sign of aggression, a fact that makes them easy to domesticate and raise commercially.

Females mate for the first time around two years, males around three years. Pregnancy lasts 324 to 345 days and results in one offspring, called a cria. Cria nurse for five or six months. The average lifespan is twenty to twenty-five years. Primary predators of wild alpacas are pumas and foxes.

Alpacas and people: When Spanish explorers arrived in Peru, they found the Incan culture to be based on textiles. In an effort to conquer the native peoples, the explorers slaughtered 90 percent of the alpaca population. As the natives went into hiding or escaped, they took with them both sexes of alpacas, thereby keeping the species alive. Today alpacas are ranch-raised for their wool. Their friendly personalities and resistance to disease make them easy to care for.

Conservation status: Alpacas are not threatened. There are about 3.5 million alpacas in the world. ■

Llama (*Lama glama*)

LLAMA
Lama glama

Physical characteristics: The average height of a llama is 3.8 feet (1.2 meters). They weigh around 309 pounds (140 kilograms). Legs are long, and the coat is a reddish-brown. Face, ears, and legs can be tainted black, white, or a mix of other colors.

Geographic range: Llamas live in Peru, Argentina, Chile, Bolivia, Ecuador, and Colombia.

Habitat: Llamas live in high-altitude grasslands up to 13,120 feet (4,000 meters).

Diet: Llamas eat grasses and salty plants.

Behavior and reproduction: Llamas do not touch one another, not even in mother-offspring relationships. They are very herd-oriented and travel in groups. Llamas live to be older than twenty years.

Llamas are believed to have numerous mates. One male can mate with up to thirty females. Pregnancy lasts about eleven months.

Llamas and people: Llama fiber is used in making ropes, cowboy hats, and rugs. Their skin is used to make leather goods, and their bones make instruments for weaving looms. Their meat is low in fat, and because they move rather slowly, llamas are easy to catch. They make great pack animals and are used throughout the world for commercial mountain treks.

Conservation status: Llamas are not threatened. There were around 2.5 million llamas throughout the world in 2004. ■

FOR MORE INFORMATION

Books:

Frisch, Aaron. *Llamas.* Mankato, MN: The Creative Company, 2003.

Karr, Kathleen. *Exiled: Memoirs of a Camel.* New York: Marshall Cavendish, 2004.

Nowak, Ronald M. "Guanaco, Llama, and Alpaca." *Walker's Mammals of the World 5.1 Online.* Baltimore: Johns Hopkins University Press, 1997. http://www.press.jhu.edu/books/walkers_mammals_of_the_world/ artiodactyla/artiodactyla.camelidae.lama.html (accessed on May 28, 2004).

Periodicals:

Freeman, Darren. "Alpaca Ranchers Spur Livestock Trend N.C. Farming Don't Worry—The Llama-Like Animals Don't Spit at People." *The Virginian Pilot* (March 28, 2004): Y1.

Web sites:

"About Alpacas." AlpacaInfo.com. http://www.alpacainfo.com/newsite/ about/history.html (accessed on May 28, 2004).

"Information About Camels." LlamaWeb. http://www.llamaweb.com/ Camel/Info.html (accessed on May 28, 2004).

CHEVROTAINS
Tragulidae

Class: Mammalia
Order: Artiodactyla
Family: Tragulidae
Number of species: 4 species

PHYSICAL CHARACTERISTICS

Chevrotains look like tiny hornless deer with small heads, tapered snouts, skinny legs, and thick bodies. From head to rump, they measure 17 to 19 inches (44 to 85 centimeters), and they weigh 4.4 to 29 pounds (2 to 13 kilograms). Their backs are rounded and somewhat higher toward their rear ends, like the backs of rats. Their ears are tiny and covered with hair, which is short and thick over their entire body. The coat is reddish brown to brown with patterns of white and brown spots and stripes on various areas, depending on the species. Males have tusk-like teeth on top, but females have small, cone-shaped canines, teeth on either side of the four front teeth with one set on each jaw. Chevrotains have three fully developed stomach chambers, which allows for efficient digestion. Each foot has four toes.

GEOGRAPHIC RANGE

Chevrotains are found in Southeast Asia and east central Africa.

HABITAT

Asian chevrotains live in rainforests, lowland forests, mangrove forests, and thickets. They prefer areas with thick vegetation during the day and venture into open area at night. The vegetation provides refuge from predators. African chevrotains live in tropical rainforests and thick growth along water courses. This species escapes predators by diving into the water.

phylum

class

subclass

order

monotypic order

suborder

▲ **family**

DIET

Chevrotains eat grasses and leaves, favoring young shoots, fallen fruits, and seeds. They have been seen eating small animals occasionally.

BEHAVIOR AND REPRODUCTION

Because they are shy and come out only at night, chevrotains are difficult to study. They are easily frightened and jump at the first sign of danger. Chevrotains are loners and socialize only during mating and while rearing young. The exception to this is the lesser Malay mouse deer, which is monogamous (muh-NAH-guh-mus), has only one mate.

Chevrotains are territorial and mark their ranges using sounds and scent marks including feces, urine, and glandular secretions. Mouse deer bleat softly, like a lamb, when alarmed. Although they will fight, bouts are short and infrequent. Males fight with their tusk-like teeth.

Females are more active than males. All chevrotain sit on their hind legs or crouch with all legs folded to rest.

Little is known about the mating system of chevrotains. Gestation, pregnancy, lasts six to nine months and results in the birth of one offspring each year. Babies are nursed, fed with mother's milk, until the age of three to six months and can stand on their own within an hour after birth. Chevrotains are able to mate after nine to twenty-six months, and this is when the young leave home. These animals live to an age of eleven to thirteen years. Their primary predators are large birds of prey and reptiles.

CHEVROTAINS AND PEOPLE

Regardless of where they live, chevrotains are hunted by native populations for food. Some people keep them as pets. Although some zoos have had success in breeding water chevrotains, these animals have proven difficult to breed in captivity.

CONSERVATION STATUS

All four species are threatened by hunting and habitat destruction. The water chevrotain is listed by the World Conservation Union (IUCN) as Data Deficient, meaning there is not enough population information to evaluate its risk, and only one subspecies is Endangered, facing a very high risk of extinction in the wild.

Lesser Malay mouse deer (*Tragulus javanicus*)

LESSER MALAY MOUSE DEER
Tragulus javanicus

Physical characteristics: The lesser Malay mouse deer is neither mouse nor deer, but it is the smallest living artiodactyl (ar-tee-oh-DACK-tuhl), weighing between 3.3 and 5.5 pounds (1.5 and 2.5 kilograms) and measuring 18 to 22 inches (45 to 55 centimeters) from head to rump. The tail is about 2 inches (5 centimeters). The large eyes are surrounded by a lighter ring of fur. The upper coat is brown tinged with orange, and the underside is white. Females are somewhat smaller than males.

Geographic range: Lesser Malay mouse deer are found in Malaysia, Cambodia, southwestern China, Indonesia, Borneo, Laos, Myanmar, Singapore, and Thailand.

Habitat: Lesser Malay mouse deer live in lowland forests. They are also found near water in thick vegetation, hollow trees, and among rocks.

Diet: Lesser Malay mouse deer eat leaves, buds, grass, and fallen fruits.

Behavior and reproduction: Recent studies suggest that this species, once believed to be nocturnal, active at night, and solitary, is actually somewhat active during the day and tends to form monogamous pairs. Lesser mouse deer are territorial and routinely mark their territory. When upset, this species will tap the ground with its hooves at a rate of seven times per second. They will also emit a shrill cry when frightened, but otherwise are silent.

Lesser Malay mouse deer are ready to breed at five to six months. Pregnancy lasts four to five months and produces one fawn, rarely two. The young can stand within thirty minutes of birth and the mother nurses her baby while standing. Offspring are weaned, removed from mother's milk, between ten and thirteen weeks. Within 55 to 155 minutes after they give birth, female lesser Malay mouse deer are able to get pregnant again.

Lifespan of the lesser Malay mouse deer is up to twelve years. Their predators include reptiles and large birds of prey such as owls and hawks.

Lesser Malay mouse deer and people: This species is hunted for its smooth skin, which is used for the production of leather goods such as wallets and handbags.

Conservation status: Although not threatened according to the IUCN, the lesser mouse deer population is threatened by habitat destruction and hunting. Their range and numbers have increased due to conservation efforts. ■

FOR MORE INFORMATION

Books:

Morris, Kathy, John Morris, and I. Nyoman Kartana. *Mouse Deer and Crocodile: An Asian Folktale.* Arlington, VA: Bamboo Books, 1999.

Web sites:

Starr, Christopher K. "Anansi the Spider Man: A West African Trickster in the West Indies." Acarology Conference, August 1999. http://users.carib-link.net/rfbarnes/anansi.htm (accessed on June 1, 2004).

Strawder, N. "*Tragulus javanicus.*" Animal Diversity Web. http://animaldiversity.ummz.umich.edu/site/accounts/information/Tragulus_javanicus.html (accessed on June 1, 2004).

"*Tragulus javanicus.*" Ultimate Ungulate. http://www.ultimateungulate.com/Artiodactyla/Tragulus_javanicus.html (accessed on June 1, 2004).

family

CHAPTER

PHYSICAL CHARACTERISTICS

Deer have long bodies and long legs. Coats are various shades of brown; some species have white fur to blend in with the arctic environment. They have an enhanced sense of smell. All are capable swimmers and fast runners. Males of nearly every species have velvet-covered antlers that they shed each year; in some species, females also have antlers. Hooves help them navigate snow, but deep snows can lead to death due to lack of mobility, which results in predation and starvation. Males are usually larger than females. Deer species vary in weight from 22 pounds (10 kilograms) to 1,764 pounds (800 kilograms).

GEOGRAPHIC RANGE

Deer are found everywhere except Australia and Africa.

HABITAT

Depending on the species, deer live in a variety of habitats. Most deer species prefer areas with thick forest undergrowth.

DIET

Deer are herbivores (plant eaters) that eat lichens (fungus found on trees), leaves, twigs, shoots, berries, and grasses. They have four stomach chambers, which allow them to chew and swallow their food and then regurgitate (vomit) it later for further chewing. This makes digestion more efficient.

phylum

class

subclass

order

monotypic order

suborder

▲ **family**

BEHAVIOR AND REPRODUCTION

Some deer are solitary (lone), but most species are polygynous (puh-LIH-juh-nus; one male to several female mates). Depending on species, they live in mother-offspring pairs or herds numbering into the tens of thousands of individuals.

Gestation (pregnancy) periods vary depending on species, but usually single births, sometimes twins, result. Calves are nursed (fed mother's milk) for a short time. Most babies are born able to walk, even run, within hours.

Predators include wolves, grizzly bears, coyotes, mountain lions, foxes, and wild cats. Life expectancy varies by species. Some deer live an average of two years, while others can live past the age of fifteen years.

DEER AND PEOPLE

A number of species are important game animals throughout the world. They are hunted for meat and sport, and the larger species are often a source of subsistence for native cultures that herd them.

CONSERVATION STATUS

Of the fifty-seven species, twenty-seven are included on the IUCN Red List. One is Extinct, died out; one is Critically Endangered, facing an extremely high risk of extinction; four are Endangered, facing a very high risk of extinction; six are Vulnerable, facing a high risk of extinction; four are Near Threatened, not currently threatened, but could become so; and eleven are considered Data Deficient, meaning there is not enough information to determine a conservation status. Reason for threats include overexploitation by humans as well as habitat destruction.

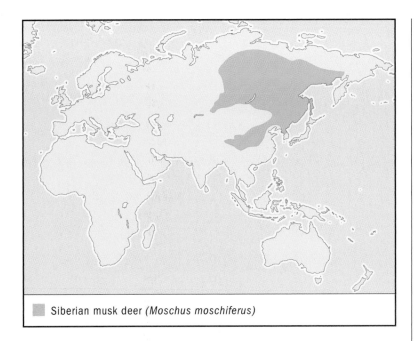

Siberian musk deer (*Moschus moschiferus*)

SIBERIAN MUSK DEER
Moschus moschiferus

Physical characteristics: The Siberian musk deer weighs 18 to 36 pounds (8 to 16 kilograms) and measures 24 to 39 inches (60 to 100 centimeters). Coat is various shades of brown, and there are fuzzy whitish yellow spots on the neck and chest, with rows of brighter spots on both sides of the body.

Geographic range: This musk deer is found in eastern Asia.

Habitat: This deer needs plenty of lichens (LIE-kenz) to eat and shelter from predators. It lives in coniferous forests with dense undergrowth and ground moss. Siberian musk deer can move easily on top of snow because of their light weight. Deep, loose snow is difficult for them to navigate and can kill them.

Diet: Lichens are the primary food source, comprising 80 percent of their diet in winter. They also eat fir needles, twigs, leaves, berries, and mushrooms in winter. Musk deer have been known to migrate up to 20 miles (35 kilometers) for food. Lichens aid digestion in summer, at which time they also eat flowers, moss, shoots, and grass.

Behavior and reproduction: Five to seven females and their offspring live together on a home range. This home range overlaps with that of a dominating male. The more important or stronger females live at the center of the range, and as old deer die, younger ones move toward the center. Musk deer are nocturnal (active at night). Although fast runners, they tire quickly, so they escape predators usually by jumping and leaping as they run.

These polygamous (puh-LIH-guh-mus) animals give birth in April, May or June, depending on the region. Fawns are hidden for up to two months. Primary predators include lynx, wolverine, foxes, wolves, tiger, bear, and the yellow-throated marten.

Siberian musk deer and people: Humans hunt this species for their musk, which is produced by an abdominal gland in males and valued for its cosmetic and medical uses.

Conservation status: Listed as Vulnerable by the IUCN due to overhunting. ■

Indian muntjac (*Muntiacus muntjak*)

INDIAN MUNTJAC
Muntiacus muntjak

Physical characteristics: Measures 35 to 53.2 inches (89 to 135 centimeters) long with a shoulder height of 15.7 to 25.6 inches (40 to 65 centimeters). Weight ranges from 33.1 to 77.2 pounds (15 to 35 kilograms), with males being larger than females. Males have small antlers about 6 inches (15 centimeters) long. Females have small knobs where antlers would be. Coat coloration is gold and white, with limbs and face being dark to reddish brown. Indian muntjacs have small ears and tusk-like upper canines measuring 1 inch (2.5 centimeters) in males.

Geographic range: Found in northeastern Pakistan, India, Sri Lanka, Nepal, southern China, Vietnam, Malay Peninsula and some nearby islands, Riau Archipelago, Sumatra and Nias Island to the west, Bangka, Belitun Island, Java, Bali, and Borneo.

Indian muntjacs eat some small animals. They catch them by biting with their canine teeth and "punching" them with their strong front legs. (© W. Perry Conway/Corbis. Reproduced by permission.)

Habitat: Indian muntjacs live in tropical rainforests, deciduous forests, and scrub forests as well as hilly areas, grasslands, and savannas. They must remain near a water source.

Diet: Feed on herbs, fruit, birds' eggs, small animals, seeds, sprouts, and grasses found at the edge of the forest or in a clearing. They catch animals by biting with their canines and punching with their strong forelegs.

Behavior and reproduction: Although they sometimes move in pairs or small groups, adults are solitary (lone). When in danger of predation, Indian muntjacs bark like dogs, sometimes for more than an hour, to scare away the predator. Pythons, jackals, tigers, leopards, and crocodiles are the primary enemies of this deer.

This deer is ready to breed between the ages of six and twelve months. After a six-month pregnancy, females give birth to one fawn, rarely two, which remains with the mother until the age of six months. Though no one is sure how long muntjacs live in the wild, this species lives about seventeen years in captivity.

Indian muntjacs and people: Muntjacs are hunted for their meat and skins, and hunters themselves make the barking sound of the muntjac to warn other hunters of approaching danger, such as a tiger. Muntjac populations are a threat when found in larger numbers because they tear bark from trees, which takes a toll on sources for humans' shelter and fuel.

Conservation status: The Indian muntjac is not considered threatened. ■

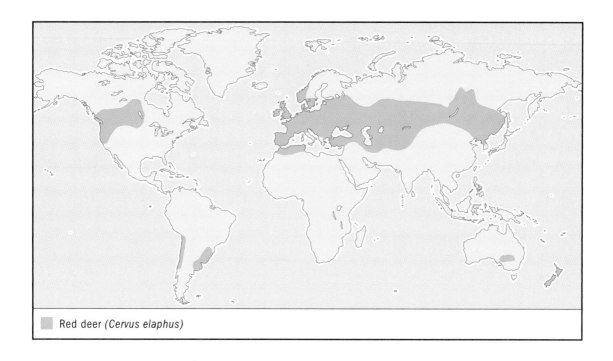

Red deer (Cervus elaphus)

RED DEER
Cervus elaphus

Physical characteristics: Males weigh up to 480 pounds (190 kilograms) and stand up to 48 inches (120 centimeters) high at the shoulder. Females weigh up to 240 pounds (110 kilograms) and stand up to 44 inches (110 centimeters) high at the shoulder. The coat is a rich red color that changes to grayish brown in the cold months. The rump sports a creamy white patch and short tail. Males have antlers that fall off from February to April each year. New ones grow in August.

Geographic range: Found in western Europe, northwest Africa, Asia to western China, and northwestern America. Red deer have been successfully introduced to New Zealand.

Habitat: Red deer prefer to live in forested areas, but in regions where forests have been cleared, this species has adapted. They can be found in open plains, marshlands, mountain terraces, and meadows.

Diet: Red deer feed mostly on twigs, leaves, and stems of broadleaf trees and shrubs, needles and branches of fir trees, herbs, lichens,

fruits, and fungi. They enjoy willow, oak, poplar, and mountain ash trees. Those found in North America depend on western hemlock, fir, western red cedar, willow, and ferns. They also eat skunk cabbage, wall lettuce, and red elderberry.

Behavior and reproduction: Active throughout a twenty-four-hour cycle, red deer are most active at dawn and dusk. They live in small groups within woodlands, where the forest covering offers more protection. In open spaces, they live in larger herds. Males and females live separately except during breeding season, which is in October. At this time, herds separate and males gather together a group of females. During breeding (also known as "rutting") season, males become more aggressive and less tolerant of one another. Rival stags will roar at one another, lock antlers, and push at each other until one stag "wins" the group of up to forty or so females. Now and then stag antlers will lock, and the two deer will starve to death. Other than this, stags rarely kill each other in the fight for dominance.

After a pregnancy of thirty-three to thirty-four weeks, females give birth to one calf, which is weaned (taken off mother's milk) between nine and twelve months. At one-and-a-half years of age, red deer are ready to mate. Stags live to the age of twelve years in the wild, females to ten. Predators include foxes, wild cats, golden eagles, and wolves, which prey on the young.

Red deer and people: This deer is hunted for its meat (venison) and for sport. Teams of red deer pulled coaches in ceremonial processions connected with the hunting goddess Diana in Ancient Rome. Humans are the red deer's primary predator today.

Conservation status: Not threatened. Red deer farming is becoming popular in all regions. Herds in Britain are large enough that they must be culled (reduced in number by selection according to those fittest for survival and reproduction) annually so they do not starve. ■

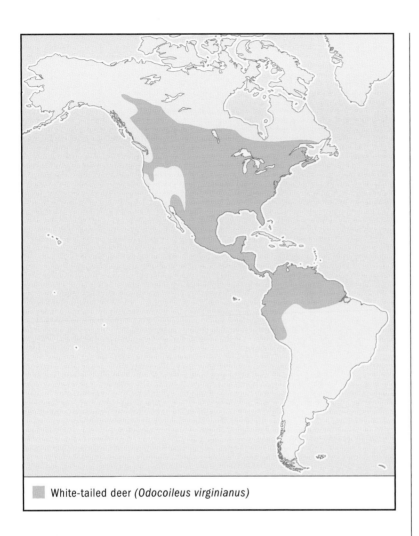

White-tailed deer (*Odocoileus virginianus*)

WHITE-TAILED DEER
Odocoileus virginianus

Physical characteristics: This is a small deer species, weighing 110 to 300 pounds (50 to 136 kilograms) and measuring 67 to 77 inches (170 to 195 centimeters) long. Summer coat is a foxy-red color. Coat changes to grayish brown in fall, and hairs grow thicker and longer. The underpart of the tail is white, as is the throat, nose, stomach, and area surrounding the eyes. Only males have antlers, but both sexes have scent glands on all four hooves. Although their eyesight and hearing are well developed, they rely on sense of smell to detect danger.

Almost 70 percent of the white-tailed deer's diet consists of tree and shrub leaves and twigs. (© Raymond Gehman/ Corbis. Reproduced by permission.)

Geographic range: This deer is found in southern Canada and all of the United States except for Hawaii, Alaska, and the southwest. Also lives throughout Central America to Bolivia.

Habitat: Although they have adapted to live in a variety of habitats ranging from swamps and farmland to forest, white-tailed deer prefer to live in areas with dense thickets (growths of bushes) and clear edges (for food).

Diet: Almost 70 percent of this deer's diet consists of tree and shrub leaves and twigs. Adults need 5 to 11 pounds (2.5 to 5 kilograms) of food daily. In winter, stored body fat allows them to subsist on 2 pounds (1 kilogram) daily. Though watering places are often at the center of home ranges, this animal can go without water if succulent (water-based) plants are available.

Behavior and reproduction: When sensing danger, this deer will stomp its hooves, snort, and point its tail up to alert other deer. Able to run at speeds of up to thirty miles per hour, these deer are also able jumpers and swimmers. Home ranges are usually less than one square mile (2.59 square kilometers). Females live alone unless they are mothers, and bucks live in small herds of three or four individuals except during mating season.

White-tailed deer are polygynous and begin breeding in late September into December. Pregnancy lasts 188 to 222 days and usually results in the birth of twins. Within hours, they nurse and walk around following the mother, though they prefer to hide until around ten days, when they begin eating on their own. They nurse until eight to ten weeks of age. Usual rate of first breeding is two years for both sexes. Mortality rate among white-tailed deer is high, around 30 to 50 percent. Most live to be two or three years old. Predators include bears, mountain lions, wolves, jaguars, and coyotes.

White-tailed deer and people: This species is the most numerous of big game animals in the world. Hunters kill about three million each year, and still the population thrives. White-tailed deer carry Lyme disease, which has become more prevalent among humans, especially in the northeastern states. Some people consider this deer a pest because it gets into yards and eats shrubs, flowers, and other ornamental vegetation.

Conservation status: White-tailed deer are not threatened.   ■

Southern pudu (*Pudu pudu*)

Physical characteristics: The smallest deer in the world weighs 20 to 33 pounds (9 to 15 kilograms) and stands 14 to 18 inches (35 to 45 centimeters) high at the shoulder. Its thick coat is a reddish brown, and the lips and insides of ears are tinged with orange. Males have short spiked antlers. Body is low to the ground. Eyes and ears are small. The tail of this deer is so small as to be almost nonexistent.

Geographic range: The pudu lives in Argentina and southern Chile.

Habitat: This deer lives in rainforests, bamboo groves, and in mountains. Prefers thickets for protection from wild cats and foxes.

Diet: The pudu eats twigs, leaves, fruits, seeds, and bark. Stands on back legs to reach food if necessary.

Behavior and reproduction: These solitary deer socialize only during mating season. They traverse the jungle via well-worn paths and form dung piles near resting places. Each pudu has a home range of 40 to 60 acres (16.2 to 24.3 hectares).

This polygynous deer mates in the fall. Pregnancy lasts about 210 days and results in the birth of a single fawn. Babies nurse for two months. Females are ready to mate at twelve months, males at eighteen. Life expectancy is eight to ten years.

Southern pudu and people: Hunted for food and sport.

Conservation status: Endangered due to habitat destruction and domestic dogs. ■

The southern pudu is the smallest deer in the world. (© Tom McHugh/Photo Researchers, Inc. Reproduced by permission.)

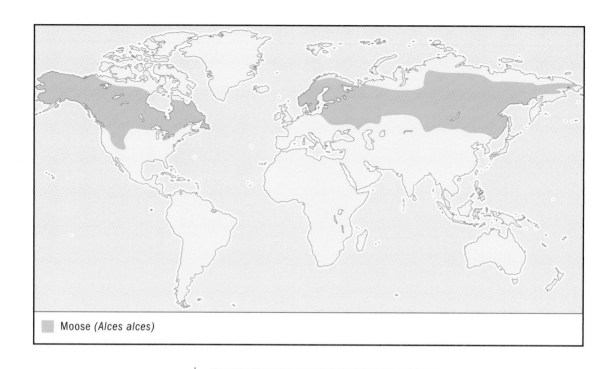

Moose (*Alces alces*)

MOOSE
Alces alces

Physical characteristics: Adults weigh 594 to 1,320 pounds (270 to 600 kilograms) and measure 7.9 to 10.5 feet (2.4 to 3.2 meters) long. The antlers of the male are longer than those of any mammal in the world and can measure up to 6.6 feet (2 meters) wide from tip to tip. The head is huge and long, with a square upper lip that hangs over the lower one. Muzzle is hairy. Coat is dark brown, fading to light brown on the long legs. Hearing and sense of smell are excellent.

Geographic range: Moose are found in North America and Eurasia.

Habitat: Moose live in forests where there is snow in winter. They like territory with ponds and lakes. Because they are not able to sweat, moose need to live in cooler climates. In summer, they cool off in water.

Diet: Moose eat bark and branches during winter and enjoy leaves, herbs, and aquatic plants in summer. In winter, adults eat 22 to 30 pounds (10 to 13 kilograms) of food each day; that amount doubles in summer and spring. Moose can also eat toxic plants.

Behavior and reproduction: Moose live alone or in small groups. No social bonding occurs. Moose can run at 35 miles per hour (56 kilometers per hour) and swim at 6 miles per hour (9.7 kilometers per hour). They tend to stay in the same area, though some migrate between favored sites, up to 186 miles (300 kilometers) in European species. Home ranges are 3.1 to 6.2 square miles (5 to 10 square kilometers).

The polygynous moose begin breeding in August. Females attract males with a loud moaning bellow, and males groan in response. Females also emit a powerful scent. Males compete for females, and after a 215- to 243-day pregnancy, a single calf is born (though twins are common). Young moose nurse until five months of age, and they begin eating food as early as three weeks. They stay with their mother until they are one year, or the next calf is born.

Almost half of all moose young die within the first year of life. Though moose live to be five to twelve years, at eight years they begin to suffer from arthritis and dental disease. Although large, moose fall prey to grizzly bears and wolves.

The antlers of the male moose are longer than those of any mammal in the world and can measure up to 6.6 feet (2 meters) wide from tip to tip. (Erwin and Peggy Bauer/Bruce Coleman Inc. Reproduced by permission.)

Moose and people: Moose meat is a main source of food for many people. In North America, more than fifty thousand moose are harvested annually for meat and sport. They are a main attraction in the ecotourism industry.

Conservation status: Moose are not threatened. ■

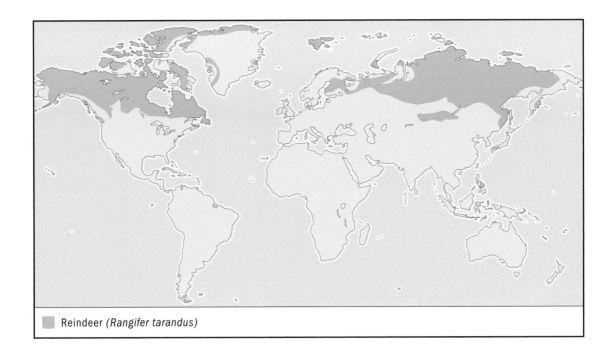

Reindeer (*Rangifer tarandus*)

REINDEER
Rangifer tarandus

Physical characteristics: Acknowledged as the tame subspecies of caribou, this animal weighs 121 to 699.6 pounds (55 to 318 kilograms) and measures 381 to 584.2 inches (150 to 230 centimeters) long. Males can be twice as big as females. Tails are short, and coat color varies from dark brown to almost white, depending on the region. Hooves are large and broad, which assist the reindeer in swimming. Both sexes have antlers.

Geographic range: Reindeer are found throughout the upper latitudes of Eurasia and North America.

Habitat: Reindeer live in arctic deserts on Arctic Ocean islands as well as on arctic tundra (treeless region of north polar areas). They like coniferous forests of pine and larch trees where woody lichens are abundant. Forest swamps and marshlands also appeal to reindeer.

Diet: The summer diet includes willows, birches, mushrooms, and grasses. In winter, reindeer eat dry plants, cotton grass, and mosses.

Reindeer shed velvet, skin covering their antlers, in fall, when they are getting ready to mate. (John Shaw/Bruce Coleman Inc. Reproduced by permission.)

The moss is especially important because it contains a chemical that acts like antifreeze and keeps body fluids from freezing. Lichens are an important source of carbohydrates and are eaten year-round.

Behavior and reproduction: Reindeer migrate in spring and fall, sometimes covering as many as 3,105 miles (6,000 kilometers) in one year. They can travel at a rate of 50 miles per hour (80 kilometers per hour). They live in mother-offspring pairs, herds, and gatherings. Typical herds include 2,500 to 3,000 individuals with a single leader. During migration, herds can reach 80,000 to 100,000 animals.

The polygynous reindeer breed in September and October, and fights between rival males are frequent. Victors "win" seven to eight females. Pregnancy lasts 192 to 246 days and result in the birth of one calf. Newborns are able to stand within an hour and can outrun a human within twenty-four hours. They nurse for one month and then begin grazing with the mother. Calves retain a strong bond with mothers for three months. Females live longer than males, sometimes past fifteen years. Average life expectancy for males is 4.5 years. Primary predators are wolves, brown bear, raven, golden eagle, and sea eagle. Calves often die during migration due to cold and exhaustion; 40 percent die in the first year, 30 percent in the second.

Adult males shed antlers soon after breeding, but females don't shed them until spring. Reindeer are able swimmers and can cross water bodies that are 75 miles (120 kilometers) wide.

Reindeer and people: Native peoples of the north depend on reindeer for their survival in terms of food and skin. A number of native cultures in America, Siberia, and Scandinavia revolve around reindeer and caribou herding. Velvet antlers are used in Asian medicine.

Conservation status: Reindeer are not threatened. ■

FOR MORE INFORMATION

Books:

Geist, Valerius. *Deer of the World: Their Evolution, Behaviour, and Ecology.* Mechanicsburg, PA: Stackpole Books, 1998.

Rue, Leonard III. *The Encyclopedia of Deer: Your Guide to the World's Deer Species, Including White Tails, Mule Deer, Caribou, Elk, Moose and More.* Stillwater, MN: Voyageur Press, 2004.

Wexo, John Bonnett, et al. *The Deer Family (Zoobooks).* Minnetonka, MN: Creative Publishing, 1999.

Web sites:

Fox, D. and P. Myers. "Cervidae." Animal Diversity Web. http://animaldiversity.ummz.umich.edu/site/accounts/information/Cervidae.html (accessed on June 3, 2004).

"Indian Muntjac." Sedgwick County Zoo. http://www.scz.org/animals/m/muntjac.html (accessed on June 3, 2004).

"Moose Biology with Kristine Bontaites." Mooseworld. http://www.mooseworld.com/biologist.htm (accessed on June 3, 2004).

"*Pudu puda.*" Ultimate Ungulate. http://www.ultimateungulate.com/Artiodactyla/Pudu_puda.html (accessed on June 3, 2004).

"Red Deer." Young People's Trust for the Environment. http://www.yptenc.org.uk/docs/factsheets/animal_facts/red_deer.html (accessed on June 3, 2004).

"Science & Nature: Animals: Red Deer, Wapiti, Elk." BBC. http://www.bbc.co.uk/nature/wildfacts/factfiles/199.shtml (accessed on June 3, 2004).

"White-tailed Deer." Natureworks. http://www.nhptv.org/natureworks/whitetaileddeer.htm (accessed on June 3, 2004).

PHYSICAL CHARACTERISTICS

Giraffes stand up to 18 feet (5.5 meters) to the top of the head and weigh 460 to 4,250 pounds (210 to 1,930 kilograms). When compared to the long neck (up to 8 feet, or 2.4 meters), the body is short. Legs are long and end in hooves the size of dinner plates. Their tails grow up to 39 inches (1 meter) and have a tassel at the end. Males are usually larger than females.

Eyes are large, and the long tongue (19 inches [45 centimeters]) is black. Both sexes have short horns of about 5 inches (13.5 centimeters) in length, though males' are thicker. Males also have a middle horn and four or more small bumps.

The okapi (oh-KOP-ee) never weighs more than 550 pounds (250 kilograms), and its head is horse-like in shape. Its neck is not as long as the giraffe's. Where the giraffe's coat is various shades of brown with patterns of cream-colored hair, the okapi's coat is dark brown with white stripes on the upper legs, white "socks" on the ankle, and dark rings at the leg joints. Both species walk with their weight supported alternately on their left and right legs, like camels. They use their necks to maintain balance.

GEOGRAPHIC RANGE

Giraffids (giraffes and okapis) are found only in sub-Saharan Africa.

DID YOU KNOW?

- Giraffes breathe twenty times a minute.
- Giraffes can run up to 35 miles per hour (60 kilometers per hour).
- Okapis weren't discovered until 1900.
- Female giraffes will return to the same site year after year to give birth.
- Newborn giraffes grow as much as an inch each day.
- The okapi is the only mammal that can clean its ears with its tongue.
- Because it takes a giraffe a long time to stand from the lying-down position, these animals will sleep using the buddy system: the herd sleeps while a designated individual keeps watch.
- The hind legs of the okapi have the same striped pattern and coloring as the zebra.
- Giraffes love the thorny acacia (uh-KAY-shah) tree and are able to eat it by closing their nostrils and producing a great deal of spit to help swallow the thorns. Their lips are protected by thick hair.
- Okapis find breeding partners by sense of smell.
- The okapi was first thought to be related to the zebra.

HABITAT

Giraffes live in savannas (tropical or subtropical community characterized by small trees and shrubs among herbs and grasses). Okapis live in tropical lowland forests.

DIET

Giraffes are browsers (eaters of shrubs, trees, and herbs) that eat mostly deciduous foliage in the rains and evergreen species during other seasons. They also eat fruit and grass now and then, and will drink water if available, but most of it comes through the plants they eat. Okapis eat buds, leaves, and branches as well as clay high in sulfur (to supplement their mineral intake).

BEHAVIOR AND REPRODUCTION

Giraffes are social whereas okapis keep to themselves. The home ranges of giraffes are large, while those of the okapi are small. The males of both species will fight other males to establish dominance, usually using their horns by swinging their long necks and butting into each other.

Giraffes are polygynous (puh-LIH-juh-nus; one male to several female mates), as okapi are believed to be. Pregnancy lasts fifteen months for the giraffe and results in the birth of a single calf. Calves nurse (drink mother's milk) for a year and supplement their diet with browse beginning at the age of one month. Females stay with the herd while males leave around the age of three years. Life expectancy is twenty to twenty-five years.

After fourteen to fifteen months of pregnancy, a single okapi calf is born deep in the forest, where it will remain hidden for weeks. It will spend up to 80 percent of its first two months in hiding. Calves nurse until the age of six months and live over thirty years in captivity.

GIRAFFES, OKAPIS, AND PEOPLE

Giraffes are poached (illegally hunted) for their hair, which is made into thread, bracelets, fly whisks, as well as for their meat and hide. Okapi breed successfully in zoos, though we know very little about their behavior in the wild.

CONSERVATION STATUS

Neither species is threatened.

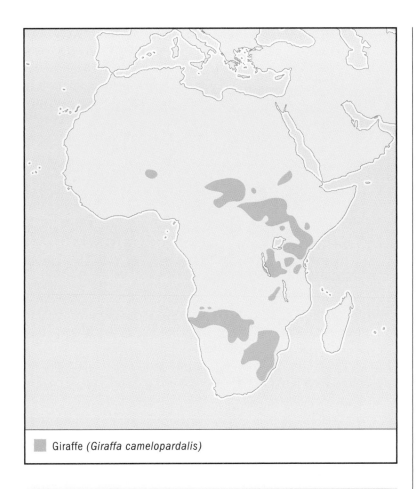

Giraffe (*Giraffa camelopardalis*)

GIRAFFE
Giraffa camelopardalis

Physical characteristics: These animals stand up to 18 feet (5.5 meters) tall and weigh between 1,200 and 4,350 pounds (550 to 1,930 kilograms). Coat patterning helps to camouflage them, and no two coats are alike.

Geographic range: Giraffes live in sub-Saharan Africa.

Habitat: Giraffes are found in dry savannas.

Diet: Giraffes feed on leaves of more than 100 tree and shrub species. They use their tongues and thin lips to select only the most

nutrient-dense leaves. Male giraffes can eat up to 145 pounds (66 kilograms) of food a day, but can also survive on as little as 15 pounds (7 kilograms) a day when food is scarce. They have four stomach chambers, which allows them to digest food more efficiently by swallowing food whole, regurgitating (vomiting), chewing, and swallowing again. They will drink water if available, but this makes them vulnerable to predators, so they often drink with a friend keeping watch.

Behavior and reproduction: Giraffes live in herds of up to twenty animals. Herds can be all-female, all-male, mixed, or female with young. Home ranges vary from 2 to 252 square miles (5 to 654 square kilometers), depending on food and water availability. Male giraffes spend 43 percent of their time each day feeding, and 22 percent walking. Females feed for more than half the day, and walk for 13 percent of the time. Giraffes rest at night. Though usually silent, giraffes will vocalize when looking for lost calves or when in danger.

Females are ready to breed at four years, and do so year-round. They give birth standing up, sometimes while walking, so the baby falls about 6 feet (2 meters) to the ground. Newborns are 6 feet (2 meters) tall and weigh between 110 and 120 pounds (50 to 55 kilograms). Babies are born with horns. Predators include hyenas, lions, leopards, and wild dogs. Giraffes use their height to detect predators while they're still in the distance.

Giraffes and people: Giraffes are hunted and poached for meat, skin, and hair. They are a main attraction in zoos.

Conservation status: The giraffe is not currently threatened, but has disappeared from its former range in western Africa. ■

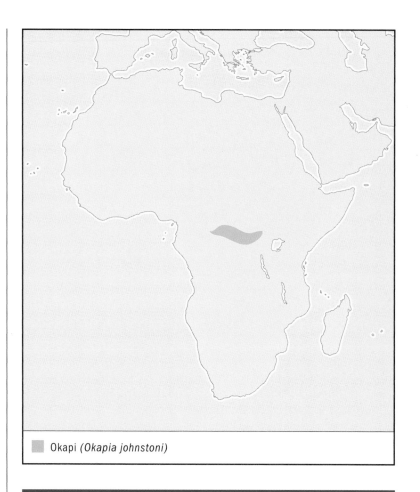

Okapi (*Okapia johnstoni*)

OKAPI
Okapia johnstoni

Physical characteristics: Okapis weigh 462 to 550 pounds (210 to 250 kilograms) and stand 5 to 5.6 feet (150 to 170 centimeters) at the shoulder. Females are taller than males.

Geographic range: Okapis are restricted to the Democratic Republic of the Congo.

Habitat: The okapi lives in tropical lowland forest near water.

Diet: Okapis feed on more than 100 species of plants, including some that are poisonous to humans. They also eat ferns, fungi, fruit,

Okapis feed on more than 100 species of plants, including some that are poisonous to humans. (© William Munoz/ Photo Researchers, Inc. Reproduced by permission.)

and grasses. Okapis ingest charcoal from trees burned by lightning. They use well-worn paths to travel between feeding sites.

Behavior and reproduction: Most active during the day. Not territorial, but males will fight for dominance. Okapis are usually silent but will make coughing sounds during rutting (mating) season. Okapi young are more vocal and make coughing and bleating sounds like a lamb. They groom one another and exhibit playful behavior.

Okapis give birth to a single calf from August to October after about fifteen months of pregnancy. Females retreat into the dense forest growth to give birth. Protective mothers warn off trespassers by beating the ground with their front legs. Lifespan is thirty years in captivity. The main predator of the okapi is the leopard.

Okapis and people: Zoos keep and breed okapis today. When the species was initially discovered, zoos lost many okapis in transport because they were unable to survive the long boat and train rides.

Conservation status: Okapis are not currently threatened, but are protected in the Democratic Republic of the Congo because their distribution range is so limited. Populations are healthy. ■

FOR MORE INFORMATION

Books:

Leach, Michael, et al. *Giraffe: Habitats, Life Cycles, Food Chains, Threats.* Milwaukee: Raintree, 2002.

Lyndaker, Susan, et al. *Okapi: Mysterious Animal of Congo-Zaire.* Austin: University of Texas Press, 1999.

Sherr, Lynn. *Tall Blondes.* Kansas City, MO: Andrews McMeel Publishing, 1997.

Periodicals:

Meadows, Robin. "A Neck Up on the Competition." *Zoogoer* (July/August 1996). http://nationalzoo.si.edu/Publications/ZooGoer/1996/4/neckuponcompetition.cfm (accessed on June 4, 2004).

Web sites:

"Okapi." The Big Zoo. http://www.thebigzoo.com/Animals/Okapi.asp (accessed on June 4, 2004).

Palkovacs, E. "*Okapi johnstoni.*" Animal Diversity Web. http://animaldiversity.ummz.umich.edu/site/accounts/information/Okapia_johnstoni.html (accessed on June 4, 2004).

PRONGHORN

Antilocapridae

Class: Mammalia

Order: Artiodactyla

Family: Antilocapridae

One species: Pronghorn
(*Antilocapra americana*)

family

CHAPTER

phylum

class

subclass

order

monotypic order

suborder

▲ **family**

PHYSICAL CHARACTERISTICS

Pronghorn measure 52.1 to 58.8 inches (132.3 to 149.4 centimeters) long and have a shoulder height of 32.7 to 37 inches (83.1 to 94 centimeters). They weigh 87 to 129 pounds (40 to 59 kilograms). These long-legged runners have stocky bodies, and their coat is various shades of brown on top, with sides and underparts creamy white. Males have brownish black patches from below the ears and downward 3 to 4 inches (7.6 to 10.2 centimeters). Pronghorn have a short mane on the back of the neck, and their tails are short (4 inches, or 10.2 centimeters). The rump is covered by two patches of white hair. This animal is able to regulate the amount of insulation provided by its coat by erecting or flattening its hairs.

Both sexes have horns covered in keratin (KARE-ah-tin; protective material that makes up hair and fingernails). There are two branches, or prongs, one curving forward and another, shorter one pointing directly back. Males shed their horns every year; females shed them irregularly. Pronghorn have superb vision. Researchers believe that the placement of their eyes high on top of their skulls allows for them to keep a watch for predators while continuing to feed on lower-elevated grounds.

GEOGRAPHIC RANGE

Found in western North America.

HABITAT

Pronghorn can be found in abundant numbers in short-grass prairies where shrubs are readily available even with snow cover.

Pronghorn   963

PRONGHORN IN COLORADO

According to NationalGeographic.com, one of the earliest mentions of the pronghorn is in the expedition diaries of explorers Meriwether Lewis and William Clark. As often happens today, they compared the pronghorn to goats, antelopes, and gazelles.

The pronghorn population has taken a rollercoaster ride in terms of numbers. From an estimated thirty to sixty million in the early 1800s, they declined to less than 15,000 by 1915. As of 2004, there are an estimated one million on the plains of North America.

According to Colorado Division of Wildlife biologist Mark Vieira, the number of pronghorn in that state fell to around 2,000 at the end of the twentieth century but has grown to a steady 55,000 as of 2004. He explained to *Rocky Mountain News* reporter Gary Gerhardt that pronghorn thrive in this region because they don't compete with cattle. The two animals eat different plants, so all have enough to eat.

Winter months have proven particularly harsh for the Colorado pronghorn population on the Pawnee National Grasslands, however. During the winter, the animals create herds of about 100 individuals. Because Colorado has suffered serious drought in the twenty-first century, there isn't enough food to go around. Vieira reported, "Our usual fawn production was fifty to sixty fawns per one hundred does. Now it's fallen to eighteen per one hundred." In addition to starvation, the lack of vegetation is prohibiting pronghorn from manufacturing antibodies necessary for warding off disease.

"We are really desperate for moisture now. If we could get two good years, we could bring the population back," Viera said. Most pronghorn live in Montana and Wyoming.

Steppes (vegetation zones characterized by shrubs, grasses, and few trees) are also popular habitats, and deserts are home to less than 1 percent of the population.

Pronghorn are usually found on treeless, flat terrain between altitudes of 3,000 to 8,000 feet (914 to 2,438 meters).

DIET

Pronghorn prefer succulent (water-based) forbs (drought-resistant herbs with broader leaves than grasses) over other food. During droughts and snowy months, pronghorn rely on shrubs to supplement their diet. They walk while they eat and seem to find food using smell as well as sight. They use their muscled

Pronghorn (*Antilocapra americana*)

lips to grab hold of plants and vegetation, bring it to their mouths, then rip the plant apart with their teeth. Pronghorn will drink water if available, but pronghorn get most of their water from succulents, plants that contain a lot of water.

BEHAVIOR AND REPRODUCTION

Pronghorn are among the fastest land animals, able to reach speeds of 53.7 miles per hour (86.5 kilometers per hour) and maintain that pace for several miles (kilometers) before exhaustion sets in. They run with their mouths open to increase oxygen intake. Pronghorn are also strong swimmers.

Pronghorn are vocal animals, and make snorting and "sneezing" sounds when sensing something unfamiliar in their habitat. Fawns make soft bleating sounds (similar to lambs) that help parents locate hidden offspring. Adult females grunt or click when approaching hidden fawns or when being pursued by bucks. Bucks roar when chasing does or other bucks. During courtship, bucks smack their lips and flick their tongues, both of which create a low sucking sound.

Pronghorn males may fight during the breeding season. (© Stephen J. Krasemann/Photo Researchers, Inc. Reproduced by permission.)

Pronghorn live in herds, sometimes loosely scattered, but always highly organized. When threatened, they'll raise their white rump hairs and snort, alerting other herd members to gather together more closely. They are active during daylight and nighttime, with peak activity occurring just after sunrise and before sunset. They spend most of their time feeding or sleeping, the latter of which they do in short spurts and frequently throughout the day.

Home ranges vary greatly and are dependent on quality of habitat, group size, season, and history of land use. Winter and summer ranges may be as far apart as 100 miles (160 kilometers). Bucks will mark their territory with urine and feces.

Pronghorn are polygynous (puh-LIH-juh-nus; one male has several female mates), and mating occurs between July and early October. Pregnancy lasts eight and a half months; a single fawn is born in the spring if this is the doe's first birth. Successive births usually result in twins, rarely triplets. By day four, fawns are able to outrun humans. Fawns nurse (drink mother's milk) until around four weeks of age, at which time they join their mothers on feeding trips.

Pronghorn are sexually mature at sixteen to seventeen months. Primary predators, animals that hunt them for food, include coyotes, wolves, and bobcats. Lifespan is seven to ten years.

PRONGHORN AND PEOPLE

Pronghorn have a long history with Native Americans. Many Indian myths involved this animal, and it was considered the personification of peace, good fortune, and speed. Pronghorn often appeared on prehistoric pottery and walls.

Late in the nineteenth century, pronghorn were slaughtered for their skins. Canada and the United States opened hunting seasons in the mid-1900s, and by the end of 2002, almost five million pronghorn had been legally harvested. This hunting season provides tons of meat and millions of dollars in profit for businesses located in pronghorn country.

Pronghorn are known to damage crops, sometimes extensively.

CONSERVATION STATUS

Pronghorn are not threatened.

FOR MORE INFORMATION

Books:

Byers, John A. *Built for Speed: A Year in the Life of Pronghorn.* Cambridge, MA: Harvard University Press, 2003.

Frisch, Aaron. *Pronghorn Antelope.* North Mankato, MN: Smart Apple Media, 2002.

Nowak, Ronald M. "Pronghorn." *Walker's Mammals of the World Online 5.1.* Baltimore: Johns Hopkins University Press, 1997. http://www.press.jhu.edu/books/walkers_mammals_of_the_world/artiodactyla/artiodactyla.antilocapridae.antilocapra.html (accessed on July 8, 2004).

O'Gara, Bart, Jim D. Yoakum, and Richard E. McCabe. *Pronghorn: Ecology and Management.* Boulder, CO: University Press of Colorado, 2004.

Periodicals:

Gerhardt, Gary. "Unique Pronghorn are a Sight to Behold; Speedy Animals Often Overlooked in Wildlife." *Rocky Mountain News* (May 1, 2004).

Tabor, Thomas C. "The Pronghorn: Back from the Edge of Oblivion." *Countryside & Small Stock Journal* (May 1, 2004).

Web sites:

"The Pronghorn." Desert USA. http://www.desertusa.com/mag99/may/papr/pronghorn.html (accessed on July 8, 2004).

"Pronghorn." Great Plains Nature Center. http://www.gpnc.org/pronghor.htm (accessed on July 8, 2004).

Class: Mammalia

Order: Artiodactyla

Family: Bovidae

Number of species: 137 to 138 species

family

CHAPTER

phylum

class

subclass

order

monotypic order

suborder

▲ **family**

PHYSICAL CHARACTERISTICS

Bovids (BOH-vidz) vary in weight, from 6.6 to over 2,867 pounds (3 to over 1,300 kilograms), with a shoulder height range of 9.85 inches to 6.56 feet (25 centimeters to 2 meters). Bodies range from slender with long legs to stocky and muscular. All bovid males have horns, as do many females. Horns are bony and covered with keratin (KARE-ah-tin; protective material that makes up hair and fingernails). Bovids do not shed the keratin layer. They have hooves and four stomach chambers, which allows for efficient digestion.

Bovids have a number of scent glands on different parts of their bodies. They secrete oil from these glands during mating season, when in danger, or to mark territory.

Bovids range in color from white to black to orange-yellow. Most are some shade of brown.

GEOGRAPHIC RANGE

Found in Africa, Europe, Asia, and North America.

HABITAT

Bovids occupy a wide variety of habitats, including grasslands, swamps, tropical forests, arctic tundra, desert, cliff faces, and mountain ledges. Most abundant in tropical forests and grasslands. They occupy different habitats at different times of the year, with migration (seasonal movement from region to region) dependent upon food supply.

DIET

Bovids are herbivores (plant eaters) with four stomach chambers. The fact that they have four chambers means they can survive on plants few other animals could digest. They feed mainly on grasses, first by winding them around their tongues and pulling them from the ground, then swallowing them. After some time has passed, bovids will regurgitate (vomit) the swallowed food, chew it, and swallow it again. Bacteria in the stomach breaks down the food and allows digestion to occur.

BEHAVIOR AND REPRODUCTION

Some species are solitary (lone) while others live in herds or groups with complex social structures. Some species are territorial and will defend their ranges year-round or only during the mating season. Others live on ranges that are used each year. Many bovids are vocal, and calls range from lion-like roars to whistles and grunts.

Bovids are primarily polygynous (puh-LIH-juh-nus; one male to several female mates). Males often defend mating territories. Most females give birth to their first young around the age of two or three years. Males usually wait until they are a little older, primarily because they have to compete with other, older males to mate. Gestation (pregnancy) times vary according to species, but usually one, sometimes two, babies are born each year. Females care for their young without the help of the father. Adult males live separately, either alone or in small herds, from the females for most of the year.

Bovid offspring nurse (drink mother's milk) for at least a month, sometimes until the age of two or three years. Predators include tigers, small cats, wolves, and leopards.

BOVIDAE AND PEOPLE

Bovids have been hunted extensively for meat, sport, and hides, some species to the point of serious threat to the population. Many species—goat, sheep, cattle, buffalo—have been domesticated (tamed) and are raised for their meat and skin.

CONSERVATION STATUS

As of 2004, 114 species are listed on the IUCN Red List of Threatened Species. Loss of habitat is the main reason for threat. Increasing human populations require more land and natural resources. Hunting has affected bovid populations as well, but to a lesser degree.

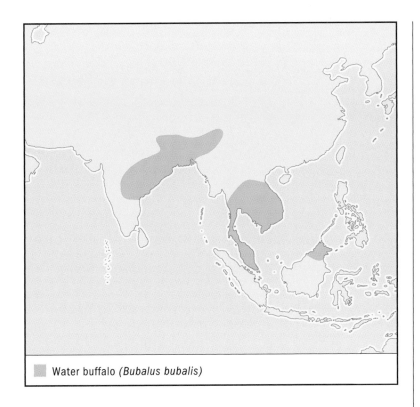

Water buffalo *(Bubalus bubalis)*

WATER BUFFALO
Bubalus bubalis

Physical characteristics: Water buffalo measure 98.4 to 118.1 inches (250 to 300 centimeters) long and stand 59 to 74.4 inches (150 to 189 centimeters) at the shoulder. They weigh between 1,543 and 2,645 pounds (700 to 1,200 kilograms), with females weighing about 20 percent less than males. They are the largest bovids, with disproportionately big feet and wide hooves. Fur is dark gray to black in wild species. Tail ends in a bushy ball of black hair. Males have crescent-shaped pointed horns that measure around 47.2 inches (120 centimeters) long. Females also have horns.

Geographic range: Found in India, Nepal, and Bhutan. A small population lives in a wildlife reserve in Thailand.

Habitat: Water buffalo live in tropical and subtropical forests as well as grasslands. They live near water, from swamps to woodlands and

Water buffalo spend part of their day in the water to stay cool and keep insects off of them. (Erwin and Peggy Bauer/Bruce Coleman Inc. Reproduced by permission.)

plains. They not only drink the water, but spend much of the day partially submerged so that they remain cool and ward off insects.

Diet: This bovid eats grasses, herbs, aquatic plants, and other vegetation.

Behavior and reproduction: Water buffalo form herds of females and offspring of up to thirty individuals. Old males are solitary. After a 300- to 340-day pregnancy, females give birth to one calf, sometimes to twins. Calves nurse for six to nine months. Female calves sometimes remain with the mother for life. Males leave around the age of three years. Females are ready to mate around eighteen months of age. This bovid will interbreed with domesticated cattle.

Water buffalo and people: Water buffalo were first domesticated in China more than seven thousand years ago. They provide meat, hides, horns, milk, and butter fat. For native cultures, they also provide an inexpensive method of power for plowing fields and transporting people.

Conservation status: Listed as Endangered, facing a very high risk of extinction, by the IUCN. Domesticated populations are abundant, but there are fewer than four thousand wild water buffalo in the world. Existing populations are small and separated by a great distance from each other, which limits reproduction. ■

American bison (*Bison bison*)

AMERICAN BISON
Bison bison

Physical characteristics: Females are 20 percent shorter in length and 40 percent less in weight than males. Males measure 85.2 to 125.2 inches (242 to 318 centimeters) long and stand 65.7 to 73.2 inches (167 to 186 centimeters) at the shoulder. They weigh between 1,199 to 1,999.5 pounds (544 to 907 kilograms). This is the largest mammal in North America. Though it appears to hold its head low, there is actually a hump over the shoulders. Legs are short and tail is medium length with a tuft of black hair on the end. Coat is brown to dark brown, and hair is longer on front and top of head, along the neck, shoulders, and forequarters. Ears are partially hidden. Both sexes have a beard of long hair as well as a mane of dark hair along the lower portion of the neck to the chest. Males have short black

horns that go out on the sides and curve upward. Females' horns are shorter, skinnier, and more curved.

Geographic range: Found in a select few parks and refuges of North America.

Habitat: This bovid needs plenty of grassland and meadow for grazing. It lives in mixed wood forests as well as prairies and plains.

Diet: The American bison is not picky about what it eats. They eat huge quantities of low-quality forage (grasses, herbs, and shrubs) and supplement their diet with berries and lichen (fungi found growing on trees). Uses head to remove snow from vegetation during winter.

Behavior and reproduction: Form mixed groups consisting of females, calves, and males aged one to three years. During mating season, adult males may join these herds. Males form groups of up to thirty animals, though they also are found alone or in pairs. During migration, herds join together and may travel more than 124 miles (200 kilometers) to find ranges where food is more plentiful. American bison like to wallow in shallow holes which they dig in the ground.

These polygynous bovids mate from July through September, with seasons varying depending on the region. Females go through 285 days of gestation and deliver a single calf in the spring, usually each year. They like to give birth in heavily concealed areas for privacy and protection, and they stay separated from the rest of the herd for a couple days. Within three hours of birth, the calf can run, and it is nursed for seven to twelve months.

American bison and people: Bison were important game animals for native populations across North Amerca. They provided meat, bones for tools, hides for blankets, leather for clothing, and sinews for twine. Today, bison is raised on ranches for its meat.

Conservation status: Bison are not considered threatened. They once ranged across half of North America and numbered in the millions. Because they are ranched throughout the continent, their population is not in danger of extinction, despite the fact that very few live in the wild. Disease and parasites are the main threats to the American bison. ■

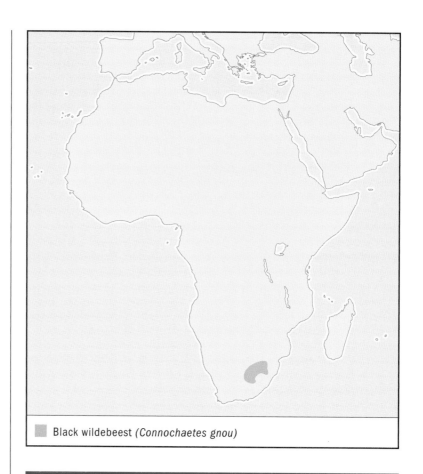

Black wildebeest (*Connochaetes gnou*)

BLACK WILDEBEEST
Connochaetes gnou

Physical characteristics: Also known as the gnu, this bovid weighs 242 to 396 pounds (110 to 180 kilograms) and measures 5.6 to 7.3 feet (170 to 220 centimeters) long. Shoulder height of 3 to 4 feet (90 to 120 centimeters). Females are slightly smaller than males. Coats are dark brown to black, with males darker than females. A short mane on neck stands up and is whitish with black tips. The beard is black.

Geographic range: The black wildebeest lives in east-central South Africa.

Habitat: This bovid lives primarily in open grassland where water is available.

Diet: Prefers short grasses but is known to browse on bushes and other vegetation to supplement the winter diet. Need to drink every one to two days.

Behavior and reproduction: Females and young form herds while males form their own groups. Males will defend territories during mating season by horn wrestling and loud vocalizations. Some are migratory.

Males "perfume" themselves for courtship by rolling in their urine and dung. They further draw attention to themselves by bellowing out a "ge-nu" call, foaming at the mouth, and dashing madly around while shaking their heads.

Mates from February through April, and after a gestation period of 240 to 270 days, females give birth to a single calf. Young walk within ten minutes of birth and are nursed for about four months. Females are ready to breed between eighteen and thirty months, males at three years. Lifespan in captivity is around twenty years. Lion and hyenas will take down lame or sick adults, and babies fall prey to wild dogs, leopards, and cheetahs.

Black wildebeest and people: Settlers viewed this bovid as a pest and did their best to kill them all. They used their tails as fly swatters.

Conservation status: Extinct in the wild, but captive black wildebeest populations are abundant, so they are not considered threatened. ■

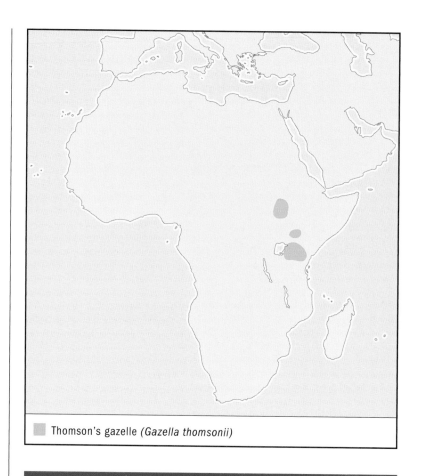

▪ Thomson's gazelle (*Gazella thomsonii*)

THOMSON'S GAZELLE
Gazella thomsonii

Physical characteristics: Weighs 29 to 66 pounds (13 to 30 kilograms) and measures 3 to 4 feet (91 to 122 centimeters) with a tail length of 6 to 8 inches (15 to 20 centimeters). Females are slightly smaller than males. Coat is reddish brown on top with a white belly. A black stripe runs from the foreleg to the hindquarters, and there is a white patch on the rump that extends to the black tail. Eyes rimmed with white that reaches to the nose along the muzzle and above the black cheek stripes. Males' horns are slightly curved and measure 11.5 to 12.0 inches (29.2 to 30.5 centimeters) and are used solely for fighting other male gazelles. Female horns are shorter and thinner and are used to defend their feeding area.

Geographic range: Found in Kenya, Ehtiopia, northern Tanzania, and southeast Sudan.

Habitat: Prefer the short grassy plains and savannas (tropical plant community characterized by shrubs and trees amidst cover of grasses and herbs) so that large herds can feed together. During the drier season, they move to the taller grasslands.

Diet: Grasses make up about 90 percent of this bovid's diet during the dry season, but it also feeds on shrubs and seeds, alfalfa, hay, and leaves.

Behavior and reproduction: This gazelle is most active early and late in the day. It rests during the hottest part of the day. Rather than fight, Thomson's gazelles will flee from predators, reaching speeds of 40 to 50 miles per hour (65 to 80 kilometers per hour). They are fantastic leapers, able to reach 30 feet (9 meters) in a single bound and up to 10 feet (3 meters) vertically. Their speed comes from long foot bones and anklebones.

They live in herds of two to twenty individuals, and members can change by the hour. Multiple herds interact with each other. Territories range from 6 to 495 acres (2 to 200 hectares) but are usually between 25 and 75 acres (10 and 30 hectares). Because they are water-dependent, they sometimes travel up to 100 miles (160 kilometers) to find water during the dry season.

Males establish territories during breeding season and mark them with urine and dung piles as well as secretions from scent glands. The polygamous (puh-LIH-guh-mus; having more than one mate at a time) Thomson's gazelle breeds twice annually. Females give birth to one offspring after a gestation lasting five to six months. Mother and baby stay separated from the herd for a couple weeks. Offspring can run by four weeks, and they nurse for four months. Predators include cheetahs, leopards, lions, and hyenas. Young gazelles are also killed by pythons, eagles, baboons, and jackals. Life span in the wild is roughly ten years.

Thomson's gazelle and people: These gazelles are hunted for food and skins.

Conservation status: Although predation is high, populations are secure because they are fast breeders. Females are ready to breed again within two to four weeks after giving birth. Thomson's gazelle is not threatened.   ∎

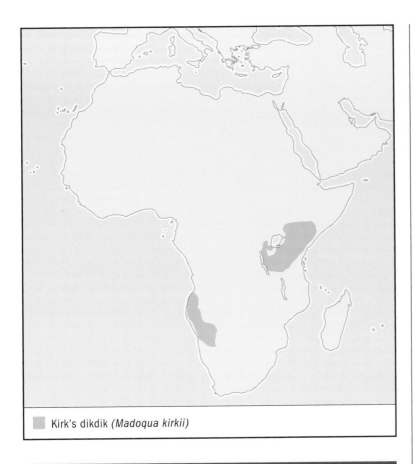

Kirk's dikdik (*Madoqua kirkii*)

KIRK'S DIKDIK
Madoqua kirkii

Physical characteristics: This small antelope measures 22.5 to 29.5 inches (57 to 75 centimeters) long and 14 to 18 inches (35 to 45 centimeters) high. It weighs just 6 to 14 pounds (2.7 to 6.5 kilograms). The fur on its back is gray with black and white flecks; face and legs are tan, and the chin, belly, and underside of the tail are white. The crest of fur on the head is yellow-orange, as are the face and legs. Ears are large, and big eyes are ringed with short white fur. Males have large glands beneath the eyes, and their sharp horns grow to be 4 inches (10 centimeters).

Geographic range: This dikdik is found in Tanzania, Kenya, Somalia, Angola, and Namibia.

Kirk's dikdik does not have to drink water—it receives enough moisture from dew and the vegetation that it eats. (Ann & Steve Toon Wildlife Photography. Reproduced by permission.)

Habitat: This dikdik lives in dry, hot regions of mixed woodland. Uses thickets and thorny bushes for cover.

Diet: Kirk's dikdik browses on herbs, leaves, evergreen shoots, fruits and berries, and flowers during the day and night. It rises on hind legs to reach food if necessary, and gets minerals by eating soil and bones and by visiting saltlicks. It does not need regular water intake.

Behavior and reproduction: This dikdik lives in pairs and defends their territory by chasing same-sex intruders. Territory is marked with urine, dung, and secretions from scent glands. Males defend territory boundaries by butting bordering vegetation and raising the hair on their heads. It makes six different vocalizations.

Pairs are monogamous (muh-NAH-guh-mus; mate only with each other) for life. After a gestation period of 166 to 174 days, females birth one young. Offspring are able to join parents after six weeks of hiding in vegetation, and they nurse until eight or ten weeks of age. Dikdiks are ready to mate between six and eight months, and females are ready to breed again within ten days of delivering their babies. Predators include eagles, pythons, lizards, lions, cheetahs, wild dogs, and hyenas. Life span in the wild is three to four years.

Kirk's dikdik and people: Common source of meat throughout its range.

Conservation status: Kirk's dikdik is not considered threatened. Total population is estimated to be from the hundreds of thousands to two million. ■

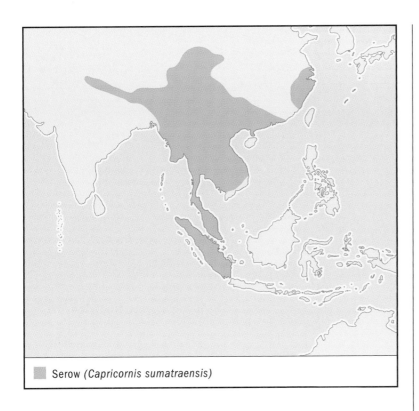

Serow (*Capricornis sumatraensis*)

SEROW
Capricornis sumatraensis

Physical characteristics: The serow weighs 110 to 300 pounds (50 to 140 kilograms) and measures 55 to 70 inches (140 to 180 centimeters) long. Stands 33 to 37 inches (85 to 94 centimeters) tall. Grayish black upperparts with whitish underparts. Horns are slim and curved back.

Geographic range: Serows are found in the Himalayas of India, Nepal, and Bhutan; western China; Southeast Asia, and Indonesia.

Habitat: Serows live in mountain forests between 6,000 and 10,000 feet (1,830 to 3,040 meters) altitude.

Diet: Eats a variety of grasses, shoots, and leaves. Does not migrate or move far in its feeding.

Behavior and reproduction: This goat-like bovid lives alone or in

Serows live in high mountain forests, between 6,000 and 10,000 feet (1,830 to 3,040 meters) altitude. (Illustration by Emily Damstra. Reproduced by permission.)

groups of up to seven individuals. They rest below rock overhangs and cliffs during the day, and have been known to swim between islands off the coast of Malaysia. Moves along well-trodden paths.

Gestation lasts for seven to eight months, with a single baby being born in September or October. Life span is about ten years.

Serow and people: Hunted for meat and body parts used in medicine.

Conservation status: Listed as Vulnerable, facing a high risk of extinction, by IUCN, primarily due to poaching (illegal hunting) and habitat loss. ■

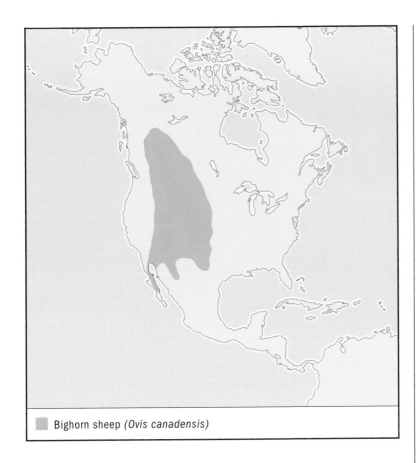

Bighorn sheep (*Ovis canadensis*)

BIGHORN SHEEP
Ovis canadensis

Physical characteristics: The maximum weight in males is 300 pounds (137 kilograms), 200 pounds (91 kilograms) in females. They measure 49 to 77 inches (124 to 195 centimeters) long, with females being smaller. Males have huge horns curling round and forward. Females' horns are much smaller and curl just a little. Coats range from reddish brown to almost black-brown with white undersides, rump, muzzle, and back of legs. They have excellent eyesight. Bighorns vocalize during mating season and when in danger.

Geographic range: Bighorn sheep are found in western North America south to desert ranges of the southwest United States and Mexico.

Bighorn sheep do not defend territories, but they will fight over a female. (Bob and Clara Calhoun/Bruce Coleman Inc. Reproduced by permission.)

Habitat: Bighorns live in deserts, but prefer mountain meadows, rocky cliffs, and mountains. They prefer regions where annual snowfall does not exceed 60 inches (152 centimeters) because they aren't able to paw through snow with their cloven (split) hooves.

Diet: Bighorns eat grasses, herbs, and shrubs. Those that live in the desert eat desert plants.

Behavior and reproduction: Bighorns live in small hers of two to nine, with mature males staying separate from the herd. They migrate to higher elevations in the summer and to sheltered valleys during the cold months.

Though males won't defend territories, they will fight each other over a female. Bighorns jump from ledge to ledge with ease and are able to climb mountains at a rate of 15 miles per hour (24.1 kilometers per hour). On level ground, they move at a rate of 30 miles per hour (48.3 kilometers per hour). They are capable swimmers.

These polygamous bovids mate in the fall. Gestation lasts 150 to 180 days and results in the birth of one or two lambs. Offspring are protected by their mothers for several months. Females are ready to mate at thirty months, males between seven and eight years. Life span in the wild averages ten years, but can reach twenty. Coyotes and mountain lions are primary predators.

Bighorn sheep and people: Prized for its majestic horns, the bighorn is hunted as a trophy as well as for meat.

Conservation status: Though population numbers are lower than they were in the nineteenth century, they are stable, and the species is not considered threatened. ■

FOR MORE INFORMATION

Books:

Geist, Val. *Buffalo Nation: History and Legend of the North American Bison.* Stillwater, MN: Voyageur Press, 2002.

Lott, Dale F. *American Bison: A Natural History.* Berkely, CA: University of California Press, 2003.

Nowak, Ronald M. "Antelopes, Cattle, Bison, bBuffalo, Goats, and Sheep." *Walker's Mammals of the World Online 5.1.* Baltimore: Johns Hopkins University Press, 1997. http://www.press.jhu.edu/books/walkers_mammals_of_the_world/artiodactyla/artiodactyla.bovidae.html (accessed on June 7, 2004).

Robbins, Ken. *Thunder on the Plains: The Story of the American Buffalo.* New York: Atheneum, 2001.

Periodicals:

Mills, James Edward. "Wisconsin Bison are Plentiful and Popular." *Wisconsin State Journal* (June 5, 2004).

Web sites:

"American Bison." NatureWorks. http://www.nhptv.org/natureworks/americanbison.htm (accessed on June 7, 2004).

"Bighorn Sheep." Desert USA. http://www.desertusa.com/big.html (accessed on June 7, 2004).

"Black Wildebeest." Singapore Zoological Gardens-Docent. (accessed on June 7, 2004).

Fox, D., and P. Myers "Bovidae." Animal Diversity Web. http://animaldiversity.ummz.umich.edu/site/accounts/information/Bovidae.html (accessed on June 7, 2004).

"Wildlives: African Animals: Dikdiks." African Wildlife Foundation. http://www.awf.org/wildlives/67 (accessed on June 7, 2004).

"Wildlives: African Animals: Thomson's Gazelle." African Wildlife Foundation. http://www.awf.org/wildlives/156 (accessed on June 7, 2004).

Species List by Biome

CONIFEROUS FOREST
American black bear
American pika
American water shrew
Asian elephant
Bobcat
Brown-throated three-toed
  sloth
Chimpanzee
Common bentwing bat
Coypu
Desert cottontail
Eastern mole
Edible dormouse
Ermine
Gambian rat
Geoffroy's spider monkey
Giant panda
Gray squirrel
Gray wolf
Greater sac-winged bat
Hairy-footed jerboa
Human
Indian crested porcupine
Kirk's dikdik
Lar gibbon
Little brown bat
Malayan moonrat
Mandrill
Moose

Mountain beaver
Mountain hare
Nine-banded armadillo
North American beaver
North American porcupine
Northern pika
Pacarana
Pallas's long-tongued bat
Pallid bat
Pileated gibbon
Puma
Red deer
Red panda
Red-shanked douc langur
Reindeer
Rhesus macaque
Serow
Siamang
Siberian musk deer
Snow leopard
Snowshoe hare
South African porcupine
Southern tree hyrax
Star-nosed mole
Striped skunk
Tasmanian devil
Three-striped night monkey
Tiger
Valley pocket gopher
Venezuelan red howler monkey

Virginia opossum
Weeper capuchin
Western barbastelle
White-tailed deer
White-throated capuchin

DECIDUOUS FOREST
Aardvark
African civet
American bison
American black bear
American least shrew
American pika
American water shrew
Ashy chinchilla rat
Asian elephant
Aye-aye
Bobcat
Bornean orangutan
Bridled nail-tailed wallaby
Brush-tailed phascogale
Brush-tailed rock wallaby
Capybara
Central American agouti
Chimpanzee
Collared peccary
Common bentwing bat
Common brush-tailed possum
Common genet

Common ringtail
Common tenrec
Common wombat
Cotton-top tamarin
Coypu
Crowned lemur
Degu
Desert cottontail
Eastern chipmunk
Eastern gray kangaroo
Eastern mole
Eastern pygmy possum
Edible dormouse
Ermine
Eurasian wild pig
European badger
Forest elephant
Forest hog
Funnel-eared bat
Gambian rat
Geoffroy's spider monkey
Giant panda
Goeldi's monkey
Gray squirrel
Gray wolf
Greater dog-faced bat
Greater glider
Greater horseshoe bat
Greater sac-winged bat
Ground pangolin
Human
Indian crested porcupine
Indian muntjac
Indian rhinoceros
Koala
Lar gibbon
Lesser Malay mouse deer
Lesser New Zealand short-
  tailed bat
Lion
Little brown bat
Lord Derby's anomalure
Lowland tapir
Malayan moonrat
Mara
Mountain beaver
Mountain hare

North American beaver
North American porcupine
Northern raccoon
Numbat
Paca
Pacarana
Pallas's long-tongued bat
Parnell's moustached bat
Pileated gibbon
Puma
Pygmy glider
Red deer
Red fox
Red kangaroo
Red panda
Red-tailed sportive lemur
Rhesus macaque
Ringtailed lemur
Rock cavy
Senegal bushbaby
Serow
Siamang
Silky anteater
South African porcupine
Southern flying squirrel
Spotted hyena
Star-nosed mole
Striped skunk
Sugar glider
Three-striped night monkey
Tiger
Valley pocket gopher
Venezuelan red howler
  monkey
Virginia opossum
Water buffalo
Weeper capuchin
Western barbastelle
Western European hedgehog
White rhinoceros
White-tailed deer
White-throated capuchin

DESERT

Australian jumping mouse
Bighorn sheep

Bobcat
Brazilian free-tailed bat
California leaf-nosed bat
Collared peccary
Damaraland mole-rat
Dassie rat
Desert cottontail
Dromedary camel
Egyptian slit-faced bat
Egyptian spiny mouse
Grant's desert golden mole
Gray wolf
Hairy-footed jerboa
Hardwicke's lesser mouse-
  tailed bat
Human
Kirk's dikdik
Lion
Mzab gundi
Naked mole-rat
North American porcupine
Pallid bat
Parnell's moustached bat
Pink fairy armadillo
Pronghorn
Puma
Red fox
Rhesus macaque
San Joaquin pocket mouse
Savanna elephant
Short-beaked echidna
Southern marsupial mole
Spotted hyena
Striped skunk
Trident leaf-nosed bat
Valley pocket gopher
Virginia opossum
White-footed sportive lemur

GRASSLAND

Aardvark
Aardwolf
African civet
Alpaca
Alpine marmot
American bison

American black bear
American least shrew
American pika
Ashy chinchilla rat
Asian elephant
Australian false vampire bat
Australian jumping mouse
Black wildebeest
Black-bellied hamster
Black-tailed prairie dog
Brazilian free-tailed bat
Bridled nail-tailed wallaby
California leaf-nosed bat
Capybara
Central American agouti
Chimpanzee
Common bentwing bat
Common genet
Common tenrec
Coypu
Degu
Dwarf epauletted fruit bat
Eastern barred bandicoot
Eastern chipmunk
Eastern gray kangaroo
Eastern mole
Egyptian rousette
Egyptian slit-faced bat
Egyptian spiny mouse
Ermine
Eurasian wild pig
Forest elephant
Gambian rat
Giant anteater
Giant kangaroo rat
Giraffe
Grant's desert golden mole
Gray wolf
Greater bilby
Greater dog-faced bat
Greater horseshoe bat
Grevy's zebra
Ground pangolin
Hardwicke's lesser mouse-tailed bat
Hispaniolan solenodon
Hispid cotton rat

Human
Indian crested porcupine
Indian muntjac
Indian rhinoceros
Kiang
Lesser New Zealand short-tailed bat
Lion
Llama
Long-tailed chinchilla
Lowland tapir
Maned wolf
Mara
Naked bat
Nine-banded armadillo
Northern pika
Numbat
Paca
Pallas's long-tongued bat
Pallid bat
Parnell's moustached bat
Pearson's tuco-tuco
Pink fairy armadillo
Pronghorn
Przewalski's horse
Puma
Red deer
Red fox
Red kangaroo
Rock cavy
Rock hyrax
San Joaquin pocket mouse
Savanna elephant
Senegal bushbaby
Short-beaked echidna
Smoky bat
Snow leopard
South African porcupine
Spix's disk-winged bat
Springhare
Star-nosed mole
Striped skunk
Tasmanian wolf
Thomson's gazelle
Tiger
Valley pocket gopher

Vampire bat
Virginia opossum
Water buffalo
Western European hedgehog
Western red colobus
White rhinoceros
Yellow-streaked tenrec

LAKE AND POND
American water shrew
Babirusa
Capybara
Central American agouti
Common hippopotamus
Coypu
Duck-billed platypus
European otter
Greater bulldog bat
Malayan tapir
Muskrat
North American beaver
North American porcupine
Prehensile-tailed porcupine
Tiger

OCEAN
Antarctic fur seal
Beluga
Blue whale
Burmeister's porpoise
California sea lion
Common bottlenosed dolphin
Dugong
Franciscana dolphin
Galápagos sea lion
Gray whale
Harbor porpoise
Harp seal
Hawaiian monk seal
Humpback whale
Killer whale
Narwhal
North Atlantic right whale
Northern bottlenosed whale
Northern elephant seal
Northern minke whale

Pygmy right whale
Pygmy sperm whale
Shepherd's beaked whale
Sperm whale
Spinner dolphin
Steller's sea cow
Walrus
West Indian manatee

RAINFOREST
Australian false vampire bat
Aye-aye
Babirusa
Bald uakari
Bennett's tree kangaroo
Bornean orangutan
Brazilian free-tailed bat
Brown-throated three-toed
  sloth
Brush-tailed rock wallaby
Central American agouti
Checkered sengi
Chevrotains
Chimpanzee
Collared peccary
Colombian woolly monkey
Common brush-tailed possum
Common ringtail
Common squirrel monkey
Common tenrec
Common tree shrew
Cotton-top tamarin
Coypu
Crowned lemur
Cuban hutia
Eastern pygmy possum
Eurasian wild pig
Forest elephant
Fossa
Funnel-eared bat
Geoffroy's spider monkey
Giant anteater
Goeldi's monkey
Greater sac-winged bat
Ground cuscus
Hispaniolan solenodon

Hoffman's two-toed sloth
Human
Indian crested porcupine
Indian flying fox
Indian muntjac
Indri
Kitti's hog-nosed bat
Lar gibbon
Lesser New Zealand short-
  tailed bat
Lord Derby's anomalure
Lowland tapir
Malayan colugo
Malayan tapir
Mandrill
Masked titi
Milne-Edwards's sifaka
Monito del monte
Mountain beaver
Musky rat-kangaroo
Naked bat
North American beaver
Northern bettong
Northern greater bushbaby
Okapi
Old World sucker-footed bat
Paca
Pacarana
Philippine tarsier
Pileated gibbon
Potto
Prehensile-tailed porcupine
Proboscis monkey
Pygmy hippopotamus
Pygmy marmoset
Pygmy slow loris
Queensland tube-nosed bat
Red mouse lemur
Red-shanked douc langur
Rhesus macaque
Ring-tailed mongoose
Rock hyrax
Rufous spiny bandicoot
Short-beaked echidna
Siamang
Siberian musk deer
Silky anteater

Silky shrew opossum
Smoky bat
Southern pudu
Spiny rat
Spix's disk-winged bat
Sugar glider
Sumatran rhinoceros
Three-striped night monkey
Valley pocket gopher
Vampire bat
Venezuelan red howler
  monkey
Virginia opossum
Water opossum
Weeper capuchin
Western gorilla
Western red colobus
Western tarsier
White bat
White-faced saki
White-tailed deer
White-throated capuchin
Yellow-streaked tenrec

RIVER AND STREAM
American water shrew
Aye-aye
Babirusa
Baiji
Black-bellied hamster
Boto
Capybara
Central American agouti
Common hippopotamus
Common squirrel monkey
Coypu
Duck-billed platypus
European otter
Ganges and Indus dolphin
Greater bulldog bat
Greater cane rat
Lowland tapir
Malayan tapir
Mountain beaver
Muskrat
North American beaver

North American porcupine
Northern raccoon
Old World sucker-footed bat
Paca
Prehensile-tailed porcupine
Pygmy hippopotamus
Smoky bat
Tiger
Virginia opossum
Water opossum
West Indian manatee
White-footed sportive lemur

SEASHORE
Antarctic fur seal
California sea lion
Cape horseshoe bat
European otter
Galápagos sea lion
Grant's desert golden mole
Greater bulldog bat
Harp seal
Hawaiian monk seal
Honey possum
Lesser New Zealand short-
tailed bat

Marianas fruit bat
Northern elephant seal
Pearson's tuco-tuco
Walrus

TUNDRA
American black bear
Ermine
Gray wolf
Hairy-footed jerboa
Human
Long-tailed chinchilla
Moose
Mountain hare
North American porcupine
Northern pika
Norway lemming
Polar bear
Red fox
Reindeer
Snowshoe hare
Striped skunk

WETLAND
American black bear

Bobcat
Bornean orangutan
Brazilian free-tailed bat
Capybara
Common squirrel monkey
Coypu
European otter
Giant anteater
Greater bulldog bat
Greater cane rat
Greater dog-faced bat
Indian flying fox
Malayan moonrat
Marianas fruit bat
North American beaver
Northern raccoon
Old World sucker-footed bat
Pacarana
Parnell's moustached bat
Proboscis monkey
Puma
Rhesus macaque
Spix's disk-winged bat
Star-nosed mole
Tiger
Valley pocket gopher

Species List by Geographic Range

AFGHANISTAN
Common bentwing bat
Dromedary camel
Eurasian wild pig
Gray wolf
Greater horseshoe bat
Hardwicke's lesser mouse-
    tailed bat
Red deer
Red fox
Rhesus macaque
Snow leopard
Trident leaf-nosed bat

ALBANIA
Blue whale
Common bentwing bat
Common bottlenosed dolphin
Edible dormouse
Eurasian wild pig
European badger
European otter
Gray wolf
Greater horseshoe bat
Humpback whale
Northern minke whale
Pygmy sperm whale
Red deer
Red fox
Sperm whale

ALGERIA
Blue whale
Common bentwing bat
Common bottlenosed dolphin
Common genet
Dromedary camel
Eurasian wild pig
European otter
Greater horseshoe bat
Humpback whale
Killer whale
Mzab gundi
Northern bottlenosed whale
Northern minke whale
Pygmy sperm whale
Red deer
Red fox
Sperm whale
Trident leaf-nosed bat

ANDORRA
European badger
Red fox

ANGOLA
Aardvark
African civet
Blue whale
Common bentwing bat

Common bottlenosed dolphin
Common genet
Dassie rat
Egyptian slit-faced bat
Gambian rat
Giraffe
Ground pangolin
Humpback whale
Kirk's dikdik
Lion
Northern minke whale
Pygmy sperm whale
South African porcupine
Sperm whale
Spinner dolphin
Spotted hyena
Springhare
Western gorilla
White rhinoceros

ANTARCTICA
Antarctic fur seal
Blue whale
Northern minke whale

ARGENTINA
Blue whale
Brazilian free-tailed bat
Brown-throated three-toed sloth

Burmeister's porpoise
Capybara
Central American agouti
Collared peccary
Common bottlenosed dolphin
Coypu
Franciscana dolphin
Giant anteater
Greater bulldog bat
Humpback whale
Killer whale
Llama
Lowland tapir
Maned wolf
Mara
Monito del monte
Northern minke whale
Pallas's long-tongued bat
Pearson's tuco-tuco
Pink fairy armadillo
Prehensile-tailed porcupine
Puma
Pygmy right whale
Red deer
Shepherd's beaked whale
Southern pudu
Sperm whale
Three-toed tree sloths
Vampire bat
Water opossum

ARMENIA
Common bentwing bat
Edible dormouse
Eurasian wild pig
European badger
Gray wolf
Red deer
Red fox

AUSTRALIA
Australian false vampire bat
Australian jumping mouse
Bennett's tree kangaroo
Blue whale
Bridled nail-tailed wallaby

Brush-tailed phascogale
Brush-tailed rock wallaby
Common bentwing bat
Common bottlenosed dolphin
Common brush-tailed possum
Common ringtail
Common wombat
Duck-billed platypus
Dugong
Eastern barred bandicoot
Eastern gray kangaroo
Eastern pygmy possum
Greater bilby
Greater glider
Honey possum
Humpback whale
Killer whale
Koala
Musky rat-kangaroo
Northern bettong
Northern minke whale
Numbat
Pygmy glider
Pygmy right whale
Pygmy sperm whale
Queensland tube-nosed bat
Red fox
Red kangaroo
Rufous spiny bandicoot
Short-beaked echidna
Southern marsupial mole
Sperm whale
Spinner dolphin
Sugar glider
Tasmanian devil
Tasmanian wolf

AUSTRIA
Alpine marmot
Common bentwing bat
Edible dormouse
Ermine
Eurasian wild pig
European badger
Greater horseshoe bat
Mountain hare

Red deer
Red fox
Western European hedgehog

AZERBAIJAN
Common bentwing bat
Edible dormouse
Eurasian wild pig
European badger
Gray wolf
Red deer
Red fox

BANGLADESH
Asian elephant
Blue whale
Common bentwing bat
Common bottlenosed dolphin
Eurasian wild pig
Ganges and Indus dolphin
Gray wolf
Greater horseshoe bat
Humpback whale
Indian crested porcupine
Indian flying fox
Indian muntjac
Indian rhinoceros
Northern minke whale
Pygmy sperm whale
Red fox
Rhesus macaque
Serow
Sperm whale
Spinner dolphin
Tiger

BELARUS
Black-bellied hamster
Edible dormouse
Ermine
Eurasian wild pig
European badger
Gray wolf
Moose
Mountain hare

Red deer
Red fox

BELGIUM
Black-bellied hamster
Blue whale
Common bottlenosed dolphin
Edible dormouse
Ermine
Eurasian wild pig
European badger
Greater horseshoe bat
Harbor porpoise
Humpback whale
Killer whale
North Atlantic right whale
Northern minke whale
Pygmy sperm whale
Sperm whale
Western European hedgehog

BELIZE
Blue whale
Brazilian free-tailed bat
Central American agouti
Collared peccary
Common bottlenosed dolphin
Funnel-eared bat
Geoffroy's spider monkey
Giant anteater
Greater bulldog bat
Greater dog-faced bat
Greater sac-winged bat
Hispid cotton rat
Humpback whale
Nine-banded armadillo
Northern minke whale
Paca
Pallas's long-tongued bat
Parnell's moustached bat
Pygmy sperm whale
Silky anteater
Sperm whale
Spinner dolphin
Spix's disk-winged bat
Vampire bat

Virginia opossum
Water opossum
White-tailed deer

BENIN
Aardvark
African civet
Blue whale
Common bottlenosed dolphin
Common genet
Gambian rat
Humpback whale
Lord Derby's anomalure
Northern minke whale
Pygmy sperm whale
Rock hyrax
Senegal bushbaby
South African porcupine
Sperm whale
Spinner dolphin

BHUTAN
Asian elephant
Common bentwing bat
Gray wolf
Greater horseshoe bat
Indian crested porcupine
Red fox
Red panda
Rhesus macaque
Serow
Snow leopard
Water buffalo

BOLIVIA
Alpaca
Ashy chinchilla rat
Boto
Brazilian free-tailed bat
Brown-throated three-toed
  sloth
Capybara
Central American agouti
Collared peccary
Coypu
Giant anteater
Goeldi's monkey

Greater bulldog bat
Greater dog-faced bat
Greater sac-winged bat
Hoffman's two-toed sloth
Llama
Lowland tapir
Maned wolf
Nine-banded armadillo
Pacarana
Pallas's long-tongued bat
Puma
Pygmy marmoset
Silky anteater
Spix's disk-winged bat
Three-toed tree sloths
Vampire bat
White-faced saki
White-tailed deer

BOSNIA AND HERZEGOVINA
Common bentwing bat
Edible dormouse
Eurasian wild pig
European badger
Greater horseshoe bat
Red deer
Red fox

BOTSWANA
Aardvark
Aardwolf
African civet
Common genet
Common hippopotamus
Damaraland mole-rat
Egyptian slit-faced bat
Giraffe
Ground pangolin
Lion
Savanna elephant
Springhare

BRAZIL
Bald uakari
Blue whale

Boto
Brazilian free-tailed bat
Brown-throated three-toed
  sloth
Burmeister's porpoise
Capybara
Central American agouti
Collared peccary
Common bottlenosed dolphin
Common squirrel monkey
Coypu
Franciscana dolphin
Funnel-eared bat
Giant anteater
Goeldi's monkey
Greater bulldog bat
Greater dog-faced bat
Greater sac-winged bat
Hoffman's two-toed sloth
Humpback whale
Killer whale
Lowland tapir
Maned wolf
Masked titi
Nine-banded armadillo
Northern minke whale
Paca
Pacarana
Pallas's long-tongued bat
Parnell's moustached bat
Prehensile-tailed porcupine
Pygmy marmoset
Pygmy right whale
Pygmy sperm whale
Red deer
Rock cavy
Silky anteater
Smoky bat
Sperm whale
Spinner dolphin
Spix's disk-winged bat
Three-striped night monkey
Three-toed tree sloths
Vampire bat
Venezuelan red howler
  monkey
Water opossum

Weeper capuchin
White-faced saki
White-tailed deer

BULGARIA
Common bentwing bat
Edible dormouse
Eurasian wild pig
European badger
Gray wolf
Greater horseshoe bat
Harbor porpoise
Red deer
Red fox

BURKINA FASO
Aardvark
African civet
Common genet
Egyptian slit-faced bat
Rock hyrax
Senegal bushbaby

BURUNDI
Aardvark
African civet
Common bentwing bat
Common genet
Egyptian slit-faced bat
Gambian rat
Lord Derby's anomalure
Senegal bushbaby
South African porcupine

CAMBODIA
Asian elephant
Blue whale
Common bentwing bat
Common bottlenosed dolphin
Dugong
Eurasian wild pig
Greater horseshoe bat
Humpback whale
Indian muntjac
Lesser Malay mouse deer

Malayan tapir
Northern minke whale
Pileated gibbon
Pygmy sperm whale
Serow
Sperm whale
Spinner dolphin

CAMEROON
Aardvark
African civet
Blue whale
Chimpanzee
Common bottlenosed dolphin
Common genet
Dwarf epauletted fruit bat
Egyptian rousette
Forest elephant
Forest hog
Gambian rat
Greater cane rat
Humpback whale
Lord Derby's anomalure
Mandrill
Northern minke whale
Potto
Pygmy sperm whale
Rock hyrax
Senegal bushbaby
South African porcupine
Sperm whale
Spinner dolphin
Western gorilla
Western red colobus

CANADA
American bison
American black bear
American least shrew
American pika
American water shrew
Beluga
Bighorn sheep
Black-tailed prairie dog
Bobcat
California sea lion

Eastern chipmunk
Eastern mole
Ermine
Gray squirrel
Gray wolf
Harbor porpoise
Harp seal
Killer whale
Little brown bat
Moose
Mountain beaver
Muskrat
Narwhal
North American beaver
North American porcupine
North Atlantic right whale
Northern bottlenosed whale
Northern raccoon
Pallid bat
Polar bear
Pronghorn
Puma
Red deer
Red fox
Reindeer
Snowshoe hare
Southern flying squirrel
Star-nosed mole
Striped skunk
Virginia opossum
Walrus
White-tailed deer

CENTRAL AFRICAN REPUBLIC

Aardvark
African civet
Chimpanzee
Common genet
Dwarf epauletted fruit bat
Egyptian rousette
Forest elephant
Gambian rat
Giraffe
Greater cane rat
Lord Derby's anomalure

Rock hyrax
Senegal bushbaby
South African porcupine
Western gorilla
White rhinoceros

CHAD

Aardvark
African civet
Common genet
Dromedary camel
Egyptian slit-faced bat
Gambian rat
Ground pangolin
Mzab gundi
Rock hyrax
Senegal bushbaby
Spotted hyena
Trident leaf-nosed bat
White rhinoceros

CHILE

Alpaca
Ashy chinchilla rat
Blue whale
Brazilian free-tailed bat
Burmeister's porpoise
Common bottlenosed dolphin
Coypu
Degu
Humpback whale
Killer whale
Llama
Long-tailed chinchilla
Monito del monte
Northern minke whale
Pallas's long-tongued bat
Pearson's tuco-tuco
Pygmy right whale
Pygmy sperm whale
Red deer
Shepherd's beaked whale
Southern pudu
Sperm whale
Vampire bat

CHINA

Asian elephant
Baiji
Blue whale
Common bentwing bat
Common bottlenosed dolphin
Dugong
Edible dormouse
Ermine
European badger
Giant panda
Gray wolf
Greater horseshoe bat
Hairy-footed jerboa
Humpback whale
Indian muntjac
Kiang
Killer whale
Lar gibbon
Lesser Malay mouse deer
Moose
Mountain hare
Northern minke whale
Northern pika
Pygmy slow loris
Pygmy sperm whale
Red deer
Red fox
Red panda
Reindeer
Rhesus macaque
Serow
Siberian musk deer
Snow leopard
Sperm whale
Spinner dolphin
Tiger

COLOMBIA

Bald uakari
Blue whale
Boto
Brazilian free-tailed bat
Brown-throated three-toed
  sloth
Capybara

Central American agouti
Collared peccary
Colombian woolly monkey
Common bottlenosed dolphin
Common squirrel monkey
Cotton-top tamarin
Funnel-eared bat
Giant anteater
Goeldi's monkey
Greater bulldog bat
Greater sac-winged bat
Hispid cotton rat
Hoffman's two-toed sloth
Humpback whale
Killer whale
Llama
Lowland tapir
Nine-banded armadillo
Northern minke whale
Paca
Pacarana
Pallas's long-tongued bat
Parnell's moustached bat
Prehensile-tailed porcupine
Pygmy marmoset
Pygmy sperm whale
Silky anteater
Silky shrew opossum
Smoky bat
Sperm whale
Spinner dolphin
Spiny rat
Spix's disk-winged bat
Three-striped night monkey
Three-toed tree sloths
Vampire bat
Water opossum
White-faced saki
White-tailed deer
White-throated capuchin

CONGO
African civet
Blue whale
Common bottlenosed dolphin
Common genet

Dwarf epauletted fruit bat
Egyptian rousette
Egyptian slit-faced bat
Forest elephant
Forest hog
Humpback whale
Lord Derby's anomalure
Northern minke whale
Potto
Pygmy sperm whale
South African porcupine
Sperm whale
Spinner dolphin
Springhare
Western gorilla

COSTA RICA
American least shrew
Blue whale
Brazilian free-tailed bat
Brown-throated three-toed
  sloth
Central American agouti
Collared peccary
Common bottlenosed dolphin
Funnel-eared bat
Geoffroy's spider monkey
Giant anteater
Greater bulldog bat
Greater dog-faced bat
Greater sac-winged bat
Hispid cotton rat
Hoffman's two-toed sloth
Humpback whale
Killer whale
Nine-banded armadillo
Northern minke whale
Paca
Pallas's long-tongued bat
Parnell's moustached bat
Puma
Pygmy sperm whale
Silky anteater
Smoky bat
Sperm whale
Spinner dolphin

Spiny rat
Spix's disk-winged bat
Three-toed tree sloths
Vampire bat
Virginia opossum
Water opossum
White bat
White-tailed deer
White-throated capuchin

CROATIA
Blue whale
Common bentwing bat
Common bottlenosed dolphin
Edible dormouse
Eurasian wild pig
European badger
Greater horseshoe bat
Humpback whale
Northern minke whale
Pygmy sperm whale
Red deer
Red fox
Sperm whale

CUBA
Blue whale
Brazilian free-tailed bat
Central American agouti
Collared peccary
Common bottlenosed dolphin
Cuban hutia
Funnel-eared bat
Greater bulldog bat
Humpback whale
Killer whale
Northern minke whale
Pallid bat
Parnell's moustached bat
Pygmy sperm whale
Sperm whale
Spinner dolphin

CYPRUS
Blue whale

Common bottlenosed dolphin
Humpback whale
Northern minke whale
Pygmy sperm whale
Sperm whale

CZECH REPUBLIC

Black-bellied hamster
Common bentwing bat
Edible dormouse
Ermine
European badger
Greater horseshoe bat
Red deer
Red fox

DEMOCRATIC REPUBLIC OF THE CONGO

Aardvark
African civet
Blue whale
Checkered sengi
Chimpanzee
Common bentwing bat
Common bottlenosed dolphin
Common genet
Common hippopotamus
Dwarf epauletted fruit bat
Egyptian rousette
Egyptian slit-faced bat
Forest elephant
Forest hog
Gambian rat
Giraffe
Humpback whale
Lord Derby's anomalure
Mandrill
Northern minke whale
Okapi
Potto
Pygmy sperm whale
Rock hyrax
South African porcupine
Sperm whale

Spinner dolphin
Western gorilla
Western red colobus
White rhinoceros

DENMARK

Blue whale
Common bottlenosed dolphin
Ermine
Eurasian wild pig
European badger
Harbor porpoise
Humpback whale
Killer whale
North Atlantic right whale
Northern minke whale
Norway lemming
Pygmy sperm whale
Red deer
Red fox
Sperm whale
Western European hedgehog

DJIBOUTI

Aardvark
Blue whale
Common bottlenosed dolphin
Common genet
Dromedary camel
Dugong
Humpback whale
Northern minke whale
Rock hyrax
Senegal bushbaby
Sperm whale
Spinner dolphin

DOMINICAN REPUBLIC

Blue whale
Brazilian free-tailed bat
Common bottlenosed dolphin
Funnel-eared bat
Greater bulldog bat
Hispaniolan solenodon

Humpback whale
Killer whale
Northern minke whale
Parnell's moustached bat
Pygmy sperm whale
Sperm whale
Spinner dolphin

ECUADOR

Blue whale
Boto
Brazilian free-tailed bat
Brown-throated three-toed sloth
Capybara
Central American agouti
Collared peccary
Common bottlenosed dolphin
Galápagos sea lion
Giant anteater
Goeldi's monkey
Greater bulldog bat
Greater dog-faced bat
Greater sac-winged bat
Hoffman's two-toed sloth
Humpback whale
Killer whale
Llama
Lowland tapir
Nine-banded armadillo
Northern minke whale
Pacarana
Pallas's long-tongued bat
Pygmy marmoset
Pygmy sperm whale
Silky anteater
Silky shrew opossum
Sperm whale
Spinner dolphin
Spiny rat
Spix's disk-winged bat
Three-toed tree sloths
Vampire bat
Water opossum
White-faced saki
White-tailed deer

EGYPT

Blue whale
Common bottlenosed dolphin
Common genet
Dromedary camel
Egyptian rousette
Egyptian slit-faced bat
Egyptian spiny mouse
Eurasian wild pig
Greater horseshoe bat
Hardwicke's lesser mouse-
  tailed bat
Humpback whale
Northern minke whale
Pygmy sperm whale
Red fox
Rock hyrax
Sperm whale
Trident leaf-nosed bat

EL SALVADOR

Blue whale
Brazilian free-tailed bat
Brown-throated three-toed
  sloth
Collared peccary
Common bottlenosed dolphin
Funnel-eared bat
Geoffroy's spider monkey
Giant anteater
Greater bulldog bat
Greater sac-winged bat
Hispid cotton rat
Humpback whale
Killer whale
Nine-banded armadillo
Northern minke whale
Paca
Pallas's long-tongued bat
Parnell's moustached bat
Pygmy sperm whale
Silky anteater
Sperm whale
Spinner dolphin
Spix's disk-winged bat
Three-toed tree sloths

Vampire bat
Virginia opossum
Water opossum
White-tailed deer

EQUATORIAL GUINEA

African civet
Blue whale
Common bottlenosed dolphin
Common genet
Forest elephant
Humpback whale
Lord Derby's anomalure
Mandrill
Northern minke whale
Potto
Pygmy sperm whale
South African porcupine
Sperm whale
Spinner dolphin
Western gorilla

ERITREA

Aardvark
Blue whale
Common bottlenosed dolphin
Common genet
Dromedary camel
Dugong
Egyptian slit-faced bat
Humpback whale
Northern minke whale
Rock hyrax
Sperm whale
Spinner dolphin

ESTONIA

Blue whale
Common bottlenosed dolphin
Ermine
Eurasian wild pig
European badger
Gray wolf
Harbor porpoise
Humpback whale

Moose
Mountain hare
Northern minke whale
Red deer
Red fox
Sperm whale

ETHIOPIA

Aardvark
Common genet
Dromedary camel
Egyptian slit-faced bat
Forest hog
Grevy's zebra
Lion
Naked mole-rat
Rock hyrax
Senegal bushbaby
Thomson's gazelle

FINLAND

Blue whale
Common bottlenosed dolphin
Ermine
Eurasian wild pig
European badger
European otter
Gray wolf
Humpback whale
Moose
Mountain hare
Northern minke whale
Norway lemming
Red fox
Reindeer
Sperm whale
Western European hedgehog

FRANCE

Alpine marmot
Blue whale
Common bentwing bat
Common bottlenosed dolphin
Common genet
Edible dormouse

Ermine
Eurasian wild pig
European badger
European otter
Greater horseshoe bat
Harbor porpoise
Humpback whale
Killer whale
North Atlantic right whale
Northern bottlenosed whale
Northern minke whale
Pygmy sperm whale
Red deer
Red fox
Sperm whale
Western European hedgehog

FRENCH GUIANA
Blue whale
Capybara
Collared peccary
Common bottlenosed dolphin
Common squirrel monkey
Funnel-eared bat
Giant anteater
Greater bulldog bat
Greater dog-faced bat
Greater sac-winged bat
Humpback whale
Lowland tapir
Nine-banded armadillo
Northern minke whale
Paca
Pallas's long-tongued bat
Parnell's moustached bat
Prehensile-tailed porcupine
Pygmy sperm whale
Silky anteater
Smoky bat
Sperm whale
Spinner dolphin
Spix's disk-winged bat
Three-toed tree sloths
Vampire bat
Water opossum
Weeper capuchin

White-faced saki
White-tailed deer

GABON
African civet
Blue whale
Common bottlenosed dolphin
Common genet
Common hippopotamus
Dwarf epauletted fruit bat
Egyptian rousette
Forest elephant
Forest hog
Humpback whale
Lord Derby's anomalure
Mandrill
Northern minke whale
Potto
Pygmy sperm whale
South African porcupine
Sperm whale
Spinner dolphin
Western gorilla

GAMBIA
Aardvark
African civet
Blue whale
Common bottlenosed dolphin
Common genet
Gambian rat
Greater cane rat
Humpback whale
Killer whale
Northern minke whale
Pygmy sperm whale
Senegal bushbaby
South African porcupine
Sperm whale
Spinner dolphin
Western red colobus

GEORGIA
Common bentwing bat
Edible dormouse

Eurasian wild pig
European badger
Gray wolf
Harbor porpoise
Red deer
Red fox

GERMANY
Alpine marmot
Black-bellied hamster
Blue whale
Common bentwing bat
Common bottlenosed dolphin
Edible dormouse
Ermine
Eurasian wild pig
European badger
Greater horseshoe bat
Harbor porpoise
Humpback whale
Killer whale
North Atlantic right whale
Northern minke whale
Northern raccoon
Pygmy sperm whale
Red deer
Red fox
Sperm whale
Western European hedgehog

GHANA
Aardvark
African civet
Blue whale
Chimpanzee
Common bottlenosed dolphin
Common genet
Dwarf epauletted fruit bat
Egyptian rousette
Forest elephant
Forest hog
Gambian rat
Humpback whale
Lord Derby's anomalure
Northern minke whale
Potto

Pygmy sperm whale
Rock hyrax
Senegal bushbaby
South African porcupine
Sperm whale
Spinner dolphin
Western red colobus

GREECE
Blue whale
Common bentwing bat
Common bottlenosed dolphin
Edible dormouse
European badger
European otter
Gray wolf
Greater horseshoe bat
Harbor porpoise
Humpback whale
Northern minke whale
Pygmy sperm whale
Red deer
Red fox
Sperm whale

GREENLAND
Blue whale
Ermine
Harbor porpoise
Harp seal
Humpback whale
Killer whale
North Atlantic right whale
Northern bottlenosed whale
Northern minke whale
Polar bear
Reindeer
Walrus

GRENADA
Nine-banded armadillo
Pallas's long-tongued bat

GUAM
Marianas fruit bat

GUATEMALA
American least shrew
Blue whale
Brazilian free-tailed bat
Central American agouti
Collared peccary
Common bottlenosed dolphin
Funnel-eared bat
Geoffroy's spider monkey
Giant anteater
Greater bulldog bat
Greater dog-faced bat
Greater sac-winged bat
Hispid cotton rat
Humpback whale
Killer whale
Nine-banded armadillo
Northern minke whale
Paca
Pallas's long-tongued bat
Parnell's moustached bat
Puma
Pygmy sperm whale
Silky anteater
Sperm whale
Spinner dolphin
Spix's disk-winged bat
Vampire bat
Virginia opossum
Water opossum
White-tailed deer

GUINEA
Aardvark
African civet
Blue whale
Chimpanzee
Common bottlenosed dolphin
Common genet
Egyptian slit-faced bat
Forest hog
Gambian rat
Humpback whale
Killer whale
Northern minke whale
Pygmy hippopotamus

Pygmy sperm whale
Rock hyrax
Senegal bushbaby
South African porcupine
Sperm whale
Spinner dolphin

GUINEA-BISSAU
Aardvark
African civet
Blue whale
Common bottlenosed dolphin
Common genet
Forest hog
Gambian rat
Humpback whale
Killer whale
Northern minke whale
Pygmy sperm whale
Rock hyrax
Senegal bushbaby
South African porcupine
Sperm whale
Spinner dolphin
Western red colobus

GUYANA
Blue whale
Boto
Capybara
Collared peccary
Common bottlenosed dolphin
Common squirrel monkey
Funnel-eared bat
Giant anteater
Greater bulldog bat
Greater dog-faced bat
Greater sac-winged bat
Humpback whale
Lowland tapir
Nine-banded armadillo
Northern minke whale
Paca
Pallas's long-tongued bat
Parnell's moustached bat
Prehensile-tailed porcupine

Pygmy sperm whale
Silky anteater
Smoky bat
Sperm whale
Spinner dolphin
Spix's disk-winged bat
Three-toed tree sloths
Vampire bat
Water opossum
Weeper capuchin
White-faced saki
White-tailed deer

HAITI
Blue whale
Brazilian free-tailed bat
Common bottlenosed dolphin
Funnel-eared bat
Greater bulldog bat
Hispaniolan solenodon
Humpback whale
Killer whale
Northern minke whale
Parnell's moustached bat
Pygmy sperm whale
Sperm whale
Spinner dolphin

HONDURAS
American least shrew
Blue whale
Brazilian free-tailed bat
Brown-throated three-toed
  sloth
Central American agouti
Collared peccary
Common bottlenosed dolphin
Funnel-eared bat
Geoffroy's spider monkey
Giant anteater
Greater bulldog bat
Greater dog-faced bat
Greater sac-winged bat
Hispid cotton rat
Hoffman's two-toed sloth
Humpback whale

Killer whale
Nine-banded armadillo
Northern minke whale
Paca
Pallas's long-tongued bat
Parnell's moustached bat
Pygmy sperm whale
Silky anteater
Sperm whale
Spinner dolphin
Spiny rat
Spix's disk-winged bat
Three-toed tree sloths
Vampire bat
Virginia opossum
Water opossum
White bat
White-tailed deer
White-throated capuchin

HUNGARY
Black-bellied hamster
Common bentwing bat
Edible dormouse
Ermine
Eurasian wild pig
European badger
Greater horseshoe bat
Red deer
Red fox

ICELAND
Blue whale
Harbor porpoise
Humpback whale
Killer whale
North Atlantic right whale
Northern bottlenosed whale
Northern minke whale
Norway lemming

INDIA
Asian elephant
Blue whale
Common bentwing bat

Common bottlenosed dolphin
Dromedary camel
Dugong
Ermine
Eurasian wild pig
Ganges and Indus dolphin
Gray wolf
Greater horseshoe bat
Hardwicke's lesser mouse-
  tailed bat
Humpback whale
Indian crested porcupine
Indian flying fox
Indian muntjac
Indian rhinoceros
Kiang
Killer whale
Lion
Northern minke whale
Pygmy sperm whale
Red fox
Red panda
Rhesus macaque
Serow
Snow leopard
Sperm whale
Spinner dolphin
Tiger
Water buffalo

INDONESIA
Asian elephant
Babirusa
Blue whale
Bornean orangutan
Common bentwing bat
Common bottlenosed dolphin
Common tree shrew
Dugong
Eurasian wild pig
European otter
Humpback whale
Indian muntjac
Killer whale
Lar gibbon
Lesser Malay mouse deer

Malayan colugo
Malayan moonrat
Malayan tapir
Naked bat
Northern minke whale
Proboscis monkey
Pygmy sperm whale
Serow
Siamang
Sperm whale
Spinner dolphin
Sumatran rhinoceros
Tiger
Western tarsier

IRAN
Blue whale
Common bentwing bat
Common bottlenosed dolphin
Dromedary camel
Dugong
Edible dormouse
Egyptian rousette
Egyptian spiny mouse
Eurasian wild pig
European badger
Gray wolf
Greater horseshoe bat
Hairy-footed jerboa
Humpback whale
Indian crested porcupine
Killer whale
Northern minke whale
Pygmy sperm whale
Red deer
Red fox
Sperm whale
Spinner dolphin
Trident leaf-nosed bat

IRAQ
Dromedary camel
Egyptian spiny mouse
Eurasian wild pig
Gray wolf
Greater horseshoe bat

Red fox
Trident leaf-nosed bat

IRELAND
Blue whale
Common bottlenosed dolphin
Ermine
Eurasian wild pig
European badger
European otter
Harbor porpoise
Humpback whale
Killer whale
Mountain hare
North Atlantic right whale
Northern bottlenosed whale
Northern minke whale
Red deer
Red fox
Sperm whale
Western European hedgehog

ISRAEL
Blue whale
Common bottlenosed dolphin
Dromedary camel
Egyptian rousette
Egyptian slit-faced bat
Egyptian spiny mouse
Eurasian wild pig
Gray wolf
Hardwicke's lesser mouse-
   tailed bat
Humpback whale
Indian crested porcupine
Northern minke whale
Pygmy sperm whale
Red fox
Rock hyrax
Sperm whale
Trident leaf-nosed bat

ITALY
Alpine marmot
Blue whale

Common bentwing bat
Common bottlenosed dolphin
Edible dormouse
Ermine
Eurasian wild pig
European badger
Gray wolf
Greater horseshoe bat
Humpback whale
Killer whale
Mountain hare
Northern minke whale
Pygmy sperm whale
Red deer
Red fox
Sperm whale
Western European hedgehog

IVORY COAST
Aardvark
African civet
Blue whale
Chimpanzee
Common bottlenosed dolphin
Common genet
Dwarf epauletted fruit bat
Egyptian rousette
Forest elephant
Forest hog
Gambian rat
Humpback whale
Lord Derby's anomalure
Northern minke whale
Pygmy hippopotamus
Pygmy sperm whale
Rock hyrax
Senegal bushbaby
South African porcupine
Sperm whale
Spinner dolphin
Western red colobus

JAMAICA
Blue whale
Brazilian free-tailed bat
Common bottlenosed dolphin

Funnel-eared bat
Greater bulldog bat
Humpback whale
Killer whale
Northern minke whale
Pallas's long-tongued bat
Parnell's moustached bat
Pygmy sperm whale
Sperm whale
Spinner dolphin

JAPAN
Blue whale
Common bentwing bat
Common bottlenosed dolphin
Dugong
Ermine
Eurasian wild pig
European badger
European otter
Gray whale
Greater horseshoe bat
Harbor porpoise
Humpback whale
Killer whale
Marianas fruit bat
Mountain hare
Northern minke whale
Northern pika
Pygmy sperm whale
Reindeer
Siberian musk deer
Sperm whale
Spinner dolphin

JORDAN
Dromedary camel
Egyptian slit-faced bat
Egyptian spiny mouse
Eurasian wild pig
Gray wolf
Hardwicke's lesser mouse-
  tailed bat
Red fox
Rock hyrax
Trident leaf-nosed bat

KAZAKHSTAN
Black-bellied hamster
Common bentwing bat
Edible dormouse
Ermine
Eurasian wild pig
European badger
Gray wolf
Hairy-footed jerboa
Moose
Mountain hare
Red deer
Red fox
Snow leopard

KENYA
Aardvark
Aardwolf
African civet
Blue whale
Common bentwing bat
Common bottlenosed dolphin
Common genet
Dugong
Egyptian rousette
Egyptian slit-faced bat
Forest hog
Gambian rat
Giraffe
Greater cane rat
Grevy's zebra
Ground pangolin
Humpback whale
Kirk's dikdik
Lion
Lord Derby's anomalure
Naked mole-rat
Northern greater bushbaby
Northern minke whale
Potto
Pygmy sperm whale
Rock hyrax
Senegal bushbaby
South African porcupine
Sperm whale
Spinner dolphin

Springhare
Thomson's gazelle

KUWAIT
Egyptian spiny mouse
Gray wolf
Trident leaf-nosed bat

KYRGYZSTAN
Common bentwing bat
Edible dormouse
Ermine
Eurasian wild pig
European badger
Gray wolf
Red deer
Red fox
Snow leopard

LAOS
Asian elephant
Common bentwing bat
Eurasian wild pig
Greater horseshoe bat
Indian muntjac
Lesser Malay mouse deer
Malayan tapir
Pileated gibbon
Pygmy slow loris
Red fox
Red-shanked douc langur
Rhesus macaque
Serow

LATVIA
Blue whale
Common bottlenosed dolphin
Ermine
Eurasian wild pig
European badger
Gray wolf
Harbor porpoise
Humpback whale
Moose
Mountain hare

Northern minke whale
Red deer
Red fox
Sperm whale

LEBANON
Blue whale
Common bottlenosed dolphin
Dromedary camel
Egyptian spiny mouse
Hardwicke's lesser mouse-
  tailed bat
Humpback whale
Northern minke whale
Pygmy sperm whale
Sperm whale
Trident leaf-nosed bat

LESOTHO
Aardvark
African civet
Common bentwing bat
Common genet
Egyptian slit-faced bat
South African porcupine

LESSER ANTILLES
Blue whale
Brazilian free-tailed bat
Common bottlenosed dolphin
Funnel-eared bat
Greater bulldog bat
Humpback whale
Killer whale
Northern minke whale
Pygmy sperm whale
Sperm whale
Spinner dolphin

LIBERIA
Aardvark
African civet
Blue whale
Common bottlenosed dolphin

Common genet
Forest elephant
Forest hog
Humpback whale
Killer whale
Lord Derby's anomalure
Northern minke whale
Pygmy hippopotamus
Pygmy sperm whale
Rock hyrax
South African porcupine
Sperm whale
Spinner dolphin
Western red colobus

LIBYA
Blue whale
Common bottlenosed dolphin
Dromedary camel
Egyptian spiny mouse
Eurasian wild pig
Greater horseshoe bat
Humpback whale
Mzab gundi
Northern minke whale
Pygmy sperm whale
Red fox
Sperm whale
Trident leaf-nosed bat

LIECHTENSTEIN
Ermine
Eurasian wild pig
Greater horseshoe bat
Red deer
Red fox

LITHUANIA
Blue whale
Common bottlenosed dolphin
Edible dormouse
Ermine
Eurasian wild pig
European badger
Harbor porpoise

Humpback whale
Moose
Mountain hare
Northern minke whale
Red deer
Red fox
Sperm whale

LUXEMBOURG
Edible dormouse
Ermine
Eurasian wild pig
European badger
Greater horseshoe bat
Red deer
Red fox

MACEDONIA
Common bentwing bat
Edible dormouse
Eurasian wild pig
European badger
Gray wolf
Greater horseshoe bat
Red deer
Red fox

MADAGASCAR
Aye-aye
Blue whale
Common bentwing bat
Common bottlenosed dolphin
Common tenrec
Crowned lemur
Dugong
Fossa
Humpback whale
Indri
Killer whale
Milne-Edwards's sifaka
Northern minke whale
Old World sucker-footed bat
Pygmy sperm whale
Red mouse lemur

Red-tailed sportive lemur
Ringtailed lemur
Ring-tailed mongoose
Sperm whale
Spinner dolphin
White-footed sportive lemur
Yellow-streaked tenrec

MALAWI
Aardvark
African civet
Checkered sengi
Common bentwing bat
Common genet
Egyptian slit-faced bat
Gambian rat
Ground pangolin
South African porcupine

MALAYSIA
Asian elephant
Blue whale
Bornean orangutan
Common bentwing bat
Common bottlenosed dolphin
Common tree shrew
Dugong
Eurasian wild pig
Humpback whale
Indian muntjac
Killer whale
Lar gibbon
Lesser Malay mouse deer
Malayan colugo
Malayan moonrat
Malayan tapir
Naked bat
Northern minke whale
Proboscis monkey
Pygmy sperm whale
Serow
Siamang
Sperm whale
Spinner dolphin
Sumatran rhinoceros

MALI
Aardvark
African civet
Common genet
Dromedary camel
Egyptian rousette
Egyptian slit-faced bat
Gambian rat
Mzab gundi
Rock hyrax
Savanna elephant
Senegal bushbaby

MARIANA ISLANDS
Marianas fruit bat

MAURITANIA
Aardvark
Blue whale
Common bottlenosed dolphin
Dromedary camel
Humpback whale
Killer whale
Northern minke whale
Pygmy sperm whale
Sperm whale
Spinner dolphin

MEXICO
American black bear
American least shrew
Bighorn sheep
Black-tailed prairie dog
Blue whale
Bobcat
Brazilian free-tailed bat
Brown-throated three-toed
  sloth
California leaf-nosed bat
California sea lion
Central American agouti
Collared peccary
Common bottlenosed dolphin
Desert cottontail
Eastern mole

Funnel-eared bat
Geoffroy's spider monkey
Gray whale
Greater bulldog bat
Greater dog-faced bat
Greater sac-winged bat
Hispid cotton rat
Humpback whale
Killer whale
Little brown bat
Muskrat
Nine-banded armadillo
North American beaver
North American porcupine
Northern elephant seal
Northern minke whale
Northern raccoon
Paca
Pallas's long-tongued bat
Pallid bat
Parnell's moustached bat
Pronghorn
Puma
Pygmy sperm whale
Silky anteater
Sperm whale
Spinner dolphin
Spix's disk-winged bat
Striped skunk
Three-toed tree sloths
Valley pocket gopher
Vampire bat
Virginia opossum
Water opossum
White-tailed deer

MOLDOVA
Black-bellied hamster
Common bentwing bat
Edible dormouse
Eurasian wild pig
European badger
Gray wolf
Greater horseshoe bat
Red deer
Red fox

MONACO

European badger
Red fox

MONGOLIA

Ermine
Eurasian wild pig
Gray wolf
Hairy-footed jerboa
Moose
Mountain hare
Northern pika
Przewalski's horse
Red deer
Red fox
Reindeer
Siberian musk deer
Snow leopard

MOROCCO

Blue whale
Common bentwing bat
Common bottlenosed dolphin
Dromedary camel
Eurasian wild pig
European otter
Greater horseshoe bat
Harbor porpoise
Hardwicke's lesser mouse-
  tailed bat
Humpback whale
Killer whale
North Atlantic right whale
Northern bottlenosed whale
Northern minke whale
Pygmy sperm whale
Red deer
Red fox
Sperm whale
Spinner dolphin
Trident leaf-nosed bat

MOZAMBIQUE

Aardvark
African civet
Blue whale
Checkered sengi
Common bentwing bat
Common bottlenosed dolphin
Common genet
Common hippopotamus
Dugong
Egyptian rousette
Egyptian slit-faced bat
Gambian rat
Ground pangolin
Humpback whale
Killer whale
Lord Derby's anomalure
Northern minke whale
Pygmy sperm whale
Rock hyrax
South African porcupine
Sperm whale
Spinner dolphin
Springhare
White rhinoceros

MYANMAR

Asian elephant
Blue whale
Common bentwing bat
Common bottlenosed dolphin
Eurasian wild pig
Gray wolf
Greater horseshoe bat
Humpback whale
Indian flying fox
Indian muntjac
Kitti's hog-nosed bat
Lar gibbon
Lesser Malay mouse deer
Malayan moonrat
Malayan tapir
Northern minke whale
Pygmy sperm whale
Red fox
Red panda
Rhesus macaque
Serow

Sperm whale
Spinner dolphin
Tiger

NAMIBIA

Aardvark
African civet
Blue whale
Common bentwing bat
Common bottlenosed dolphin
Common genet
Common hippopotamus
Damaraland mole-rat
Dassie rat
Egyptian slit-faced bat
Giraffe
Grant's desert golden mole
Ground pangolin
Humpback whale
Killer whale
Kirk's dikdik
Northern minke whale
Pygmy sperm whale
Rock hyrax
Savanna elephant
Sperm whale
Springhare

NEPAL

Asian elephant
Common bentwing bat
Eurasian wild pig
Ganges and Indus dolphin
Gray wolf
Greater horseshoe bat
Indian crested porcupine
Indian muntjac
Indian rhinoceros
Kiang
Red fox
Red panda
Rhesus macaque
Serow
Snow leopard
Water buffalo

NETHERLANDS
Black-bellied hamster
Blue whale
Common bottlenosed dolphin
Ermine
Eurasian wild pig
European badger
Harbor porpoise
Humpback whale
Killer whale
Northern minke whale
Northern raccoon
Pygmy sperm whale
Red deer
Red fox
Sperm whale
Western European hedgehog

NEW ZEALAND
Blue whale
Brush-tailed rock wallaby
Common bottlenosed dolphin
Common brush-tailed possum
Dugong
Humpback whale
Killer whale
Lesser New Zealand short-
  tailed bat
Northern minke whale
Pygmy right whale
Pygmy sperm whale
Shepherd's beaked whale
Sperm whale

NICARAGUA
American least shrew
Blue whale
Brazilian free-tailed bat
Brown-throated three-toed
  sloth
Central American agouti
Collared peccary
Common bottlenosed dolphin
Funnel-eared bat
Geoffroy's spider monkey

Giant anteater
Greater bulldog bat
Greater dog-faced bat
Greater sac-winged bat
Hispid cotton rat
Hoffman's two-toed sloth
Humpback whale
Killer whale
Nine-banded armadillo
Northern minke whale
Paca
Pallas's long-tongued bat
Parnell's moustached bat
Pygmy sperm whale
Silky anteater
Sperm whale
Spinner dolphin
Spiny rat
Spix's disk-winged bat
Three-toed tree sloths
Vampire bat
Virginia opossum
Water opossum
White bat
White-tailed deer
White-throated capuchin

NIGER
Aardvark
Dromedary camel
Egyptian slit-faced bat
Gambian rat
Mzab gundi
Rock hyrax
Senegal bushbaby
Trident leaf-nosed bat

NIGERIA
Aardvark
African civet
Blue whale
Chimpanzee
Common bottlenosed dolphin
Common genet
Dwarf epauletted fruit bat

Egyptian rousette
Egyptian slit-faced bat
Gambian rat
Humpback whale
Lord Derby's anomalure
Northern minke whale
Potto
Pygmy sperm whale
Rock hyrax
Senegal bushbaby
South African porcupine
Sperm whale
Spinner dolphin
Western gorilla
Western red colobus

NORTH KOREA
Blue whale
Common bentwing bat
Common bottlenosed dolphin
Eurasian wild pig
Humpback whale
Killer whale
Northern minke whale
Northern pika
Pygmy sperm whale
Red deer
Siberian musk deer
Sperm whale
Spinner dolphin

NORWAY
Blue whale
Common bottlenosed dolphin
Ermine
Eurasian wild pig
European badger
European otter
Harbor porpoise
Humpback whale
Killer whale
Moose
Mountain hare
North Atlantic right whale
Northern bottlenosed whale

Northern minke whale
Norway lemming
Polar bear
Red deer
Red fox
Reindeer
Sperm whale
Western European hedgehog

OMAN
Blue whale
Common bottlenosed dolphin
Dromedary camel
Dugong
Egyptian rousette
Egyptian spiny mouse
Gray wolf
Humpback whale
Killer whale
Northern minke whale
Pygmy sperm whale
Rock hyrax
Sperm whale
Spinner dolphin
Trident leaf-nosed bat

PAKISTAN
Blue whale
Common bentwing bat
Common bottlenosed dolphin
Dromedary camel
Dugong
Eurasian wild pig
Ganges and Indus dolphin
Gray wolf
Greater horseshoe bat
Hardwicke's lesser mouse-
  tailed bat
Humpback whale
Indian flying fox
Indian muntjac
Indian rhinoceros
Kiang
Killer whale
Northern minke whale

Pygmy sperm whale
Red fox
Rhesus macaque
Snow leopard
Sperm whale
Spinner dolphin
Trident leaf-nosed bat

PANAMA
American least shrew
Blue whale
Brazilian free-tailed bat
Brown-throated three-toed
  sloth
Capybara
Central American agouti
Collared peccary
Common bottlenosed dolphin
Funnel-eared bat
Geoffroy's spider monkey
Giant anteater
Greater bulldog bat
Greater dog-faced bat
Greater sac-winged bat
Hispid cotton rat
Hoffman's two-toed sloth
Humpback whale
Killer whale
Nine-banded armadillo
Northern minke whale
Northern raccoon
Paca
Pallas's long-tongued bat
Parnell's moustached bat
Puma
Pygmy sperm whale
Silky anteater
Smoky bat
Sperm whale
Spinner dolphin
Spiny rat
Spix's disk-winged bat
Three-toed tree sloths
Vampire bat
Water opossum
White bat

White-tailed deer
White-throated capuchin

PAPUA NEW GUINEA
Blue whale
Common bentwing bat
Common bottlenosed dolphin
Dugong
Ground cuscus
Humpback whale
Killer whale
Northern minke whale
Pygmy sperm whale
Rufous spiny bandicoot
Short-beaked echidna
Sperm whale
Spinner dolphin
Sugar glider

PARAGUAY
Brazilian free-tailed bat
Brown-throated three-toed
  sloth
Capybara
Collared peccary
Coypu
Giant anteater
Greater bulldog bat
Maned wolf
Nine-banded armadillo
Paca
Pallas's long-tongued bat
Prehensile-tailed porcupine
Three-toed tree sloths
Vampire bat
Water opossum

PERU
Alpaca
Ashy chinchilla rat
Bald uakari
Blue whale
Boto
Brazilian free-tailed bat
Burmeister's porpoise

Capybara
Central American agouti
Collared peccary
Common bottlenosed
  dolphin
Giant anteater
Goeldi's monkey
Greater bulldog bat
Greater dog-faced bat
Greater sac-winged bat
Hoffman's two-toed sloth
Humpback whale
Killer whale
Llama
Lowland tapir
Maned wolf
Nine-banded armadillo
Northern minke whale
Pacarana
Pallas's long-tongued bat
Parnell's moustached bat
Pearson's tuco-tuco
Pygmy marmoset
Pygmy sperm whale
Silky anteater
Sperm whale
Spinner dolphin
Spix's disk-winged bat
Vampire bat
Water opossum
White-faced saki
White-tailed deer

PHILIPPINES
Blue whale
Common bentwing bat
Common bottlenosed
  dolphin
Dugong
Humpback whale
Naked bat
Northern minke whale
Philippine tarsier
Pygmy sperm whale
Sperm whale
Spinner dolphin

POLAND
Black-bellied hamster
Blue whale
Common bentwing bat
Common bottlenosed
  dolphin
Edible dormouse
Ermine
Eurasian wild pig
European badger
Greater horseshoe bat
Harbor porpoise
Humpback whale
Moose
Northern minke whale
Red deer
Red fox
Sperm whale

PORTUGAL
Blue whale
Common bentwing bat
Common bottlenosed
  dolphin
Common genet
Eurasian wild pig
European badger
European otter
Greater horseshoe bat
Harbor porpoise
Humpback whale
Killer whale
North Atlantic right whale
Northern bottlenosed whale
Northern minke whale
Pygmy sperm whale
Red deer
Red fox
Sperm whale
Western barbastelle
Western European hedgehog

PUERTO RICO
Blue whale
Brazilian free-tailed bat

Common bottlenosed
  dolphin
Funnel-eared bat
Greater bulldog bat
Humpback whale
Killer whale
Northern minke whale
Pygmy sperm whale
Sperm whale
Spinner dolphin

QATAR
Egyptian spiny mouse

ROMANIA
Black-bellied hamster
Common bentwing bat
Edible dormouse
Eurasian wild pig
European badger
Gray wolf
Greater horseshoe bat
Harbor porpoise
Red deer
Red fox

RUSSIA
Beluga
Black-bellied hamster
Blue whale
Common bentwing bat
Common bottlenosed
  dolphin
Edible dormouse
Ermine
Eurasian wild pig
European otter
Gray whale
Gray wolf
Harbor porpoise
Harp seal
Humpback whale
Killer whale
Moose
Mountain hare
Narwhal

Northern minke whale
Northern pika
Northern raccoon
Polar bear
Red deer
Red fox
Reindeer
Siberian musk deer
Snow leopard
Sperm whale
Tiger
Walrus
Western European hedgehog

RWANDA
Aardvark
African civet
Chimpanzee
Common bentwing bat
Common genet
Egyptian slit-faced bat
Gambian rat
Lord Derby's anomalure
Rock hyrax
Senegal bushbaby
South African porcupine

SAUDI ARABIA
Blue whale
Common bottlenosed dolphin
Dromedary camel
Dugong
Egyptian slit-faced bat
Egyptian spiny mouse
Gray wolf
Hardwicke's lesser mouse-
    tailed bat
Humpback whale
Indian crested porcupine
Northern minke whale
Pygmy sperm whale
Rock hyrax
Sperm whale
Spinner dolphin
Trident leaf-nosed bat

SENEGAL
Aardvark
African civet
Blue whale
Chimpanzee
Common bottlenosed dolphin
Common genet
Egyptian slit-faced bat
Gambian rat
Hardwicke's lesser mouse-
    tailed bat
Humpback whale
Killer whale
Northern minke whale
Pygmy sperm whale
Rock hyrax
Senegal bushbaby
South African porcupine
Sperm whale
Spinner dolphin
Western red colobus

SIERRA LEONE
Aardvark
African civet
Blue whale
Chimpanzee
Common bottlenosed dolphin
Common genet
Egyptian slit-faced bat
Forest hog
Gambian rat
Humpback whale
Killer whale
Lord Derby's anomalure
Northern minke whale
Potto
Pygmy hippopotamus
Pygmy sperm whale
Rock hyrax
Senegal bushbaby
South African porcupine
Sperm whale
Spinner dolphin
Western red colobus

SINGAPORE
Lesser Malay mouse deer

SLOVAKIA
Black-bellied hamster
Edible dormouse
Ermine
European badger
Greater horseshoe bat
Red deer
Red fox

SLOVENIA
Blue whale
Common bentwing bat
Common bottlenosed dolphin
Edible dormouse
Ermine
Eurasian wild pig
European badger
Greater horseshoe bat
Humpback whale
Northern minke whale
Pygmy sperm whale
Red deer
Red fox
Sperm whale

SOMALIA
Aardwolf
African civet
Blue whale
Common bentwing bat
Common bottlenosed dolphin
Common genet
Dromedary camel
Dugong
Egyptian slit-faced bat
Humpback whale
Kirk's dikdik
Naked mole-rat
Northern greater bushbaby
Northern minke whale
Pygmy sperm whale

Rock hyrax
Senegal bushbaby
South African porcupine
Sperm whale
Spinner dolphin

SOUTH AFRICA
Aardvark
Aardwolf
African civet
Black wildebeest
Blue whale
Cape horseshoe bat
Common bentwing bat
Common bottlenosed dolphin
Common genet
Damaraland mole-rat
Dassie rat
Egyptian rousette
Egyptian slit-faced bat
Gambian rat
Giraffe
Grant's desert golden mole
Ground pangolin
Humpback whale
Killer whale
Northern minke whale
Pygmy right whale
Pygmy sperm whale
Rock hyrax
Savanna elephant
Shepherd's beaked whale
South African porcupine
Southern tree hyrax
Sperm whale
Spinner dolphin
Springhare

SOUTH KOREA
Blue whale
Common bentwing bat
Common bottlenosed dolphin
Eurasian wild pig
Humpback whale
Killer whale

Northern minke whale
Pygmy sperm whale
Sperm whale
Spinner dolphin

SPAIN
Alpine marmot
Blue whale
Common bentwing bat
Common bottlenosed dolphin
Common genet
Edible dormouse
Eurasian wild pig
European badger
European otter
Gray wolf
Greater horseshoe bat
Harbor porpoise
Humpback whale
Killer whale
North Atlantic right whale
Northern bottlenosed whale
Northern minke whale
Pygmy sperm whale
Red deer
Red fox
Sperm whale
Western barbastelle
Western European hedgehog

SRI LANKA
Asian elephant
European otter
Indian crested porcupine
Indian flying fox
Indian muntjac

SUDAN
Aardvark
African civet
Blue whale
Chimpanzee
Common bottlenosed dolphin
Common genet

Common hippopotamus
Dromedary camel
Dugong
Dwarf epauletted fruit bat
Egyptian slit-faced bat
Gambian rat
Giraffe
Greater cane rat
Ground pangolin
Humpback whale
Northern minke whale
Pygmy sperm whale
Rock hyrax
Senegal bushbaby
South African porcupine
Sperm whale
Spinner dolphin
Spotted hyena
Thomson's gazelle
Trident leaf-nosed bat
White rhinoceros

SURINAME
Blue whale
Collared peccary
Common bottlenosed dolphin
Common squirrel monkey
Funnel-eared bat
Giant anteater
Greater bulldog bat
Greater dog-faced bat
Greater sac-winged bat
Humpback whale
Lowland tapir
Northern minke whale
Paca
Pallas's long-tongued bat
Parnell's moustached bat
Prehensile-tailed porcupine
Pygmy sperm whale
Silky anteater
Smoky bat
Sperm whale
Spinner dolphin
Spix's disk-winged bat
Three-toed tree sloths

Vampire bat
Water opossum
Weeper capuchin
White-faced saki
White-tailed deer

SWAZILAND
Aardvark
African civet
Common bentwing bat
Common genet
Egyptian slit-faced bat
Gambian rat
Giraffe
Ground pangolin
South African porcupine

SWEDEN
Blue whale
Common bottlenosed dolphin
Ermine
Eurasian wild pig
European badger
Gray wolf
Harbor porpoise
Humpback whale
Moose
Mountain hare
Northern minke whale
Norway lemming
Red deer
Red fox
Sperm whale
Western European hedgehog

SWITZERLAND
Alpine marmot
Common bentwing bat
Edible dormouse
Ermine
Eurasian wild pig
European badger
Greater horseshoe bat
Mountain hare
Red deer

Red fox
Western European hedgehog

SYRIA
Blue whale
Common bottlenosed dolphin
Dromedary camel
Egyptian spiny mouse
Eurasian wild pig
Gray wolf
Greater horseshoe bat
Hardwicke's lesser mouse-
  tailed bat
Humpback whale
Northern minke whale
Pygmy sperm whale
Red deer
Red fox
Sperm whale
Trident leaf-nosed bat

TAJIKISTAN
Common bentwing bat
Edible dormouse
Ermine
Eurasian wild pig
European badger
Gray wolf
Greater horseshoe bat
Red deer
Red fox
Snow leopard

TANZANIA
Aardvark
African civet
Blue whale
Checkered sengi
Chimpanzee
Common bentwing bat
Common bottlenosed dolphin
Common genet
Common hippopotamus
Dugong
Egyptian rousette

Egyptian slit-faced bat
Gambian rat
Giraffe
Greater cane rat
Ground pangolin
Humpback whale
Killer whale
Kirk's dikdik
Lion
Lord Derby's anomalure
Northern greater bushbaby
Northern minke whale
Pygmy sperm whale
Rock hyrax
Senegal bushbaby
South African porcupine
Sperm whale
Spinner dolphin
Springhare
Thomson's gazelle

THAILAND
Asian elephant
Blue whale
Common bentwing bat
Common bottlenosed dolphin
Common tree shrew
Dugong
Eurasian wild pig
Greater horseshoe bat
Humpback whale
Indian muntjac
Kitti's hog-nosed bat
Lar gibbon
Lesser Malay mouse deer
Malayan colugo
Malayan moonrat
Malayan tapir
Northern minke whale
Pileated gibbon
Pygmy sperm whale
Red fox
Rhesus macaque
Serow
Sperm whale

Spinner dolphin
Water buffalo

TOGO
Aardvark
African civet
Blue whale
Common bottlenosed dolphin
Common genet
Forest hog
Gambian rat
Humpback whale
Lord Derby's anomalure
Northern minke whale
Pygmy sperm whale
Rock hyrax
Senegal bushbaby
South African porcupine
Sperm whale
Spinner dolphin

TRINIDAD AND TOBAGO
Pallas's long-tongued bat
Prehensile-tailed porcupine
Silky anteater
Smoky bat
Vampire bat

TUNISIA
Blue whale
Common bentwing bat
Common bottlenosed dolphin
Common genet
Dromedary camel
Eurasian wild pig
European otter
Greater horseshoe bat
Humpback whale
Killer whale
Northern minke whale
Pygmy sperm whale
Red deer
Red fox
Sperm whale
Trident leaf-nosed bat

TURKEY
Blue whale
Common bentwing bat
Common bottlenosed dolphin
Edible dormouse
Egyptian rousette
Eurasian wild pig
European badger
Gray wolf
Greater horseshoe bat
Harbor porpoise
Humpback whale
Northern minke whale
Pygmy sperm whale
Red deer
Sperm whale

TURKMENISTAN
Common bentwing bat
Edible dormouse
Eurasian wild pig
European badger
Gray wolf
Greater horseshoe bat
Hairy-footed jerboa
Red deer
Red fox

UGANDA
Aardvark
African civet
Checkered sengi
Chimpanzee
Common bentwing bat
Common genet
Dwarf epauletted fruit bat
Egyptian rousette
Egyptian slit-faced bat
Forest hog
Gambian rat
Giraffe
Greater cane rat
Ground pangolin
Lord Derby's anomalure
Potto

Senegal bushbaby
South African porcupine
White rhinoceros

UKRAINE
Alpine marmot
Black-bellied hamster
Common bentwing bat
Edible dormouse
Ermine
Eurasian wild pig
European badger
Gray wolf
Greater horseshoe bat
Harbor porpoise
Moose
Red deer
Red fox

UNITED ARAB EMIRATES
Dromedary camel
Egyptian spiny mouse
Gray wolf
Trident leaf-nosed bat

UNITED KINGDOM
Blue whale
Common bottlenosed dolphin
Ermine
Eurasian wild pig
European badger
European otter
Greater horseshoe bat
Harbor porpoise
Humpback whale
Killer whale
Mountain hare
North Atlantic right whale
Northern bottlenosed whale
Northern minke whale
Pygmy sperm whale
Red deer
Red fox
Sperm whale

Western barbastelle
Western European hedgehog

UNITED STATES
American bison
American black bear
American least shrew
American pika
American water shrew
Beluga
Bighorn sheep
Black-tailed prairie dog
Blue whale
Bobcat
Brazilian free-tailed bat
California leaf-nosed bat
California sea lion
Collared peccary
Common bottlenosed dolphin
Desert cottontail
Eastern chipmunk
Eastern mole
Ermine
Giant kangaroo rat
Gray squirrel
Gray whale
Gray wolf
Harbor porpoise
Hawaiian monk seal
Hispid cotton rat
Humpback whale
Killer whale
Little brown bat
Moose
Mountain beaver
Muskrat
Narwhal
Nine-banded armadillo
North American beaver
North American porcupine
North Atlantic right whale
Northern bottlenosed whale
Northern elephant seal
Northern minke whale
Northern raccoon
Pallid bat

Polar bear
Pronghorn
Puma
Pygmy sperm whale
Red deer
Red fox
Reindeer
San Joaquin pocket mouse
Snowshoe hare
Southern flying squirrel
Sperm whale
Spinner dolphin
Star-nosed mole
Steller's sea cow
Striped skunk
Valley pocket gopher
Virginia opossum
Walrus
West Indian manatee
White-tailed deer

URUGUAY
Blue whale
Brazilian free-tailed bat
Burmeister's porpoise
Capybara
Collared peccary
Common bottlenosed dolphin
Coypu
Franciscana dolphin
Giant anteater
Humpback whale
Killer whale
Maned wolf
Northern minke whale
Pearson's tuco-tuco
Prehensile-tailed porcupine
Pygmy right whale
Red deer
Sperm whale
Vampire bat

UZBEKISTAN
Common bentwing bat
Edible dormouse

Eurasian wild pig
European badger
Gray wolf
Hairy-footed jerboa
Red deer
Red fox
Snow leopard

VENEZUELA
Blue whale
Boto
Brazilian free-tailed bat
Capybara
Collared peccary
Colombian woolly monkey
Common bottlenosed dolphin
Common squirrel monkey
Funnel-eared bat
Giant anteater
Greater bulldog bat
Greater dog-faced bat
Greater sac-winged bat
Hispid cotton rat
Hoffman's two-toed sloth
Humpback whale
Lowland tapir
Northern minke whale
Paca
Pacarana
Pallas's long-tongued bat
Parnell's moustached bat
Prehensile-tailed porcupine
Puma
Pygmy sperm whale
Silky anteater
Silky shrew opossum
Smoky bat
Sperm whale
Spinner dolphin
Spix's disk-winged bat
Three-striped night monkey
Three-toed tree sloths
Vampire bat
Venezuelan red howler
  monkey
Water opossum

Weeper capuchin
White-tailed deer

VIETNAM
Asian elephant
Blue whale
Common bentwing bat
Common bottlenosed dolphin
Dugong
Eurasian wild pig
Greater horseshoe bat
Humpback whale
Indian muntjac
Malayan tapir
Northern minke whale
Pygmy slow loris
Pygmy sperm whale
Red fox
Red-shanked douc langur
Rhesus macaque
Serow
Sperm whale
Spinner dolphin

YEMEN
Blue whale
Common bottlenosed dolphin
Dromedary camel
Dugong
Egyptian rousette

Egyptian slit-faced bat
Egyptian spiny mouse
Gray wolf
Hardwicke's lesser mouse-
    tailed bat
Humpback whale
Northern minke whale
Pygmy sperm whale
Rock hyrax
Sperm whale
Spinner dolphin
Trident leaf-nosed bat

YUGOSLAVIA
Alpine marmot
Blue whale
Common bentwing bat
Common bottlenosed dolphin
Edible dormouse
Ermine
Gray wolf
Greater horseshoe bat
Humpback whale
Northern minke whale
Pygmy sperm whale
Red deer
Sperm whale

ZAMBIA
Aardvark

Aardwolf
African civet
Checkered sengi
Common bentwing bat
Common genet
Common hippopotamus
Egyptian rousette
Egyptian slit-faced bat
Gambian rat
Giraffe
Ground pangolin
Lord Derby's anomalure
South African porcupine
Spotted hyena
Springhare

ZIMBABWE
Aardvark
African civet
Common bentwing bat
Common genet
Damaraland mole-rat
Egyptian rousette
Egyptian slit-faced bat
Gambian rat
Ground pangolin
Savanna elephant
South African porcupine
Spotted hyena
Springhare

Index

Italic type indicates volume number; **boldface** type indicates entries and their pages; (ill.) indicates illustrations.

A

Aardvarks, *1:* 9, *4:* **804–7,** 805 (ill.), 806 (ill.)

Aardwolves, *3:* 580, **649–56,** 654 (ill.), 655 (ill.)

Abderitidae, *1:* 39

Abrocoma cinerea. See Ashy chinchilla rats

Abrocomidae. *See* Chinchilla rats

Acomys cahirinus. See Egyptian spiny mice

Acrobates pygmaeus. See Pygmy gliders

Acrobatidae. *See* Feather-tailed possums

Afghan pikas, *5:* 1206

African chevrotains, *4:* 927

African civets, *3:* 631–33, 631 (ill.), 632 (ill.)

African elephants, *4:* 813, 815, 816, 819

African heart-nosed bats, *2:* 280

African hedgehogs, *2:* 218

African hunting wolves, *3:* 584

African linsangs, *3:* 629

African mole-rats, *5:* 998, **1103–10**

African rhinoceroses, *4:* 850

African sheath-tailed bats, *2:* 305

African wild cats, *3:* 658

African wild dogs, *3:* 583

African Wildlife Foundation, *4:* 876

Afrotheria, *2:* 216, *5:* 1224

Agouti paca. See Pacas

Agouti taczanowskii. See Mountain pacas

Agoutidae. *See* Pacas

Agoutis, *5:* **1153–59,** 1160

Ai. See Brown throated three-toed sloths

Ailuropoda melanoleuca. See Giant pandas

Ailurus fulgens. See Red pandas

Aizen, Marcelo, *1:* 44

Alces alces. See Moose

Alexander, Shana, *4:* 811

Almiquis. *See* Cuban solenodons

Alouatta seniculus. See Venezuelan red howler monkeys

Alpaca Owners and Breeders Association, *4:* 918

Alpacas, *4:* **916–26,** 921 (ill.), 922 (ill.)

Alpine marmots, *5:* 1017–18, 1017 (ill.), 1018 (ill.)

Amazon river dolphins. *See* Botos

Amazonian manatees, *4:* 829, 841

Ambergris, *4:* 760

American beavers. *See* North American beavers

American birch mice, *5:* 1047

American bison, *4:* 973–75, 973 (ill.), 974 (ill.)

American black bears, *3:* 593, 596–98, 596 (ill.), 597 (ill.)

American Cetacean Society, *4:* 707

American chipmunks, *5:* 1008

American leaf-nosed bats, *2:* **345–57,** 359

American least shrews, *2:* 250–51, 250 (ill.), 251 (ill.)

American pikas, *5:* 1206, 1208–9, 1208 (ill.), 1209 (ill.)

American shrew-moles, *2:* 256

American water shrews, *2:* 252–53, 252 (ill.), 253 (ill.)

Amico, Guillermo, *1:* 44

Andean night monkeys, *3:* 511

Anomalures, Lord Derby's, *5:* 1072–74, 1072 (ill.), 1073 (ill.)

Anomaluridae. *See* Scaly-tailed squirrels

Anomalurus derbianus. See Lord Derby's anomalures

Brown bats
  big, 2: 276, 417
  little, 2: 417–18, 417 (ill.),
    418 (ill.)
Brown bears, 3: 593
Brown four-eyed opossums,
  1: 28
Brown greater bushbabies,
  3: 436
Brown hyenas, 3: 649–50
Brown long-eared bats, 2: 278
Brown mouse lemurs. See Red
  mouse lemurs
Brown throated three-toed
  sloths, 1: 189, 192–94, 192
  (ill.), 193 (ill.)
Brown's hutias, 5: 1188, 1189
Brush-tailed phascogales,
  1: 59–60, 59 (ill.), 60 (ill.)
Brush-tailed porcupines,
  5: 1111
Brush-tailed possums. See
  Common brush-tailed
  possums
Brush-tailed rock wallabies,
  1: 142–43, 142 (ill.), 143 (ill.)
Bubalus bubalis. See Water
  buffaloes
Buena Vista Lake ornate
  shrews, 2: 216, 249
Buffaloes, 4: 969–87
Buffy headed marmosets,
  3: 497
Buffy tufted-ear marmosets,
  3: 497
Bulldog bats, 2: 364–70
Bumblebee bats. See Kitti's
  hog-nosed bats
Bureau of Land Management,
  4: 851
Burmeister's porpoises, 4: 730,
  731, 734–35, 734 (ill.), 735
  (ill.)
Burramyidae. See Pygmy
  possums
Burrowing bettongs, 1: 130
Burrowing pikas, 5: 1201,
  1206

Bush dogs, 3: 583
Bush hyraxes, 4: 821
Bushbabies, 3: 423, 424, 425,
  436–43
Bushmeat, 4: 889

C

Cacajao calvus. See Bald uakaris
Caenolestes fuliginosus. See
  Silky shrew opossums
Caenolestidae. See Shrew
  opossums
Caldwell, William Hay, 1: 5
California Fish and Game
  Commission, 5: 1042
California leaf-nosed bats,
  2: 348–49, 348 (ill.), 349 (ill.)
California sea lions, 3: 677–79,
  677 (ill.), 678 (ill.)
Callicebus personatus. See
  Masked titis
Callimico goeldii. See Goeldi's
  monkeys
Callitrichidae. See Goeldi's
  monkeys; Marmosets;
  Tamarins
Camazotz, 2: 347
Camelidae. See Alpacas;
  Camels; Guanacos; Llamas;
  Vicuñas
Camels, 4: 916–26
Camelus dromedarius. See
  Dromedary camels
Cane rats, 5: 1097–1102
Canidae, 3: 580, 583–92
Canis lupus. See Gray wolves
Cape horseshoe bats,
  2: 336–37, 336 (ill.), 337 (ill.)
Cape pangolins. See Ground
  pangolins
Caperea marginata. See Pygmy
  right whales
Capricornis sumatraensis. See
  Serows
Capromyidae. See Hutias
Capromys pilorides. See Cuban
  hutias

Capuchins, 3: 426, 487–95
Capybaras, 5: 996–98,
  1147–52, 1149 (ill.), 1150
  (ill.)
Caribbean monk seals, 3: 581,
  691
Caribou, 4: 951
Carnassial teeth, 3: 581
Carnivora. See Land
  carnivores; Marine carnivores
Carnivores, land and marine,
  3: 578–82
Carnivorous marsupials,
  Australasian, 1: 51–55, 75
Carrizo Plain Natural Heritage
  Reserve, 5: 1042
Casiraguas, 5: 1182
Caspian seals, 3: 691
Castor canadensis. See North
  American beavers
Castoridae. See Beavers
Cats, 3: 578, 579, 582, 657–72
  domestic, 3: 658
  marsupial, 1: 56–63
  wild, 3: 581, 658
Cattle, 4: 890, 969–87
Cavies, 5: 996, 999, 1000,
  1139–46
Caviidae. See Cavies; Maras
Cebidae. See Capuchins;
  Squirrel monkeys
Cebuella pygmaea. See Pygmy
  marmosets
Cebus capucinus. See White-
  throated capuchins
Cebus olivaceus. See Weeper
  capuchins
Central American agoutis,
  5: 1156–58, 1156 (ill.), 1157
  (ill.)
Ceratotherium simum. See
  White rhinoceroses
Cercartetus nanus. See Eastern
  pygmy possums
Cercopithecidae. See Old
  World monkeys
Cervidae. See Deer
Cervus elaphus. See Red deer

Dog-faced bats, greater,
2: 309–10, 309 (ill.), 310 (ill.)
Dogs, 3: 578, 580, 581, **583–92**
  prairie, 5: 998, 1015–16,
  1015 (ill.), 1016 (ill.)
  raccoon, 3: 583, 629
Dolichotis patagonum. See
Maras
Dolphins, 4: 703–8, 729,
737–48
  baiji, 4: 714–18, 716 (ill.),
  717 (ill.)
  boto, 4: 724–28, 726 (ill.),
  727 (ill.)
  Franciscana, 4: 719–23,
  721 (ill.), 722 (ill.)
  Ganges and Indus,
  4: 709–13, 711 (ill.), 712
  (ill.)
Domestic cats, 3: 658
Domestic dogs, 3: 585
Domestic horses, 4: 848, 849,
852, 855–56
Domestic livestock, 4: 890
Domestic pigs, 4: 893, 894
Donkeys, 4: 856
Dormice, 5: 1087–92
Douc langurs, red-shanked,
3: 537, 544–45, 544 (ill.),
545 (ill.)
Dourocouli. *See* Night
monkeys
Dracula (Stoker), 2: 279, 346
Dromedary camels, 4: 917,
919–20, 919 (ill.), 920 (ill.)
Dromiciops australis. See
Monitos del monte
Dromiciops gliroides. See
Monitos del monte
Dryland mouse opossums,
1: 25
Duck-billed platypus, 1: 1–6,
15–23, 20 (ill.), 21 (ill.)
Dugong dugon. See Dugongs
Dugongidae. *See* Dugongs; Sea
cows
Dugongs, 4: 828–32, 833–40,
838 (ill.), 839 (ill.)

Dunnarts, 1: 54, 58
Dwarf epauletted fruit bats,
2: 293–94, 293 (ill.), 294 (ill.)
Dwarf gymnures, 2: 220
Dwarf lemurs, 3: 444–49
Dwarf mongooses, 3: 638

E

Eagles, Philippine, 2: 270
Eared hutias, 5: 1189
Eared seals, 3: 579, 582,
673–83, 690
Earless seals. *See* True seals
Earth pigs. *See* Aardvarks
Eastern barred bandicoots,
1: 80, 83–84, 83 (ill.), 84 (ill.)
Eastern black gibbons, 3: 552
Eastern chipmunks,
5: 1013–14, 1013 (ill.), 1014
(ill.)
Eastern gray kangaroos,
1: 138–39, 138 (ill.), 139 (ill.)
Eastern moles, 2: 214, 216,
256, 258–59, 258 (ill.), 259
(ill.)
Eastern Pacific gray whales,
4: 781
Eastern pumas, 3: 658, 667
Eastern pygmy possums,
1: 150, 152–53, 152 (ill.),
153 (ill.)
Eastern red colobus monkeys,
3: 537
Eastern tarsiers, 3: 481
Eastern tube-nosed bats. *See*
Queensland tube-nosed bats
Eastern yellow-billed hornbills,
3: 638
Echidnas, 1: 1–6, 7–14
Echimyidae. *See* Spiny rats
Echinosorex gymnura. See
Malayan moonrats
Echolocation, in bats, 2: 280
Echymipera rufescens. See
Rufous spiny bandicoots
Ectophylla alba. See White bats
Edentata, 1: 181

Edible dormice, 5: 1090–91,
1090 (ill.), 1091 (ill.)
Egg-laying mammals, 1: 5
  See also specific species
Egyptian mongooses, 3: 639
Egyptian rousettes, 2: 290–92,
290 (ill.), 291 (ill.)
Egyptian slit-faced bats,
2: 319–21, 319 (ill.), 320 (ill.)
Egyptian spiny mice,
5: 1060–61, 1060 (ill.), 1061
(ill.)
Electroreceptors, 1: 4, 19
Elegant water shrews, 2: 248
Elephant seals, 3: 684, 691
  northern, 3: 691, 695–97,
  695 (ill.), 696 (ill.)
  southern, 3: 578
Elephant shrews. *See* Sengis
Elephantidae. *See* Elephants
Elephants, 4: 808–19, 821, 885
Elephas maximus. See Asian
elephants
Emballonuridae. *See* Ghost
bats; Sac-winged bats;
Sheath-tailed bats
Emotions, in elephants, 4: 811
Endangered Species Act (U.S.)
  on gray wolves, 3: 587
  on Sirenia, 4: 831
English Nature Greater
  Horseshoe Bat Project, 2: 331
Epauletted fruit bats, dwarf,
2: 293–94, 293 (ill.), 294 (ill.)
Equidae. *See* Asses; Horses;
Zebras
Equus caballus przewalskii. See
Przewalski's horses
Equus grevyi. See Grevy's
zebras
Equus kiang. See Kiangs
Eremitalpa granti. See Grant's
desert golden moles
Erethizon dorsatum. See North
American porcupines
Erethizontidae. *See* New
World porcupines

Greater dog-faced bats,
2: 309–10, 309 (ill.), 310 (ill.)

Greater dog-like bats. *See*
Greater dog-faced bats

Greater gliders, *1*: 157–58, 157
(ill.), 158 (ill.)

Greater gliding possums,
1: **154–60**

Greater horseshoe bats, 2: 331,
333–35, 333 (ill.), 334 (ill.)

Greater marsupial moles. *See*
Southern marsupial moles

Greater New Zealand short-
tailed bats, 2: 372, 373

Greater sac-winged bats,
2: 307–8, 307 (ill.), 308 (ill.)

Green ringtails, *1*: 154

Grevy's zebras, *4*: 857–59, 857
(ill.), 858 (ill.)

Grieving elephants, *4*: 811

Grooming, mutual, *3*: 517

Ground cuscuses, *1*: 119–20,
119 (ill.), 120 (ill.)

Ground pangolins, 5: 993–95,
993 (ill.), 994 (ill.)

Ground sloths, lesser Haitian,
1: 183

Ground squirrels, 5: 998,
1008, 1009, 1010

Guadalupe fur seals, *3*: 674

Guanacos, *4*: **916–26**

Guano, 2: 401

Guardatinajas. *See* Pacas

Guatemalan black howler
monkeys, *3*: 527

Guenons, *3*: 424, 425

Guinea pigs. *See* Cavies

Gundis, 5: **1081–86**

Gunn's bandicoots. *See* Eastern
barred bandicoots

Gymnures, 2: 214, **218–24**

H

Hairless bats, 2: 399

Hairy-footed jerboas,
5: 1048–49, 1048 (ill.), 1049
(ill.)

Hairy-nosed wombats, *1*: 102,
103, 111, 112, 113, 115 (ill.)

Haitian solenodons. *See*
Hispaniolan solenodons

Hamsters, 5: 996, 997, 1051,
1058–59, 1058 (ill.), 1059 (ill.)

Harbor Branch Oceanographic
Institution, *4*: 831

Harbor porpoises, *4*: 730, 731,
732–33, 732 (ill.), 733 (ill.)

Hardwicke's lesser mouse-
tailed bats, 2: 301–3, 301
(ill.), 302 (ill.)

Hares, 5: **1200–1204, 1213–22**
See also Springhares

Harp seals, *3*: 692–94, 692
(ill.), 693 (ill.)

Hawaiian monk seals, *3*: 582,
691, 698–700, 698 (ill.), 699
(ill.)

Heart-nosed bats, 2: 280, 323

Heart-winged bats, 2: 325

Hector's dolphins, *4*: 737–38,
740

Hedgehog tenrecs, 2: 233–34

Hedgehogs, 2: 213, 215, 216,
218–24

Hees. *See* Pacas

Hemicentetes semispinosus. *See*
Yellow-streaked tenrecs

Herpestidae. *See* Fossa;
Mongooses

Herpestinae, *3*: 637

Heterocephalus glaber. *See*
Naked mole-rats

Heteromyidae. *See* Kangaroo
mice; Kangaroo rats; Pocket
mice

Hexaprotodon liberiensis. *See*
Pygmy hippopotamuses

Highland tuco-tucos, 5: 1167,
1168

Hildebrandt's horseshoe bats,
2: 330

Hippopotamidae. *See*
Hippopotamuses

Hippopotamus amphibius. *See*
Common hippopotamuses

Hippopotamuses, *4*: 703, 821,
887, **907–15**

Hippos. *See* Hippopotamuses

Hipposideridae. *See* Old World
leaf-nosed bats

Hispaniolan solenodons,
2: 240, 242, 243–44, 243
(ill.), 244 (ill.)

Hispid cotton rats, 5: 1064–65,
1064 (ill.), 1065 (ill.)

Hoffmann's two-toed sloths,
1: 183, 186–87, 186 (ill.),
187 (ill.)

Hog-nosed bats, Kitti's,
2: 276, **312–15,** 313 (ill.),
314 (ill.)

Hogs
    forest, *4*: 895–96, 895
    (ill.), 896 (ill.)
    Philippine warty, *4*: 894
    pygmy, *4*: 892, 894
    See also Nine-banded
    armadillos

Hollow-faced bats. *See* Slit-
faced bats

Hominidae. *See* Great apes;
Humans

Homo sapiens. *See* Humans

Honey badgers, *3*: 614

Honey possums, *1*: 101, 102,
167–71, 168 (ill.), 169 (ill.)

Hoofed mammals. *See* Ungulates

Hooker's sea lions, *3*: 674

Hoolock gibbons, *3*: 552

Hoover hogs. *See* Nine-banded
armadillos

Hopping mice, 5: 997

Hornbills
    eastern yellow-billed,
    3: 638
    red-billed, *3*: 638

Horses, *4*: 821, 848, 849–53,
854–64

Horseshoe bats, 2: **330–38,**
339, 340

Hose's palm civets, *3*: 630

Howler monkeys, *3*: 425,
526–35

Loxodonta cyclotis. See Forest elephants

Lutra lutra. See European otters

Lynx, Iberian, *3:* 581, 658

Lynx rufus. See Bobcats

M

Macaca mulatta. See Rhesus macaques

Macaques, *3:* 424, 426, 536
    Japanese, *3:* 423
        Mentawai, *3:* 537
        rhesus, *3:* 426, 546–47, 546 (ill.), 547 (ill.)

MacInnes' mouse-tailed bats, *2:* 300

Macroderma gigas. See Australian false vampire bats

Macropodidae. *See* Kangaroos; Wallabies

Macropus giganteus. See Eastern gray kangaroos

Macropus rufus. See Red kangaroos

Macroscelidea. *See* Sengis

Macroscelididae. *See* Sengis

Macrotis lagotis. See Greater bilbies

Macrotus californicus. See California leaf-nosed bats

Madagascar hedgehogs, *2:* 218

Madagascar sucker-footed bats. *See* Old World sucker-footed bats

Madoqua kirkii. See Kirk's dikdiks

Magellanic tuco-tucos, *5:* 1168

Mahogany gliders, *1:* 163

Malabar civets, *3:* 581, 629

Malagasy civets, *3:* 630

Malagasy mongooses, *3:* 637

Malagasy ring-tailed mongooses, *3:* 641, 642

Malay mouse deer, lesser, *4:* 928, 930–32, 930 (ill.), 931 (ill.)

Malayan colugos, *2:* 269, 270, 272–74, 272 (ill.), 273 (ill.)

Malayan flying foxes, *2:* 275–76

Malayan flying lemurs. *See* Malayan colugos

Malayan moonrats, *2:* 218, 223–24, 223 (ill.), 224 (ill.)

Malayan porcupines, *5:* 1114

Malayan tapirs, *4:* 871–73, 871 (ill.), 872 (ill.)

Malaysian sun bears, *3:* 593, 594

Manatees, *4:* 828–32, **841–47**

Mandrills, *3:* 423–25, 536, 548–49, 548 (ill.), 549 (ill.)

Mandrillus sphinx. See Mandrills

Maned sloths, *1:* 191

Maned wolves, *3:* 590–91, 590 (ill.), 591 (ill.)

Mangabeys, *3:* 424, 425

Manidae. *See* Pangolins

Manis temminckii. See Ground pangolins

Maras, *5:* 999, **1139–46,** 1144 (ill.), 1145 (ill.)

Marcano's solenodons, *2:* 242

Marianas fruit bats, *2:* 286–87, 286 (ill.), 287 (ill.)

Marine carnivores, *3:* **578–82**

Marine Mammal Protection Act, *4:* 707, 740, 797

Marking territory, *1:* 163

Marmosets, *3:* 423, 424, 425, **496–508**

Marmota marmota. See Alpine marmots

Marmots, *5:* 1008, 1017–18, 1017 (ill.), 1018 (ill.)

Marsupial cats, *1:* **56–63**

Marsupial mice, *1:* **56–63**

Marsupial moles, *1:* **94–98**

Marsupials
    Australasian carnivorous, *1:* **51–55,** 75
    New World, *1:* 26

Martens, *3:* 579, 614

Masked palm civets, *3:* 629

Masked titis, *3:* 523–24, 523 (ill.), 524 (ill.)

Massoutiera mzabi. See Mzab gundis

Mastiff bats, *2:* 276, **399–408**

Meat, wild, *4:* 889

Mechanoreceptors, *1:* 19

Mediterranean monk seals, *3:* 581, 691

Megachiroptera, *2:* 275, 276–77, 278–79, 282

Megadermatidae. *See* False vampire bats

Megalonychidae. *See* Two-toed tree sloths; West Indian sloths

Megaptera novaeangliae. See Humpback whales

Melbourne Water Department, *1:* 22

Meles meles. See European badgers

Melville, Herman, *4:* 761, 788

Mentawai macaques, *3:* 537

Mephitis mephitis. See Striped skunks

Mexican free-tailed bats. *See* Brazilian free-tailed bats

Mexican funnel-eared bats, *2:* 378, 380–81, 380 (ill.), 381 (ill.)

Mice, *5:* 996–1000, **1051–68**
    birch, *5:* **1044–50**
    jumping, *5:* **1044–50,** 1062–63, 1062 (ill.), 1063 (ill.)
    kangaroo, *5:* **1036–43**
    marsupial, *1:* **56–63**
    pocket, *5:* 998, **1036–43**
    See also Dormice

Michoacan pocket gophers, *5:* 1032

Microbiotheria. *See* Monitos del monte

Microbiotheriidae. *See* Monitos del monte

Microbiotherium species, *1:* 44

on western barbastelles,
  2: 416
on western gorillas, 3: 570
on white bats, 2: 356
on woolly monkeys,
  3: 534
on Xenarthra, 1: 181
World Wildlife Fund, 4: 797
Wroughton free-tailed bats,
  2: 402

X

Xenarthra, *1: 178–82*

Y

Yapoks. *See* Water opossums
Yellow-bellied gliders, *1:* 163
Yellow-breasted capuchins,
  3: 488
Yellow-footed rock wallabies,
  1: 101
Yellow golden moles, 2: 226
Yellow-streaked tenrecs,
  2: 237–38, 237 (ill.), 238 (ill.)
Yellow-tailed woolly monkeys,
  3: 527
Yellow-winged bats, 2: 324,
  325

Yellowstone National Park,
  3: 587
Yerbua capensis. See Springhares

Z

Zalophus californianus. See
  California sea lions
Zalophus wollebaeki. See
  Galápagos sea lions
Zebras, *4:* 848–50, 852,
  854–64
Zenkerella species, *5:* 1069
Ziphiidae. See Beaked whales